The Secrets,

Chastisement,

&

Triumph

Of the Two Hearts of Jesus & Mary

And What Heaven Is Calling Us to Do

Kelly Bowring

Two Hearts Press, LLC
www.TwoHeartsPress.com

Nihil Obstat: Msgr. Adelito A. Abella, Archdiocesan Censor
Imprimatur: Ricardo J. Cardinal Vidal, Archbishop of Cebu
April 2, 2009

The author recognizes and gladly accepts that the final authority regarding the supernatural character of the apparitions, locutions, and heavenly messages in this book rests always and finally with the Magisterium of the Catholic Church.

Library of Congress Control Number: 2007910278

Published by: Two Hearts Press, LLC, Cumming, GA, USA
Printed in the United States of America
ISBN-13: 978-0-9802292-1-9
ISBN-10: 0-9802292-1-9

Note on recent printings of 1st edition:
As Can. 829 states: "Approval or permission to publish a work is valid only for the first edition, but not for new editions or translations." This book is in its first edition, which received the 2009 imprimatur. This being so, the publisher wishes to indicate that the author made minor text additions to recent printings – mostly updates, not significant to the overall text, and not concerning faith and morals. A list is provided at the end of this book.

To order copies of this book:

Please call (24/7)
1-800-BookLog (266-5564)

Or fax orders to
1-419-281-6883

Or order on our website at
www.TwoHeartsPress.com

D E D I C A T E D
T O
Help of Christians
&
Salvation of Believers

WHAT PEOPLE ARE SAYING ABOUT THIS BOOK:

May This Book Reach As Many People As Possible!
Rev. Fr. Mhar Vincent Balili, Secretary of Cardinal Vidal

BOOK OF THE YEAR!
I recommend you get this book and read it.
I would even go so far as to say I implore you to read it.
Jerry Morin, Director, Servants to the World

Highly Recommended! A Must Read!
This book will probably sell like 'hot cakes'.
Deacon John Giglio, Internet Blog Host

A Book You Will Read More Than Once - You have my word!
I COULD NOT put it down. It kept my interest from beginning to end... Do yourself a favor and get this book. I promise you will not be disappointed.
Fr. Neil Buchlein, Pastor of Ascension Catholic Church in Hurricane, West Virginia, and Marian Internet Host

A Real Page-Turner!
This book needs to be read by every Catholic.
It will inspire you! I cannot praise it enough.
David T. Little, President, World St. Thomas More Society

The BEST book that I have read in the last 5 years, possibly, in the last 10!
Anthony P. Rocha, St. Stanislaus Parish, Bay City, MI

THE BEST CATHOLIC BOOK I HAVE EVER READ!
Don Riemer, Adoration Coordinator, St. Mary's Milwaukee, WI

4

CONTENTS

The Woman
& the Adversary

℘

I will put enmity between you (Satan)
and the woman (Mary),
and between your seed and her seed;
he shall bruise your head, and you shall bruise his heel.
Genesis 3:15

And a great portent appeared in heaven,
a woman (Mary) clothed with the sun,
with the moon under her feet,
and on her head a crown of twelve stars.
Revelation 12:1

It will never be too late to have recourse to Jesus and Mary.
Jesus to Lucia of Fatima

This book is *not* about the end of the world. This book is about hope and renewal. It is about the time we are living in now – a time of crisis and upheaval that will lead to divine renewal – like no other time in history. This book is about heavenly prophecy and about preparing for what is to come upon humanity in our time.

In the Bible, Jesus Christ and His Apostles foretell the apocalyptic times. Today, Christ and His Mother have been appearing from Heaven through apparitions and miraculous events that are occurring throughout the world to tell us that we are living in the times prophesied in the Bible. God is warning us that our times are *a thousand times worse than at the time of the flood* and that His divine mercy wants to bring humanity to reconciliation and restoration.

Increasingly in recent times, God has been communicating with the human race, particularly through the Blessed Mother, offering us a single and important heavenly message for our times. All of the major Marian revelations and apparitions of the past century, and in an ever-more culminating way, have been calling humanity to prepare for the times we are now approaching. It makes sense that the most important issue of our times is the one that Heaven has been focusing on, and repeating with greater emphasis, over the past century – and it's all about *our* time. This being so, one could say that **this message from Heaven is in some ways *the most important issue of our day*.** This book discusses biblical prophecy within the context of Tradition, Church teaching, and private revelation. It brings together themes of various sources of heavenly prophecies and presents them in a unified way to offer a comprehensive overview of God's plan for these most important times. God is calling us to prepare for the time of His justice and renewal, and this book discusses God's plan for *our* times.

Church Support for Heavenly Messages

Our Blessed Mother is coming from Heaven to give apparitions and messages to her children all over the world in this time. In this Age of Mary, the Mother of God is speaking to *us*. How are we to respond to her call? Catholics are not required to believe in a miraculous origin for the events of apparitions and locutions, even in those approved by the Church. The Church designates such approved events as *"worthy of belief."* While the faithful are not required in the strict sense to assent to and honor Marian apparitions, on the other hand, a dismissive approach is not helpful.

Since Jesus is sending His Mother from Heaven to speak with us, to warn us, to call us to conversion and holiness, as her spiritual children, it rightly behooves us to respond with child-like simplicity, and **to say *"yes"* to our heavenly Mother and thus to listen to and obey what she is asking of us**. This does not mean that we become imprudent. Discernment and prayer is always needed, with obedience to the Church. The best approach is to be cautious and discerning, but open and welcoming, of heavenly prophecy. St. Paul says: *"Do not quench the Spirit, do not despise prophesying, but test everything; hold fast what is good."*[1]

There have been many books and articles written about apparitions and prophecy. Some books focus on a particular apparition, while this book seeks to discuss heavenly prophecy from several, solid prophetic sources – so as to provide stronger evidence that such messages really are from God and to provide a more comprehensive picture of the overall heavenly plan for our time. This book seeks to weave pieces of the tapestry of heavenly prophecy together to make a whole and complete picture of what Heaven is saying to us. Other books offer speculations concerning prophecies. It is essential to make a distinction between prophetic messages from God and the speculations people draw from them. A simple review of the commentary concerning prophecy that is available quickly leads us to see that bad speculation is not lacking. But it is important not to discount authentic heavenly messages altogether simply because of bad or false speculations related to them. This book seeks to avoid such confusion by minimizing speculation and by focusing on the prophecies themselves.

There have been hundreds of reported apparitions in our times.[2] Some apparitions are Church approved, others are not fully approved and not otherwise condemned, and others, are still occurring, which usually means that they are not yet eligible for officially recognized approval until after they are completed. Some apparitions are also disapproved or condemned by the Church, deemed not to be super-natural in origin or not worthy of belief. The final and decisive judgment of apparitions, including those discussed in this book, belongs exclusively to the Supreme Magisterium of the Church. This author accepts any decision of the Magisterium fully, from the moment it shall be pronounced.

It is important to note that it is not against the Church or her canon law to read and meditate on reliable apparitions and their messages, even on the ones that have not been officially fully approved by the Church, provided they have not been condemned and do not in any way disagree with doctrine and Church teaching. Pope Urban VIII also gave sound advice about following reported, reliable heavenly apparitions, saying: *"In cases like this, it is better to believe than not to believe, for, if you believe, and it is proven true, you will be happy that you have believed, because Our Holy Mother asked it. If you believe, and it should be proven false, you will receive all blessings as if it had been true, because you believed it to be true."*

The criteria used to establish reliability for devotion lies in the sources. This book discusses various heavenly prophesies and messages by using three groups of reliable sources: 1) the Bible, the Popes, and the Saints; 2) Major and well-known Church-approved apparitions, like Fatima and Lourdes, where the Blessed Mother has appeared from Heaven; and 3) Various reported heavenly prophecies from lesser known or more recent sources which have received positive recognition from the Church.

This book relies on solid sources that are trustworthy. This can also be said of the third group of sources as mentioned above. Within this third group of sources, *this book only includes sources that have currently received a positive statement from a Bishop of the Church* (though this does not mean to imply that they have received full-Church approval yet). Before we go on to discuss the prophecies and details provided by this third group of sources as we will later do in this book, it is important to discuss in what way they particularly have been judged to be reliable sources in the first place. We will now briefly mention the current support of the Church's Bishops, as the successors of Peter who have the authority of the Church in these matters, concerning the following reported and lesser known prophecies and heavenly events: Medjugorje, La Salette, Our Lady of America, Garabandal, Akita, Our Lady of Good Success, Our Lady of All Nations, as well as concerning Fr. Gobbi, Anne, Audrey Santo, and Luisa Piccarreta.

Medjugorje

Our Lady has been reportedly appearing and giving messages in Medjugorje since 1981. The Vatican's Secretary of State Cardinal Tarcisio Bertone wrote an official letter confirming that **private pilgrimages to Medjugorje are permitted**. He also stated that the opinions of Bishop Ratko Peric, the current Bishop of Mostar, who has spoken negatively about these apparitions, are to be treated strictly *"as his personal opinion"* and thus as having no official authority. In April, 2008, it became public that the question of the authenticity of the apparitions of Medjugorje shifted directly into the hands of the Vatican. The apparitions will not be accepted or rejected by local or regional Church officials until they are directed how and when to do so by Rome. *"I can confirm it,"* states Monsignor Mato Zovkic, vicar general of the Sarajevo archdiocese. Headed by Cardinal Vinko Puljić, the national commission based in Sarajevo was formed after the Vatican took away the authority of discernment from the local bishop, who usually rules on such matters. And now the national commission has also been subjected to higher Church authorities. The vicar emphasized that the national commission no longer plans to take action until it hears direct instructions from the Vatican.[3] Thus, the Church is currently permitting the faithful to read, meditate on, and spread the messages of Medjugorje, and to make private pilgrimages there.

Blessed John Paul II wrote in his own hand, *"I thank Sophia (a friend) for everything concerning Medjugorje. I, too, go there everyday as a pilgrim in my prayers."* He also said: *"Medjugorje is the hope for the entire world, the spiritual heart of the world."*

Blessed Mother Teresa, again in her own hand, wrote: *"We are all praying one Hail Mary before Holy Mass to Our Lady of Medjugorje!"*

Fr. Gabriele Amorth, official exorcist of the Diocese of Rome who has performed more than 30,000 exorcisms, wrote, *"Medjugorje is a fortress against Satan. Satan hates Medjugorje because it is a place of conversion, of prayer, of transformation of life."*

Hundreds of cardinals and bishops, and tens of thousands of priests, have either personally visited Medjugorje as pilgrims or expressed their appreciation for this fountain of grace, and that the vast majority explicitly proclaims that the Blessed Mother is appearing in

Medjugorje, so says Denis Nolan in his book: *Medjugorje and the Church*. Numerous bishops and cardinals have expressed appreciation for this book. For example, Cardinal Francis Arinze has written from the Vatican: *"May God Bless you for the great diligence put into producing this well documented work which I shall read with great interest."*

There have been some recent positive developments as well. In January 2010, Cardinal Christoph Schönborn of Vienna, a long-time personal supporter of Medjugorje, was in Medjugorje on a "private" visit and celebrated midnight New Year's Eve Mass in the parish church lending his personal support to the visionaries. In early 2010, the Vatican appointed Cardinal Ruini to lead a commission to study the supernatural events reportedly going on there.

So, to date, there are over 10,000 messages from Heaven; over 300,000 bishops, priests, and religious have gone to Medjugorje; and over 30 million people have visited there since the apparitions began!

La Salette

Our Lady appeared and gave messages in La Salette. The secrets of Our Lady of La Salette were recently published in April, 2002, in a book, with a Bishop's *imprimatur,* entitled *Discovery of the Secret of La Salette,* by Fathers René Laurentin and Michel Corteville, intended for the general public on authenticity of the Secret of La Salette.

The last version of the secret, the longest, that of 1879, received the *imprimatur* of Bishop Zola, bishop of Lecce, Italy.

Our Lady of America

In the United States, Our Lady has given messages for our times and for our country. This devotion to the Blessed Virgin Mary under the title of Our Lady of America enjoys canonical approval through former Archbishop of Cincinnati, Ohio, the late Paul Francis Leibold. Through his written correspondence and public actions, Archbishop Leibold approved for public devotion this private apparition of the Blessed Virgin Mary to Sister Mary Ephrem (Mildred Neuzil). Archbishop Leibold approved Sister's initial writings and placed his imprimatur on the design of the medal.

Furthermore, many other Bishops have also shown their approval by their promotion of this devotion. The Most Reverend Raymond L. Burke, (former) Archbishop of Saint Louis, a canon lawyer, issued a letter opinion on Our Lady of America. In his letter dated May 31, 2007, he reviewed the history of Our Lady of America and the actions of Archbishop Leibold approving this devotion. From Archbishop Burke: *"What can be concluded canonically is that the devotion was both approved by Archbishop Leibold and, what is more, was actively promoted by him. In addition, over the years, other Bishops have approved the devotion and have participated in public devotion to the Mother of God, under the title of Our Lady of America."[4]*

Sr. Mary Ephram was told by Our Lady of America: *"America, the United States in particular, is being given the tremendous, yet privileged opportunity to lead all nations in a spiritual renewal never before so necessary, so important, so vital."* Mary said that she was coming to America now as a last resort. Sr. Mary Ephram wrote that Mary *"promised that **greater miracles than those granted at Lourdes and Fatima** would be granted here in America, the United States in particular, if we would do as she desires."* Mary promised *"miracles of the soul."* Our Lady taught Sr. Mary Ephram to pray: *"By the Holy and Immaculate Conception, O Mary, deliver us from evil."* On the fifty-third anniversary of Our Lady of America, Our Lady told Sr. Mary Ephram: *"From the beginning of time **every prophecy, every vision**, throughout the centuries, **will have its fulfillment in Our Lady of America and her message of the Indwelling Trinity living in every soul**, which will renew the whole world and destroy Lucifer and all the evil spirits in the fight he is making against the Indwelling Trinity."*

Garabandal

Our Lady reportedly appeared in Garabandal giving messages and prophecies. The Archbishop of Oviedo, Carlos Osoro Sierra, who is Apostolic Administrator of the region of Garabandal (Santander, Spain), said in May 2007: *"I respect the apparitions and have known of authentic conversions… I encourage you to continue maintaining this devotion to our Mother."*

Visionary Conchita was received in a private audience with Pope Paul VI, who said: *"Conchita I bless you and with me the whole Church blesses you."*

Akita

Our Lady appeared to a Catholic nun in Akita and spoke of prophecies to come. On April 22, 1984, after an investigation of over ten years, Bishop John Shojiro Ito of Niigata declared: *"I recognize the supernatural character of a series of mysterious events concerning the (weeping) statue of the Holy Mother Mary... Consequently, I authorize ... the veneration of the Holy Mother of Akita."* The Bishop also stated: *"As for the content of the messages received... when one thinks of the actual state of the world, the warning seems to correspond to it in many points."*

Our Lady of Good Success

Centuries ago, Our Lady appeared to a Catholic nun and gave her little-known prophecies that were to occur in our day at the end of the twentieth century. Bishop Salvador de Ribera of Quito gave ecclesiastical approval of this devotion on February 2, 1611, the day of the formal institution of the official devotion. This message, particularly the novena prayer, received ecclesiastical approval again recently by Archbishop Carlos Maria of Quito (July 31, 1941).

Our Lady of All Nations

Our Lady appeared in Amsterdam and asked for the Church to declare a final Marian dogma. On October 4, 1997, the Bishop and Auxiliary Bishop of the Diocese of Haarlem-Amsterdam declared the following: *"I am pleased to support the veneration of Mary under the title "Lady of All Nations," which Bishop Bomers and myself have approved for the Diocese of Haarlem-Amsterdam. I am furthermore pleased to encourage the action of the Lady of All Nations, the goal of which is spreading her image and prayer throughout the world. This prayer has already received more than sixty imprimaturs and is translated into over sixty languages."* This statement was signed: Jozef M. Punt, Auxiliary Bishop, Diocese of Haarlem-Amsterdam, Haarlem, Netherlands, October 4, 1997.

On May 31, 2002, Jozef M. Punt, Bishop of Haarlem/Amsterdam, officially recognized the supernatural origin of the apparitions, thereby approving the apparitions, saying: *"I have come to the conclusion that the apparitions of the Lady of All Nations in Amsterdam consist of a supernatural origin... The devotion to the Lady of All Nations can help us, in my sincere conviction, in guiding us on the right path during the present serious drama of our times, the path to a new and special outpouring of the Holy Spirit, Who alone can heal the great wounds of our times."*

Fr. Gobbi of the Marian Movement of Priests

Fr. Stefano Gobbi has reportedly received internal messages called locutions from Mary. An interior locution is a mystical word or message received interiorly by a person while in prayer and which to them is clearly not from their own mind or spirit, but in this case, from Mary. As with all mystical phenomenons, the final judgment of the claimed mysticism of Fr. Gobbi rests with the Church.[5] His book, *"To the Priests, Our Lady's Beloved Sons,"* has received the *Imprimatur* of three Cardinals: the late Cardinal Echeverria of Ecuador, Cardinal Vidal of the Philippines and Cardinal Mikaï of Thailand. It also has the *Imprimatur* of many archbishops and bishops worldwide. Fr. Gobbi founded the Marian Movement of Priests as a private association of Catholic clergy and lay associate members.

"Anne" & Direction for Our Times

"Anne" reportedly receives messages from Heaven through interior locution. She has been asked by Our Lord to remain anonymous, is entirely obedient to the Church, and has the approval of her local bishop, Bishop Leo O'Reilly of the Diocese of Kilmore in Ireland. Bishop Emeritus Federico Escaler, S.J. from the Philippines also granted his Imprimatur, in September 2005. Her messages, which are distributed by *Direction For Our Times*, are one of a heavenly call to action. They are urgent messages from God announcing that He is reclaiming His kingdom from the darkness that has spread over the earth. Through Anne, Jesus is asking us to join Him as lay apostles, helping Him in the great work of renewal that will convert millions of people worldwide.

Audrey Santo

Audrey Santo was blessed to receive many miraculous phenomenon and events during her short life at her home in the United States. As an example of extraordinary events, during a Mass being celebrated by Bishop Flanagan in the presence of Audrey, while by her bed in her home, a consecrated Communion Host miraculously bled.

Bishop McManus of Worcester, in a supportive way, wrote after Audrey died, about her, saying: *"We may never fully understand the causes of various paranormal events which have been reported... God works in mysterious ways."* In 2008, he recognized a foundation for the promotion of the cause of her canonization.

Luisa Piccarreta

Servant of God Luisa Piccarreta, a twentieth century mystic, received many messages from God concerning His Holy Will. On October 29, 2005, Archbishop Giovan Battista Pichierri concluded the Diocesan phase for the Cause of Beatification and Canonization of the Servant of God, Luisa Piccarreta, Little Daughter of the Divine Will. The Cause has now been officially transferred to the Vatican for the

Roman phase of the beatification process; and the two Vatican designated theologians assigned to review her writings have both recently granted them a positive recognition (summer 2010). *"I know my days will not end until I see her exalted to the honor of the altar as, without any shadow of doubt, she deserves,"* says Archbishop Guiseppe Carata, Archbishop Emeritus of Trani/Bari/Bisceglie and co-founder of the canonically approved Luisa Piccarreta Association. Luisa's extraordinary confessor for over 17 years and the ecclesiastical approver (*nihil obstat*) of her initial mystical writings himself has already become a canonized saint, St. Hannibal Mary di Francia. Concerning the heavenly messages given through Luisa, Our Lord declared: ***"Spread these writings! Spread these writings!"*** He is saying the same to us today!

We will discuss the messages received from these sources, as well as the other two groups of sources mentioned above, throughout this book.

Heavenly Prophesies

& Heaven's Call to Respond

This book has two main themes. First, it chronicles how the divine prophesies of our times will unfold in three phases: the time of **the secrets (chapter 1)**, the period of **the chastisement (chapter 3)**, **and** era of **the triumph of Jesus and Mary (chapter 5)**. It should be noted that for a continuous, uninterrupted portrayal of prophetic events to come, these three chapters may be read together. We are today experiencing a crescendo of heavenly prophesies about our times and concerning what is to come. As coming from such vast and differing sources, these heavenly prophesies are interwoven in this book, to show a consistency without contradiction and to give a full picture of God's plan for our times. It is however most important to recognize at this point that the future is unpredictable, as no man knows the future.[6] There is always an element of contingency with prophecy, such that its fulfillment may be altered through the response of man and the mercy of God. Ultimately, the future lies in God's Providence. To remain balanced, we must look always to the Lord, and place all of our trust in Him. Jesus promises: *"When the Spirit of truth comes... he will declare to you the things that are to come."*[7]

Second, beyond simply discussing prophetic events to come, this book is a call to prepare -- to answer *the heavenly call of Our Lady to her spiritual children to assist her in crushing the head of Satan* in three ways: by following Church authority and teaching by answering the heavenly call of **faith and conversion (chapter 2)**, by offering our lives in sacrifice as witnesses of **hope and consecration (chapter 4)**, and by uniting with the Two Hearts of Jesus and Mary in a life of **love and reparation (chapter 6)**. As God has been gradually revealing what is to come, He has also been *calling us* to focus our preparation on the spiritual rather than the physical, and on prayer rather than on fear. And in many ways, this second part of the book is the most important, as it directly affects the first part, which God seems to have conditioned upon our response of faith, our prayers of hope, and our acts of love. This book will discuss God's plan for us during the preparation, the crisis, and the great divine renewal to come in our times.

Unlike any other time in the history of the Church, the Blessed Mother has been appearing from Heaven through apparitions to various chosen persons in our times. She has been appearing all over the world and to such a large number of people that this time has been called *The Age of Mary*. These modern Marian apparitions reveal messages, not just about the crisis that is coming, but about *what we are being called to do about it.* Pope John Paul II, as Karol Cardinal Wojtyla, spoke these words during a visit to the United States in 1976:

> **We are now standing in the face of the greatest historical confrontation humanity has gone through.** *I do not think that wide circles of the American society or wide circles of the Christian community realize this fully.* **We are now facing the final confrontation between the Church and the anti-Church,** *of the Gospel versus the anti-Gospel.* **This confrontation lies within the plans of Divine Providence**... *It is a test of 2,000 years of culture and Christian civilization with all of its consequences for human dignity, individual rights, human rights and the rights of nations.*[8]

At the same time, we must not be surprised that *"these very grave signs, which [Our Lady] is giving [us] today, are neither accepted nor given credence (by many), but on the contrary are openly opposed and rejected."*[9] This has not been helpful, and seems to actually assist the Adversary. Fr. Gobbi of the Marian Movement of Priests reportedly received messages (locutions) from Our Lady from 1973 to 1997, and through him Mary gave the following advice: ***"Do not be surprised, beloved ones, that my Adversary has done everything he can to obstruct this work of mine.*** *His favorite weapon is to sow doubts and perplexity about what I am doing in the Church. He tries to base these doubts on reasons which are seemingly solid and justifiable. Thus he instills a certain critical attitude toward whatever I tell you, even before you have received and understood my words."*[10]

The Apocalypse

We are living in the times spiritually prophesied by the beloved Apostle of Jesus, St. John, in the last book of the Bible, the Book of Revelation (*The* Apocalypse). It appears by many accounts, such as we shall discuss, that the cosmic disruptions foretold beginning in Revelation Chapter Four have begun. About this time which has begun, Revelation threatens: *"For the great day of [His] wrath has come, and who can stand before it?"*[11] The Apocalypse is unfolding and will unfold in our lifetime, and soon. **The first series of apocalyptic events** include the seven seals and the seven angels with their seven trumpets (Revelation 4-11). These disruptions provoked by God's justice include natural and human calamities that cause great destruction, caused by the spiritual rottenness and excessive decadence of the sins of humanity. This in turn will lead to external invasions, all of which will cause the annihilation of a third of humanity (Revelation 9:18). Even despite these things, Revelation warns that much of mankind will refuse to repent.[12] At this time, the Church will go through a great persecution, but she shall remain strong from within with a faithful remnant (Revelation 11), and the Two Witnesses of Revelation will actively attest to her in truth and love.

The Two Witnesses

The faithful are being warned about this time, and how to prepare for it, both from the Book of Revelation and from modern heavenly prophesies. **God has given His prophetic Word and has especially sent His divine Son's Mother as the Prophetess of our times** to prepare and console us during this time of struggle, persecution and oppression, and to reassure us that we are invited to share in the victory of *"the Woman and her Son"* against the wickedness and snares of Satan and his minions (Revelation 12). **This is the time of the triumph of the Immaculate Heart of Mary, the Woman of Revelation, and of the Church.**

The prophecy of the Two Witnesses spoken of in the Book of Revelation has been interpreted, in a spiritual sense, to refer to the heavenly revelations and call of the Two Hearts of Jesus and Mary.

The Two Hearts Message and Devotion is the last great request of God to bring us His love and mercy in these critical times, before the Great Tribulation that will come before the New Time of Peace.

So many of the signs of these Two Witnesses that have been given in our times have been rejected, scorned and ignored. This reminds us of the eleventh chapter of Apocalypse regarding the Two Witnesses who in a spiritual sense represent Mary and Jesus with the apostolic mission in our times of Elijah (representing prophecy) and Moses (representing the divine law). In our times of mercy, God is giving us the remedy of hope. God is offering us peace, reconciliation, and infinite love. We who are faithful should not fear, as the Lord wishes to console us through the Two Hearts.

The devil has declared war on the faithful offspring of the Church and on the spiritual children of Mary.[13] In our time, the *"Dragon"* of Revelation has now begun to attack the *"Woman"* of the Church and make war against her, but the children of the *"Woman"* who is Mary have already gone with her into the desert of prayer to draw strength for the battle. And these consecrated souls will continue to cause Satan to be thwarted at every turn.

In **the second series of apocalyptic events**, Satan will more and more in our time make war against the *"saints"* with the use of the beast, the false prophet, and the rise of a new Babylon (Revelation 13-19), the latter of which will be called *"the great city"* and The Mother of Harlots and of the Abominations of the Earth (Revelation 17). By her sorcery the nations will be deceived; they will commit *"fornication"* with her, and the merchants will become rich through her abundance. In this new Babylon, there will be found the blood of prophets, saints, and all those slain on the earth. Revelation tells us of their plan and of their ultimate defeat: *"They will make war on the Lamb, and the Lamb will conquer them, for he is Lord of lords and King of kings, and those with him are called and chosen and faithful."*[14] Despite the evil undertakings of the New Babylon, a remnant faithful will continue to worship the Lord – while remaining faithful to the Church's teachings, obedient in keeping the Lord's commandments, and zealous in spreading the Gospel (Revelation 14), as part of the New Evangelization. **"Here is a call for the endurance and faith of the saints... those who keep the commandments of God and the faith of Jesus."**[15]

Armageddon

After the Great Persecution, then God will avenge His persecuted faithful ones and call sinners to repentance by bringing upon humanity seven final plagues (Revelation 15-16), the first of which according to Fr. Gobbi is already prefigured in the form of cancer and AIDS.[16] The faithful of God will be called at this point to *"come out of Babylon"* lest they too receive the final plagues. The spirits of demons will retaliate by bringing together the world's leaders to a battle at the place called Armageddon. WWI, Hitler, Communism, 09-11-01, the great

However, neither malady was the cause of his collapse. Instead, he had just received **a vision of the future of the Church**. After a few minutes spent in what seemed like a coma, he revived and remarked to those around him, *"Oh, what a horrible picture I was permitted to see!"* During Pope Leo's ecstasy, he heard two voices, one deep and coarse, which he understood to be Satan challenging the other voice, Jesus. The conversation reportedly went like this:

Satan: *"Given enough time and enough power, I can destroy your Church."*

Jesus: *"How much time and how much power?"*

Satan: *"100 years and a greater power over those who will give themselves to my service."*

Jesus: *"You have the time and you will have the power."*

What Leo XIII saw, as described later by those who talked to him at the time of his vision, was a period of about one hundred years when the power of Satan would reach its zenith. That period has become known as The Hundred Years' Reign of Satan. Leo XIII was so shaken by the vision of the depravity of moral and spiritual values both inside and outside the Church that he immediately composed a prayer that he then had said at the end of each Mass celebrated in the Catholic Church. **The Prayer of St. Michael the Archangel** was hence said continuously, until the Mass was revised in the Second Vatican Council. It is still an important part of the Rosary prayer today. Pius XI had asked that it be prayed for the conversion of Russia, and John Paul II spoke of the continued importance of this prayer in our times, saying: *"The Book of Revelation refers to [the] battle, recalling before our eyes the image of St. Michael the Archangel (Revelation 12:7). Pope Leo XIII certainly had a very vivid recollection of this scene when, at the end of the [nineteenth] century, he introduced a special prayer to St. Michael throughout the Church. Although this prayer is no longer recited at the end of Mass, **I ask everyone not to forget [the St. Michael Prayer] and to recite it to obtain help in the battle against forces of darkness and against the spirit of this world.***"[20] We must remember that while the devil has real power granted him by God, though it is not limitless, the Lord is all-powerful and His mercy and compassion are infinite.

The *Woman of Revelation*, the devil's foe, has not remained distant or indifferent. She has not remained quiet. Instead, Our Lady has become more and more active by way of intercession, visions, and locutions to various people throughout the world in our times, over the last century and particularly in the last few years. The Lord had told us in Scripture that in the end times He would pour out His Spirit on all mankind and that His children would prophesy, with dreams and *visions given to many*, to give humanity hope and encourage us by displaying portents in heaven and on earth.[21] These are His Signs, and they have begun to occur throughout the world in our day. The Lord has sent His Mother as the Prophetess of our times to give us dreams and visions of prophecy with miraculous portents in the skies and on the earth.

God's Warnings of Love

In the history of our salvation, God often warns His people about what is to come – He told Abraham that Israel would be in slavery for 400 years, He told Moses that Israel would be in the desert for 40 years, and He told Peter that he would deny Him three times. God did this to give His people hope in the midst of crisis and punishment. He promised that after such difficult times, He would intervene and save His people. And so shall it be in our times.

In our times, Christ is sending His own Mother to warn us and to call us to conversion in this most dramatic moment in history. God is offering us secrets of our times and of what is to come upon us, especially concerning periods of crisis, precisely to give us hope, to call us to be prepared, and to console us, with His promise that in the end He will bring His people through to safety and to a great new day. The best response we can possibly make is to confirm whose side we are on by acts of conversion, consecration, and reparation to the Lord with the assistance of Our Lady's holy love.

PREFACE
The Woman & The Adversary

Jesus, Mary, I love you, save souls.
Let us eternally adore the Holy Sacrament through Mary.
To the Two Hearts of Jesus and Mary be honor and glory.
Let the Kingdom of the Divine Will (Fiat) come!

Prayer to St. Michael

Saint Michael the Archangel,
defend us in battle;
be our protection against the wickedness
and snares of the devil.
May God rebuke him,
we humbly pray;
and do thou, O Prince of the heavenly Host,
by the power of God,
cast into hell Satan
and all the other evil spirits who prowl about the world
seeking the ruin of souls. Amen.

I

FAITH FOR BEFORE

I desire for you to comprehend that I want to realize here…
a meeting of hearts.
I desire for my, Jesus', and YOUR heart **to become one heart**
of love and peace.
Our Lady of Medjugorje

I was already convinced that Mary
leads us to Jesus, her Son.
Now I am convinced that in this time
Jesus leads us also to Mary, His mother.
John Paul II

Now the Spirit expressly says that **in latter times** *some will depart from*
the faith by giving heed to deceitful spirits and doctrines of demons
through the pretensions of liars…
But understand this,
that in the last days there will come times of stress.
For men will be **lovers of self**, **lovers of money**, *proud, arrogant,*
abusive, disobedient to their parents, ungrateful, unholy, inhuman,
implacable, slanderers, profligates, fierce, haters of good, treacher-
ous, reckless, swollen with conceit, **lovers of pleasure** *rather than*
lovers of God, holding the form of religion but denying the power of it.
Avoid such people.
1 Timothy 4:1-2, 2 Timothy 3:1-5

The Secrets
&
Age of Prophecy

CB

Surely the Lord God does nothing,
without revealing His secret to His servants the prophets.
Amos 3:7

Pray that you may comprehend the greatness of this message
which I am giving you…
Read Sacred Scripture, live it,
and pray to understand the signs of the time.
Our Lady of Medjugorje

The new springtime that will follow this time of great tribulation
will be wondrous. John Paul II, who has been called the greatest
evangelist in recent times and the Great Initiator and Angel of the New
Evangelization, of planetary evangelization, prophesied about the era
of peace to come as we crossed the threshold of hope into the Third
Christian Millennium.[1] I recall personally how inspiring he was when

my wife and I were present at World Youth Day in Denver (1993), when he called out to us with a proclamation and mission, saying: *"**Do not be afraid** to go out on the streets and into public places like the first apostles who preached Christ and the good news of salvation in the squares of cities, towns, and villages. This is no time to be ashamed of the Gospel... **It is the time to preach** it from the rooftops."*

John Paul II called the time just before the beginning of the Third Christian Millennium *"a New Advent, a season of expectation,"* a time of great graces and mercy. It was ***"the dawn of a new era of evangelization,"*** of which *"the tears of (the twentieth) century have prepared the ground for a new springtime of the human spirit."* About what is soon to come, John Paul said, *"God is preparing a great springtime for Christianity."* He reminded us that *"even if in the world evil should prevail over goodness, even if contemporary humanity should deserve a new 'flood' on account of its sins,"* we must steadfastly hope in the *"new Pentecost"* to come. He said that even now we must be about the work *"of building a new civilization, the civilization of love."* Giving some details of areas to focus on, he said: *"As the new evangelization unfolds, it must include a special emphasis on the family and the renewal of Christian marriage, [and it also] calls for followers of Christ who are unconditionally pro-life."* Entrusting ourselves to Divine Providence, John Paul reminded us that **this is no time *"for despair or pessimism or inertia."*** [2]

Highly regarded French anthropologist, René Girard, seems to agree with John Paul when he made a hopeful assessment about the near future, stating: *"I believe that we are on the eve of a revolution in our culture that will go beyond any expectation, and that the world is heading toward a change in respect of which the Renaissance will seem like nothing. [We are headed toward] a world that will seem and be as Christian as today it seems scientific."*[3] But, before the day of peace, there will come the day of justice and tribulation. We again hear John Paul the Great calling us to the great commission of our times: *"Do not be afraid! Open wide the doors to Christ."*

Our Lady of Good Success

God has been warning of the times we are currently living in for centuries through His prophets, mystics, and visionaries. About four hundred years ago, a religious, Ven. Mother Mariana de Jesus Torres, whose body is now incorrupt, received Church-approved private revelations from the Virgin Mary under the title of Our Lady of Good Success. Mother Mariana de Jesus was a mystic, prophetess, seer, and victim soul, who lived in Quito, Ecuador during its foundation as a Colony of Spain. Through her, Our Lady prophesies how the faithful would lose the Faith and how Satan will be allowed to reign *especially and specifically in the twentieth century.*[4] Dear reader, do you understand that hundreds of years ago, Our Lady gave warning to a nun about the evil times to come so far into the future? And that those times are *now!*

What is so amazing about the prophetic messages of Our Lady of Good Success is how detailed and accurate they were concerning our times, even though they were given from Heaven in the seventeenth century. Mary warned that various unfaithful religious, who, *"under the appearance of virtue and bad-spirited zeal, would turn upon Religion, who nourished them at her breast."* Our Lady prophesied details about the loss of faith, the failure of Church leaders to hand on the truths of Faith, the resulting spiritual and doctrinal crisis that would ensue, and the rampant lack of regard the faithful would have for the Sacraments, and that all this would occur universally during the twentieth century. Our Lady also said that these little-known heavenly messages would not be known by the faithful until the time when they were already being fulfilled. And only now they are becoming known! Mary prophesied as follows:

> *During this time... the Sacrament of **Anointing of the Sick** will be little esteemed. Many people will die without receiving it – either because of the negligence of their families or their false sentimentality that tries to protect the sick from seeing the gravity of their situations, or because they will rebel against the spirit of the Catholic Church, impelled by the malice of the devil. Thus many souls will be deprived of innumerable graces, consolations and the strength they need to make that great leap from time to eternity.*

> *As for the Sacrament of **Matrimony**, which symbolizes the union of Christ with His Church, it will be attacked and*

profaned in the fullest sense of the word. Masonry, which will then be in power, will enact iniquitous laws with the objective of doing away with this Sacrament, making it easy for everyone to live in sin, encouraging the procreation of illegitimate children born without the blessing of the Church. The effects of secular education will increase, which will be one reason for the lack of priestly and religious vocations.

*The Sacred Sacrament of **Holy Orders** will be ridiculed, oppressed and despised... The demon will try to persecute the Ministers of the Lord in every possible way and he will labor with cruel and subtle astuteness to deviate them from the spirit of their vocation, corrupting many of them. These corrupted priests, who will scandalize the Christian people, will incite the hatred of the bad Christians and the enemies of the Roman, Catholic and Apostolic Church to fall upon all priests. This apparent triumph of Satan will bring enormous sufferings to the good Pastors of the Church.*

*Moreover, in these unhappy times, there will be **unbridled luxury** which, acting thus to snare the rest into sin, will conquer innumerable frivolous souls who will be lost. Innocence will almost no longer be found in children, nor modesty in women, and in this supreme moment of the need of the Church, **those who should speak will fall silent.***

*But know, beloved daughter, that when your name is made known in the twentieth century, **there will be many who will not believe, claiming that this devotion is not pleasing to God.***

A simple humble faith in the truth of My apparitions to you, My predilect child, will be reserved for humble and fervent souls docile to the inspirations of grace, for Our Heavenly Father communicates His secrets to the simple of heart, and not to those whose hearts are inflated with pride, pretending to know what they do not, or self-satisfied with empty knowledge.

The secular Clergy will leave much to be desired because priests will become careless in their sacred duties. Lacking the divine compass, they will stray from the road traced by God for the priestly ministry, and they will become attached to wealth and riches, which they will unduly strive to obtain. How the Church will suffer during this dark night! Lacking a Prelate and Father to guide them with paternal love, gentleness, strength, wisdom and prudence, many priests will lose their spirit, placing their souls in great danger. This will mark the arrival of my hour.

Therefore, clamor insistently without tiring and weep with bitter tears in the privacy of your heart, imploring our Celestial Father that, for love of the Eucharistic Heart of my

Most Holy Son and His Precious Blood shed with such gener-osity and the profound bitterness and sufferings of His cruel Passion and Death, He might take pity on His ministers and bring to an end those Ominous times, sending to this Church the Prelate who will restore the spirit of its priests.

*As these heresies spread and dominate, the precious light of Faith will be extinguished in souls by the **almost total cor-ruption** of customs. During this period, **there will be great physical and moral calamities**, both public and private.*

In this seventeenth century apparition of Our Lady of Good Success, she spoke of *our* times. Our Lady warned that during our time, a worldwide campaign against the virtues of chastity and purity would succeed in ruining the youth. Our Lady of Good Success spoke of the extent of this tragedy, saying, *"**There will be almost no virgin souls in the world**... During these unfortunate times, evil will invade childhood innocence."* Further, Our Lady of Good Success warned that there will be laxity and gross negligence from *"**those who possess great wealth who will indifferently stand by** and witness the Church being op-pressed, virtue being persecuted, and the triumph of the demon,"* and they will thus make themselves guilty of *not "piously employing their riches for the destruction of this evil and the restoration of the Faith."*

The Crisis in the Family

In the Church-approved apparitions of **Our Lady of America (twentieth century)**, **Jesus spoke about the growing crisis of the family**, saying:

I am not loved in the homes of men. And because I am not loved, the Divine Trinity refuses to dwell therein.

Children are not taught to love Me, because those who have charge over them have no time or patience to do so.

***Woe to the parents** who set a bad example to their children! Terrible will be their judgment. I will demand a strict account of every soul entrusted to their care.*

Woe to parents who teach their children how to gain materially in this world and neglect to prepare them for the next!

***Woe to children** who disobey and show disrespect towards their parents!*

"Honor thy father and thy mother." On this shall they be judged most severely.

***Blessed are the homes** that honor My Name and the Name of My Father.*

Blessed are the homes where I am loved, for there the Holy Trinity dwells.

Blessed are the parents and children who have made a home for God in their hearts.[5]

Reason to Believe

The Renewal will indeed begin soon, and Heaven wants to give great graces, for all good things, especially in this time of preparation. In our times as never before in history, God wishes to establish the Triumph and Reign of the Two Hearts – the Triumph of the Sorrowful and Immaculate Heart of Mary and the Reign of the Eucharistic and Sacred Heart of Jesus. He is calling us to live in union with His holy and divine Will at every moment so as to continually experience His holy and divine Love. The heart is a symbol of love and it is the symbol of the whole person. We honor the interior life of Jesus and Mary by honoring their united hearts. We adore and love the Most Sacred Heart of Jesus; and Mary's heart was united to the God-Man's Heart. The same wound wounded these two Hearts, united as one.

The great renewal will restore the true Faith. It will be built upon the Sacred Scriptures, salvation history, and the four pillars of the Faith as taught by the *Catechism of the Catholic Church* (the Creed, the Sacraments, Morality, and Prayer), as safeguarded by the teaching authority of the Church, that is, the Pope and the Bishops in union with him (the Magisterium).

The Two Hearts Devotion is practiced through acts of conversion, consecration, and reparation in relation with the Two Hearts of Jesus and Mary. The Lord has come among us with His Mother as our rest and consolation. Like the two great witnesses of old, Moses (the Law) and Elijah (the prophets), the Two Hearts of Jesus and Mary today are prophesying to us in a united ministry of our times.[6] They tell us that the most important preparation for this *new springtime* is the Devotion to the Two Hearts.

Devotion to the
Eucharistic & Sacred Heart of Jesus

Devotion to the Eucharistic and Sacred Heart focuses on adoration of the Incarnate Word, especially His Eucharistic Heart, which, out of love for us, He allowed to be pierced for our sins. The *Catechism* teaches that *"Jesus knew and loved us each and all during his life, his agony, and his Passion and gave himself up for each of us... He has loved us all with a human heart."*[7] His human Heart is the chief symbol of His love. **The Second Person of the Trinity knows and loves each of us with His human Heart!** In the Agony in the Garden and in His Passion, Jesus felt *every* one of our sins, in His Heart and Soul and to the depth of His Person. The Heart of Jesus symbolizes His love for us as the God-Man. Pius XII said: *"We cannot reach the Heart of God save through the Heart of Christ... Christ gave more to God than was required to compensate for the offense of the whole human race... through the infinite treasure of His merits by the shedding of His Precious Blood, [He] was able to restore completely that pact of friendship between God and man."*[8] Jesus redeemed us by taking our sins upon Himself, in His Heart. His Heart is the symbol of His unconditional love for the human race and through His Heart of

Love He redeemed the whole human race. Jesus longs to give us the most sublime secrets of His Heart, as He did St. John, the Apostle. His Heart is the *"Holy of Holies,"* the place of God's tender and sweet affection for us. Jesus wants to give us His Heart, and He wants our heart in return – an exchange of hearts in love. St. Bonaventure wrote: *"Who is there who would not love this wounded Heart? Who would not love, in return, Him Who loves so much?"*

Saints on the Sacred Heart

The Church has always venerated the Two Hearts. St. John is the first devotee of the Sacred Heart, besides of course the Blessed Mother, as seen in his resting his head on the Heart of Christ at the Last Supper, plunging his heart into the Heart of the Source of Life.[9] The next day, he also received Jesus' Mother into his heart as well. To understand this, Origen states that we must put ourselves in John's place: *"No one can grasp the meaning of the Gospel of John if he has not thrown himself on the breast of Jesus and has not received from Jesus, Mary, as Mother."*[10] In the thirteenth century, St. Gertrude received a vision of St. John, who told her: *"Let us rest on His breast in which are hidden all the treasures of blessedness."* Then he took her to our Lord and both placed themselves on our Lord's Heart. This is where she discovered the Inexhaustible Treasure He was hiding in His Heart. When she asked the Evangelist why wasn't this treasure given before or why hadn't the Evangelist spoken of this Treasure, St.

John said: *"My mission was to deliver to the Church, in her first age, a simple word on the uncreated Word of God the Father that would afford the whole of humanity enough to contemplate until the end of the world, yet without any person ever succeeding in fully grasping it. But to tell of the pulsations of the Heart of Jesus has been reserved for modern times so that, in hearing of these things, the world already old and growing cold in the love of God, may be rekindled and grow warm again."*[11]

Another Apostle, St. Thomas, continued the Devotion to the Sacred Heart, which is exemplified when he places his finger in Christ's side and believes. The Church Fathers also commented on the Sacred Heart. St. Irenaeus writes: *"The Church is the fountain of the living water that flows to us from the Heart of Christ."*[12] St. Justin Martyr writes: *"We, Christians, are the true Israel which springs from the side of Christ, for we are carved out of His Heart as from a rock."*[13] Jesus has written our names on His Heart. Like Sts. Catherine of Siena and Teresa of Avila, Blessed Henry Suso (d.1366), a Dominican, once had a vision of an Angel taking his heart from him and uniting it in rapturous love to the Heart of Jesus. The Carthusian, Ludolph of Saxony (d.1378), wrote: *"Our Lord's Heart was wounded with the wound of love for our sake, so that, loving Him in return, we might enter through that open wound into His Heart and there live inflamed with His love, just as iron cast into the fire becomes incandescent."* St. Catherine of Siena, one day said to Our Lord:

Sweet, Spotless Lamb, You were dead when Your Side was opened. Why, then, did You allow that Your Heart should be thus wounded and opened by force?

Our Lord answered:

For several reasons, of which I will tell you the principal. My desires regarding the human race were infinite and the actual time of suffering and torture was at an end. Since my love is infinite, I could not therefore by this suffering manifest to you how much I loved you. That is why I willed to reveal to you the secret of my Heart by letting you see It open, that you might well understand that It loved you far more than I could prove to you by a suffering that was over.

Thomas à Kempis contemplates the mystery of the pierced Heart, saying to himself: *"Enter then, enter thou, my soul, into the side of the crucified Lord, pass through the holy wound into the most loving Heart of Jesus, which out of love was pierced by the lance, that thou may rest in the clefts of the Rock (Cant. 2:14) from the trouble of the world."*[14] Many Protestants have a high regard for the Sacred Heart Devotion. In 1642, the Puritan Protestant, Thomas Goodwin, published a book about the Sacred Heart which was later reprinted by John Wesley, the founder of the Methodists. All we can say is: *"Heart on the Cross. Heart on the Cross."*[15]

Disciple of the Sacred Heart

A strong divine call to promote the Sacred Heart Devotion occurred when St. Margaret Mary Alacoque, the beloved disciple of the Sacred Heart, received visions of the Sacred Heart in the seventeenth century. The God-Man came to emphasize anew His compassion and mercy. Jesus told her of *"His great desire of being loved by men and of **withdrawing them from the path of ruin into which Satan hurls such crowds** of them, [one] that made Him form the design of manifesting His Heart to men, with all the treasures of love, of mercy, of grace, of sanctification and salvation."* Jesus asked to be honored in the symbol of His Heart of flesh which loves us so much.

The Lord wants to bless His people through devotion to His Sacred Heart. In the seventeenth century, Jesus asked St. Margaret Mary in an apparition for the consecration of France to His Sacred Heart. But, the French king refused to do the consecration. If the French had made the consecration, the terrible outcome of the French Revolution would have been averted. It was finally made by another king one hundred years later, but a little too late. In another account, in the eighteenth century, the Bubonic plague wiped out over half of Marseille's (France) population of 90,000 in a matter of months. It was only after the Archbishop consecrated the city to the Sacred Heart of Jesus that the plague suddenly ended without any medical means or vaccinations. This devotion has proven to be as powerful as the faith one has in the promises Jesus gave concerning it, both then and today.

Apostle of Divine Mercy

Jesus, I trust in You.
O Sacred Heart of Jesus, I place all my trust in You.
O Blood and Water, which gushed forth from the
Heart of Jesus as a fount of Mercy for us,
I trust in You.

Our Lord also appeared many times to St. Faustina, the twentieth century Polish nun who became His Apostle of Mercy. She received many private revelations from Jesus and Mary, especially concerning the Devotion to His Sacred Heart, the Fount of Mercy. He asked for her to share His great desire to give humanity His mercy, which comes to us in several ways in these latter times. Jesus revealed to her the divine decree for the Feast of Divine Mercy, which the Church has approved for the Second Sunday of Easter. He also expressed His desire to be venerated through the Image of His Sacred Heart, saying: *"I promise that the soul that will venerate this image will not perish. I also promise victory over its enemies already here on earth, especially at the hour of death. I myself will defend it as My own glory... By means of this image I shall grant many graces to souls. It is to be a reminder of the demands of My mercy, because even the strongest faith is of no avail without works."*[16] Jesus asks us to imitate Him in being merciful – in deeds, in words, and in prayer.

In this regard of the need for faith to be united with works of charity and mercy, Our Lord reminds us that we pray, *"Forgive us our sins as we forgive those who sin against us,"*[17] and to remember that *"the measure with which you measure will be measured out to you."*[18] The

Image of the pierced Side of Christ Whose Heart is pouring out Blood and Water from the Cross reminds us that Calvary is love in action, the extension of mercy. Jesus tells us, *"As I have loved you so also should you love one another."*[19] Faith without works cannot bring about salvation, as James says: *"So faith by itself, if it has no works, is dead."*[20] Jesus is asking us to live our lives in love, and to sacrifice them for others through good works of prayer and mercy. Jesus asks that we intercede to Him for nine days before the Feast of Divine Mercy (Second Sunday of Easter) for the **nine groups of people most in need of mercy and who have a right to His mercy**, which are as follows: 1) all mankind, especially sinners; 2) the souls of priests and religious; 3) all devout and faithful souls; 4) those who do not believe in Jesus and those who do not yet know Him; 5) the souls of separated brethren; 6) the meek and humble souls and the souls of children; 7) the souls who especially venerate and glorify Jesus' mercy; 8) the souls who are detained in purgatory; and 9) the souls who have become lukewarm. Jesus promises through our prayers to immerse each of them in the ocean of His mercy and grace. About the spiritually lukewarm particularly, He says: *"These souls cause Me more suffering than any others; it was from such souls that My soul felt the most revulsion in the Garden of Olives."* There is no worse state to be in than to be lukewarm.[21]

John Paul II remarked that this Devotion is *for everyone,* saying:

> ***There is nothing that man needs more than Divine Mercy*** *– that love which is benevolent, which is compassion-*

ate, which raises man above his weakness to the infinite heights of the holiness of God... (This) Message of Divine Mercy that Christ himself chose to pass on to our generation through [St.] Faustina is a message that is clear and understandable for everyone. Anyone can come here, look at this image of the merciful Jesus, His Heart radiating grace, and hear in the depths of his own soul what [St.] Faustina heard: 'Fear nothing. I am with you always' (Diary, 586). And if this person responds with a sincere heart: 'Jesus, I trust in you' (from the diary) he will find comfort in all his anxieties and fears. In this dialogue of abandonment, there is established between man and Christ a special bond that sets love free. And 'there is no fear in love, but perfect love casts out fear' (1 Jn 4:18).

God's Final Gift

The Perfect Devotion centered on the Heart of Christ is a final gift of Christ's love for humanity in these evil times, as St. Margaret Mary confirms: ***"This devotion (of His Sacred Heart is) the last effort of His love that He will grant to men in these latter ages, in order to withdraw them from the empire of Satan*** *which He desires to destroy."* God has waited until our times to draw our special attention to His Heart because He wants His Heart to be the remedy of our souls in these times, to rouse us from our lethargy so that we will become inflamed with Divine Love and seek consolation in His Most Compassionate Heart. God is asking our help in the destruction of *Satan's empire*. And it is through sacrifice and mercy that Satan will be defeated, and then will come justice. Jesus said to St. Faustina:

You will prepare the world for My final coming.[22]

Speak to the world about My mercy... It is a sign for the end times. After it will come the Day of Justice. While there is still time, let them have recourse to the fountain of My mercy.[23]

Tell souls about this great mercy of Mine, because the awful day, the day of My justice, is near.[24]

He who refuses to pass through the door of My mercy must pass through the door of My justice.[25]

I am prolonging the time of mercy for the sake of sinners. But woe to them if they do not recognize this time of My visitation.[26]

Before the Day of Justice, I am sending the Day of Mercy.[27]

In addition to these words of Our Lord, the Mother of Mercy, the Blessed Virgin, said:

You have to speak to the world about His great mercy and ***prepare the world for the Second Coming*** *of Him who will come, not as a merciful Savior, but as a just Judge. Oh how terrible is that day! Determined is the day of justice, the day of divine wrath. The angels tremble before it. Speak to* *souls about this great mercy while it is still the time for grant-ing mercy.*[28]

Devotion to the Heart of Jesus is not separate from Jesus Himself. He is love, which is mainly expressed through the symbol of the heart. The Devotion to the Heart of Jesus is a devotion of love. He longs to give us His Heart. We are invited to sacrifice ourselves, to share in His pains and joys for humanity, to surrender ourselves, to console Him for the ingratitude and indifference of His people, to make amends on behalf of God's people to establish His Kingdom on earth. Jesus in turn gives us His Heart through Mary – His love, His feelings and thoughts, His happiness and pains. His divine Love is our only comfort and desire. We offer all our sufferings to the Father with the sufferings of the Divine Heart to assist in building His Kingdom of Love. The lance pierced the Lord's side, entering His Heart, and thus by this the world was redeemed. Now, from His Heart, love gushes forth to bless us with grace, make us holy, and help us to join Him in saving the world. We join the Lord in becoming victims of love for the salvation of the world.

The Eucharistic Heart

The great plan of God for us, in these times especially, is that we live from Eucharist to Eucharist, and not just Sunday to Sunday, but from daily Eucharist to daily Eucharist. That is how the early Church lived, as the Book of Acts attests: *"And day by day, attending the temple together and breaking bread... with glad and generous hearts, praising God and having favor with all the people."*[29] The Church's *Catechism* even recommends that we receive the Eucharist daily, saying: *"The Church strongly encourages the faithful to receive the holy Eucharist on Sundays and feast days, or more often still, even daily."*[30] With the Eucharist at the center of our daily lives, we will live lives of great joy and holiness. St. Faustina wrote before she died in the 1930's: *"All the good that is in me is due to Holy Communion ...I feel this holy fire has transformed me completely...O Lord, my heart is a temple in which you dwell continually."* And as a result of the continual abandonment of her human will to the Divine Will, St. Faustina received the grace of *preserving the Sacred Species in her body from one Communion to the next.* Let this be our goal as well.

Devotion to the
Sorrowful & Immaculate Heart of Mary

In loving the Eucharistic and Sacred Heart, we also reflect upon the Sorrowful and Immaculate Heart, as it was her who gave to us the Sacred Heart. These two hearts are in perfect harmony. The Second Vatican Council says that Mary's spiritual motherhood of all souls *"will last without interruption until the eternal fulfillment of all the* elect. *Assumed into Heaven she did not set aside this saving role.*" St. Bernard, in words which tell us at the same time how the Two Hearts were one in suffering, confirms saying:

> *The martyrdom of the Virgin Mary, implicit in Simeon's prophecy, is put before us in the story of Our Lord's Passion. That venerable old man, Simeon, said of the Infant Jesus: 'This Child is set for a sign that will be contradicted;' and to Mary: 'A sword will pierce your soul.'*

> *Blessed Mother, a sword did pierce your soul. For no sword could penetrate your Son's flesh without piercing your soul. After your own Son Jesus gave up His life — He was yours in a special sense though He belongs to all — the cruel lance, which opened His side and would not spare Him in death though it could do him no injury, could not touch His soul. But it pierced your soul. His soul was no longer there, but yours could not be set free, and it was pierced by a sword of sorrow. We rightly speak of you as more than a martyr, for the anguish of mind You suffered exceeded all bodily pain.*

The mystical union of the Hearts of Jesus and Mary began at the moment of Jesus' conception and continues into eternity, never to be parted. The Heart of Jesus was conceived from the heart of Mary in some ways even before the Incarnation, as St. Augustine comments: Mary *"first conceived (the Heart of) Christ in her heart, and only then in her womb."*[31] The union of the Two Hearts in actuality began in the womb of the Virgin of Nazareth at the Incarnation and reached its pinnacle at the Cross in the work of Redemption.

Our Lord requested to Sr. Lucia of Fatima that the Two Hearts be represented *side by side,* as they are in the Miraculous Medal image. In the Sacred Heart image, Christ appears, taking His Hand to open His side to disclose His utterly affectionate and lovable Heart, while reaching with His other Hand in an expression of giving toward us. And the Immaculate Heart image is usually portrayed in this way as well. Both hearts, united in love, seek to share their hearts with us. Mary's time has come. Christ wants us to focus on her heart together with His, and if we offend her, we offend Him. The Miraculous Medal Image shows the Two Hearts united side by side; and the Angel Prayer of Fatima has us call on the Two Hearts together for reparation and conversion. The Angel of Fatima said: ***"The Hearts of Jesus and Mary are attentive to the voice of your supplication."***

Many lay associations of our times dedicated to Our Lady, including the *Militia Immaculata* and the Legion of Mary, support the union of the Two Hearts and call on Mary as *Mediatrix of all Grace.* They foster Marian-Eucharistic devotion. United, but with distinction, we adore the Heart of Jesus the God-Man while venerating the heart of Mary the Mother of God. This Devotion is the highest expression of the Catholic religion and the summary of the whole work of Redemption. The Church advocates that this devotion of devotions of the Two Hearts be enthroned in all homes and families of the Catholic world, in a principal place as on a throne, to sanctify and renew the Christian morality of our families, to give us a deep knowledge of Christ and a lively faith of mind, heart, and conduct!

It is not enough to speak only of the union of the Two Hearts, but more, we must speak of the *alliance*[32] of love they share in being united in the work of Redemption and in the Renewal of our times. The definitive alliance of the Two Hearts means that Jesus and Mary are united in *"an intimate and indissoluble bond"*[33] in the work of Redemption, and *"that she with Christ redeemed mankind."*[34] This is true at Calvary and it is true in the Holy Mass: *"The oblation of Mary at the foot of the Cross, united to the oblation of Jesus as High Priest and Victim is renewed in every Holy Sacrifice of the Mass."*[35] Thus, we can say that the Mass is the Memorial of Jesus' Sacrifice, and it is the Sacrifice in which Mary is united with Him in an alliance; and that by participating in the Mass, we join our sacrifice in union with them to the Father.[36] John Paul II stated that one of most important titles of Mary is *Mother of the Eucharist*: She is present at every Mass; Our Lady of the Most Blessed Sacrament and the Eucharistic Lord Jesus are united as one in an alliance of love.

The Two Hearts united Sacrifice on Good Friday redeemed the world. At Calvary, they were one wounded Heart, feeling the same pain and love. This does not mean that they are both placed on the same level. Mary's heart is human and Jesus' Heart is that of the God-Man. Jesus is the Redeemer and He invited Mary to cooperate with Him in His work of Redemption. By the will of God, Mary was inseparably joined with her Son in the work of Redemption. Devotion to the Sorrowful and Immaculate Heart of Mary focuses on venerating the Mother of Jesus as our Mother, especially her Sorrowful Heart of love. John Paul II said: *"Devotion to Mary's Immaculate Heart expresses our reverence for her maternal compassion, both for Jesus and for all of us, her spiritual children, as she stood at the foot of the Cross... devotion to Mary's heart has prime importance, for through love of her Son and of all of humanity she exercises a unique instrumentality in bringing us to him."*[37] Thus, John Paul also stated: *"In the History of Salvation therefore the Two Hearts are inseparably united, and this definitive alliance is integral to the Church's doctrine... to her piety and the liturgical celebration... and to her pastoral pedagogy."*[38] Bl. Mother Teresa of Calcutta explains the relation between the Two Hearts, saying: *"The Heart of Mary is the door which leads us directly to Jesus. She is the gate through which we enter His Sacred Heart. Each 'Hail Mary' we pray opens our heart to His love and leads us into a deeper union with the Eucharistic Heart of Jesus."*[39]

Uniting Our Hearts with the United Hearts

Further, *we* are invited in this Devotion of the United Hearts to take our heart and give it to Jesus through Mary and to have their hearts incarnated in our heart. This will be the Second Incarnation of Christ – in our hearts in these times through Mary. There are three protagonists at the foot of the Cross, all united in a Covenant of Hearts. *"This Covenant of Hearts, forged at the foot of the Cross, embraces the heart of Mary, of Jesus and of the disciple whom Jesus loves – John.* "[40] And John represents us. With their help, we though at various times dejected and suffering all sorts of pains, resist the beatings of life's storm, to aid in the work of salvation. With them, and with them within us, we become ministers of compassion and mercy in a world devoid more and more of both. We are invited *"to penetrate by the wounded side into the very Heart of Christ."*[41] This is one of the greatest Mysteries of the Gospels!

In the love of these Two Hearts, we will find all strength and con-solation, if we completely surrender our heart to them in love. United with Jesus and Mary, we are called to make reparation and atonement for the sins of humanity in these times. We are invited to join them in the divine love Crusade to establish the Kingdom of Truth, Love, and Mercy. The Crusade of love and penance must begin *now* in this decisive crisis in history, or else the road embarked on by humanity can only take it to total destruction and to the spiritual murder of a great part of humanity.[42] Jesus wants this Devotion to light up all souls. He is saying to us: Love the Two Hearts and love with the Love of the Two Hearts, and then *you* will *know* the Love of the Two Hearts, both now and for eternity. At the wedding Feast of the Lamb with the Church in Heaven, our union with the Two Hearts will be complete and perfect. To do this, we must adopt the sentiments of Jesus and Mary – *"to forgive as [they] forgive and ask pardon as [they] did; to remain silent in the face of infamous remark, as [Jesus] did before Pilate, and, yet, to feel such zeal and bravery as to become capable of chasing the money changers out of the Temple of God with a whip; to live to do the Will of the Father as [they] did; to love so much as to even give your life for others; and to allow your body to be crushed, and with joy, to give oneself as food, so others can feed on that bread.* "[43]

The Heavenly Prophetess of the Latter Times

In recent times and especially in our day, Mary has come as the Prophetess of our times to call her children to faithfulness and to prepare us for what is to come. A renewed Church is coming after the storm of the purification, chastisement, and tribulation; and the Church will become strong and united as in a second Pentecost. But, *you* are needed now to help make this happen, to contribute in a special way during this time of preparation and upheaval. She is calling you to remain a faithful soul who grows in prayer and holiness. Marian apparitions often offer a stipulation that *if* humanity does not convert and return to God, *then* there will be devastation and punishment. So, **we are being called to help Mary to avert the times of upheaval**, or to at least lessen them. In her apparitions, Mary often invites the faithful to practice the various Marian devotions with frequency and heartfelt love.

Sr. Lucia of Fatima (beginning in the year 1917) was given profound insights concerning God's plan for our times. She wrote:

*God is giving **two last remedies to the world**. These are* ***the Holy Rosary and the Devotion to the Immaculate Heart of Mary**... the **two means to save the world are prayer and sacrifice**... the Most Holy Virgin in these last times in which we live has given **a new efficacy to the recitation of the Rosary** to such an extent that there is no problem, no matter how difficult it is, whether temporal or above all spiritual, in the personal life of each one of us, of our families, of the families of the world, or of the religious communities, or even of the life of peoples and nations that cannot be solved by the Rosary. **There is no problem I tell you, no matter how difficult it is, that we cannot resolve by the prayer of the Holy Rosary**. With the Holy Rosary, we will save ourselves. We will sanctify ourselves. We will console Our Lord and obtain the salvation of many souls. Finally, devotion to the Immaculate Heart of Mary, Our Most holy Mother, consists in considering Her as the seat of mercy, of goodness and of pardon and as the certain door by which we are to enter Heaven. (12/26/57) We must pray a great deal and beg God not to chastise us and to save us in time and for eternity. (6/58)*

The main themes of Our Lady's warnings from Fatima are summarized as follows:

1. Punishment of the World: Our Blessed Mother can no longer restrain the hand of her Divine Son from striking the world with a just punishment for its many crimes. *"They must* *not continue to offend Our Lord, Who is already too much offended.*"

2. **Amendment of Life:** "*I have come to warn the faithful to amend their lives and ask pardon for their sins.*"

3. **Five Warnings:** "*If my requests are not granted, Russia will spread her errors throughout the world, provoking wars and persecutions against the Church. Many good people will be martyred, there will come another great war, and various nations will be destroyed.*" (*WWII broke out only decades later and afterwards Russia spread Communism across the world, as she had prophesied.*)

4. **Reason for War:** "*Wars are a punishment for the sins of mankind.*"

5. **Sins of the Flesh:** "*More souls go to Hell because of the sins of the flesh than for any other reason.*"

6. **Immodest Fashions:** "*Certain fashions are being introduced that offend Our Lord very much.*"

7. **Sinful Marriages:** "*Many marriages are not good; they do not please Our Lord and are not of God.*"[44]

One scholar on Fatima summarizes Our Lady of Fatima's messages, saying: "*Our Lady of Fatima... came to recall in all its vigor the most traditional Catholicism, that of the Gospel, the Catholicism of a St. Louis Marie Grignon de Montfort or a Saint Maximilian Kolbe, right in [our times]. This Catholicism consists in the love of God and the hatred of satan, meaning the love of the Cross, and tender devotion to Mary, contempt for the world and self-renunciation, prayer and sacrifice; in short the divine eternal Wisdom in all its vigor, in all its force and with all its supernatural attractions. "*[45] Just before she died, little Bl. Jacinta of Fatima, whose body is now incorrupt, pleaded with Lucia, saying: *"Lucia, **tell everybody that God gives graces through the Immaculate Heart of Mary.** Tell them to ask graces from her, and that the Heart of Jesus wishes to be venerated together with the Immaculate Heart of Mary. Ask them to plead for peace from the Immaculate Heart of Mary, for **the Lord has confided the peace of the world to her.**"*

Our Lady of America and Her Prophecy

Our Lady of America appeared to Sister Mary Ephrem (Mildred Neuzil), of the Precious Blood Sisters, who was later a Contemplative of the Indwelling Trinity. Sister Mary Ephrem, deceased on January 10th, 2000, said she was asked by the Blessed Virgin Mary to draw a picture according to the vision of Our Lady of America. Our Lady instructed that a statue of her be constructed accordingly, and that the statue be placed after a solemn procession into the National Shrine of the Immaculate Conception, in Washington, D.C. Our Lady said that if this is done, the United States of America would turn back toward morality and the national shrine would become a place of *"wonders."* Let us turn to Our Lady of America and ask for her to be enshrined in the National Basilica of the United States, that this prophecy might be fulfilled.

Our Lady says: *"I am Our Lady of America. **I desire that my children honor me, especially by the purity of their lives.**"* She speaks of the pivotal role of the United States -- for good or for evil – in our times, saying:

> ***It is the United States that is to lead the world to peace**, the peace of Christ, the peace that He brought with Him from heaven... **Dear children, unless the United States accepts and carries out faithfully the mandate given to it by heaven to lead the world to peace, there will come upon it and all nations a great havoc of war and incredible suffering**. If, however, the United States is faithful to this mandate from heaven and yet fails in the pursuit of peace because the rest of the world will not accept or cooperate, then the United States will not be burdened with the punishment about to fall.*
>
> *Weep, then, dear children, weep with your mother over the sins of men... Intercede with me before the throne of mercy, for sin is overwhelming the world and punishment is not far away.*
>
> ***It is the darkest hour**, but if men will come to me, my Immaculate Heart will make it bright again with the mercy which my Son will rain down through my hands. **Help me save those who***

will not save themselves. *Help me bring once again the sunshine of God's peace upon the world.*

If my desires are not fulfilled much suffering will come to this land. ***My faithful one, if my warnings are taken seriously and enough of my children strive constantly and faithfully to renew and reform themselves in their inward and outward lives, then there will be no nuclear war.*** *What happens to the world depends upon those who live in it. There must be much more good than evil prevailing in order to prevent the holocaust that is so near approaching. Yet I tell you, my daughter, even should such a destruction happen because there were not enough souls who took my warning seriously, **there will remain a remnant, untouched by the chaos who, having been faithful in following me and spreading my warnings**, will gradually inhabit the earth again with their dedicated and holy lives.*[46]

Our Lady of America is calling the United States to lead the world, to establish peace, to restore the virtue of purity, and to protect the family. She calls for us to renew the family by inviting the Most Holy Trinity to be the center of the Christian family, and to recognize the Holy Family of Joseph, Mary, and Jesus as the model of family life. Let us honor Our Lady of America as she requests, so that she might bring faith and hope to our world and to families.

Mother of the Sorrowful Heart

Around the same time as Fatima, Our Lord appeared to Franciscan Tertiary, Belgian mystic, stigmatist, and the Apostle of the Devotion to the Sorrowful and Immaculate Heart of Mary, Berthe Petit. Through her, Jesus gives us a striking message about this devotion to His Mother's Heart, as He says:

> *It is hearts that must be changed. This will be accomplished only by the Devotion [to the Sorrowful and Immaculate Heart of Mary] proclaimed, explained, preached and recommended everywhere.* ***Recourse to My Mother under the title I wish for her universally, is the last help I shall give before the end of time****... The safety of your country, internal peace and confidence in* **My Church will revive** *through the spread of the Devotion and the Consecration which I wish in order that the Sorrowful and Immaculate Heart of My Mother, united in all to My Heart, may be loved and glorified. Deliverance will thus be the work of our two Hearts...* ***The clear light to be granted, through recourse to My Mother, will bring about, above all, the conversion of a multitude of straying and sinful souls****... This devotion to the Sorrowful and Immaculate Heart of My Mother* **will restore faith and hope** *to broken hearts and to ruined families; it* **will help to repair the destruction;** *it* **will sweeten sorrow.** *It will be a new strength for My Church.*

And Our Lady adds, saying: *"I call myself, 'Mother of the Sorrowful Heart.' This title willed by my Son, is dear to me above all others. According as it is spread everywhere, there will be granted graces of mercy, spiritual renewal and salvation."*

Marian Gifts from Heaven

In the course of the Church's history, Our Lady has given humanity various gifts from Heaven to assist the faithful with new forms of prayer and means of grace. These are great heavenly gifts from our spiritual Mother. We will now discuss four of her great gifts.

The Most Holy Rosary

The Rosary is the greatest Marian prayer. It is the compendium of the Gospel in prayer, and the most highly recommended prayer of the Church, second to the Liturgy and the Mass. For hundreds of years, praying the Rosary has been a significant way of fulfilling Mary's biblical prophecy, *"Henceforth all generations will call me blessed."*[47] Our Lady came and asked St. Dominic (*c.* 1220) to spread devotion to the Rosary. And one day while St. Dominic was exorcising some demons, they spoke saying: *"Now that we are forced to speak we must also tell you this: Nobody who perseveres in saying the Rosary will be damned, because [Mary] obtains for her servants the grace of true contrition for their sins and by means of this they obtain God's forgiveness and mercy."*

The Rosary entails the three types of prayer as follows:

1. The Rosary is a **vocal prayer**, prayed on the Rosary beads, the sweet chain that links us with God – beginning with the *Creed* on the crucifix as a profession of faith; saying the *Our Father* to share intimacy with Him; the ten *Hail Marys*, which repeat the biblical words of the Angel Gabriel and St. Elizabeth and to share in the jubilation of the greatest miracle in history, followed by the Name of Jesus, and finishing by calling on the Mother of God to intercede for us at the two most important moments of our lives – now and at the hour of our death; and the *Gloria* which takes us into Trinitarian contemplation and calls us to glorify the Trinity, at the end of each decade. Then, the *Fatima Prayer* accompanies the *Gloria* to offer the decade for the souls in need of God's mercy. To honor Our Lady, the Rosary ends with a *Hail, Holy Queen* and may include other prayers including a prayer for the Pope's intentions as part of the plenary indulgence.

2. The Rosary is a prayer of **meditation**. During the Rosary, we meditate in silence on mysteries of Christ's life

as seen through Mary's eyes. These are the twenty mysteries of the Rosary. We think about each mystery, then how to apply it to our own life, and conclude with some resolution to put the meditation into practice so it can bear fruit in our lives. As *a compendium of the Gospel*, the Rosary makes present the saving mysteries of our salvation.

3. The Rosary is a prayer of **contemplation**, especially in that it brings us into intimate and personal communion with God. God brings us into Himself and shares Himself with us through the Rosary. We discover His wisdom and love and experience His presence through the Rosary.

Many Saints have been great advocates of the Rosary. St. Louis de Montfort said: *"The Rosary is a **priceless treasure** inspired by God,"* and *"With Rosaries in your hands, you will conquer...and you shall overcome all the adversities which Satan is trying to inflict on the Catholic Church."* St. Teresa of Avila appeared to one of her religious sisters from Heaven to tell her of the great worth of the Hail Mary, saying: *"I would be willing to return to a life of suffering until the end of time to merit the degree of glory which God rewards one devoutly recited Hail Mary prayer."* St. Pio of Pietrelcina, the stigmatist priest, said: *"The Rosary is **THE WEAPON**."*

Through the Rosary, we attend **the School of Mary**, contemplating the Face of Christ. John Paul II, in his Apostolic Letter on *The Most Holy Rosary* (2002), said about the Rosary: *"The Rosary, though clearly Marian in character, is at heart a Christocentric prayer."* And Mary bestows on us Christ's grace as though from her very hands. We might even say that when we hold the Rosary, we are holding her hands. She conforms us to Christ. In his letter on the Rosary, John Paul quotes Bl. Bartolo Longo, a Satanist who converted to Catholicism through the Rosary and built the Marian shrine of Our Lady of Pompeii, who says: *"Just as two friends, frequently in each other's company, tend to develop similar habits, so too, by holding familiar converse with Jesus and the Blessed Virgin, by meditating on the mysteries of the Rosary and by living the same life in Holy Communion, we can become, to the extent of our lowliness, similar to them."*

John Paul places the Rosary at the heart of authentic evangelization. He promises: *"The Rosary retains all its power and continues to be a valuable pastoral resource for every good evangelizer."* He continues, calling for the Rosary as the remedy against present darkness and foes: *"At times when Christianity itself seemed under threat, its deliverance was attributed to the power of this prayer, and Our Lady of the Rosary was acclaimed as the one whose intercession brought salvation."* He is undoubtedly referring to the Battle of Lepanto. On October 7, 1571, the Christian fleet under the leadership of Don Juan of Austria, celebrated confession, received Holy Communion and an Apostolic Blessing, and prayed the Rosary during the three hours before going into battle against the much larger invading Muslim fleet. And against the odds, they were victorious. After winning victory, the Pope declared the Feast of Our Lady of Victory, which soon became the Feast of Our Lady of the Rosary. Similar victories ensued. In 1683, King John Sobieski III and his 30,000 soldiers, while invoking Jesus and Mary and praying the Rosary, fought and defeated the 200,000 Muslim Turks who were attacking Vienna and Western Europe. In 1716, Emperor Charles VI, appealing to Our Lady of the Rosary, conquered the attacking Muslim Turks at Peterwarden. There was another similar victory at Corfu in 1717. The Pope then extended the Feast of the Holy Rosary to the whole Church. In recent times, Leo XIII exhorted the Rosary to fight rationalism and liberalism; and Pius XI and Pius XII exhorted it against Communism. John Paul II called us to fight the great darkness of *our* times with the daily Rosary prayer.

John Paul calls the Rosary a prayer of peace and a prayer of the family. *"The Rosary is by its nature a prayer for peace... As a prayer for peace, the Rosary is also, and always has been, a prayer of and for the family...* **The family that prays together stays together***... To pray the Rosary for children, and even more, with children, training them from earliest years to experience this daily 'pause for prayer' with the family... is a spiritual aid that which should not be underestimated."* In his letter, he recommended that families gather together every evening to pray the Rosary, even with the youngest children. St. Pius X says: **"If you want peace in your heart, in your home, in your** *country, assemble together every night and say the Rosary.*" It is good to pray the Rosary at any time and even while alone, but it is better to pray it with others. St. Louis de Montfort notes in *The Secret of the Rosary* that one who says his Rosary alone only gains the merit of that one Rosary. But if he says it together with others, he gains the merit of each Rosary. This is the law of public prayer.

While St. Dominic established the Holy Rosary devotion, Bl. Alan de la Roche restored it to popular practice. Our Lord said to Bl. Alan de la Roche in 1460: *"You are crucifying me again now because you have all the learning and understanding that you need to preach my Mother's Rosary and you are not doing so. If you only did this you could teach many souls the right path and lead them away from sin – but you are not doing it and so you, yourself, are guilty of the sins that they commit."* Our Lady spoke to him, saying: *"After the Holy Sacrifice of the Mass, there is nothing in the Church that I love as much as the Rosary."* He then preached the Rosary with great success until his death. Could Our Lord and Our Lady be asking the same of us today – *to pray and to spread* the great devotion to the daily Rosary? I think so!

Many know of **Bl. Mother Teresa of Calcutta** who founded the Missionaries of Charity to bring Christ to the poorest of the poor, but few know that she was inspired to found the new congregation as *"the call within the call"* due to a mystical experience she received of three visions of Jesus and Mary, at the center of which was **the call to teach**

the Holy Rosary. She describes the three visions in her own words, published after her death, saying:

1)   *I saw a very big crowd – all kinds of people – very poor and children were there also. They all had their hands lifted towards me – standing in their midst. They called out "Come, come, save us – bring us to Jesus."*

2)   *Again that great crowd – I could see great sorrow and suffering in their faces – I was kneeling near Our Lady, who was facing them. – I did not see her face but I heard her say "Take care of them – Fear not.* **Teach them to say the Rosary – the family Rosary and all will be well.** *– Fear not – Jesus and I will be with you and your children."*

3)   *The same great crowd – they were covered in darkness. Yet I could see them. Our Lord on the Cross. Our Lady at a little distance from the Cross – and myself as a little child in front of her. Her left hand was on my left shoulder – and her right hand was holding my right arm. We were both facing the Cross. Our Lord said – "I have asked you. They have asked you and she, My Mother has asked you. Will you refuse to do this for me – to take care of them, to bring them to me?*

It was soon after this that her work of founding the Missionaries of Charity was approved and begun, founded on the divine call to teach the *"great crowd"* to pray the family Rosary.[48]

The Brown Scapular

The Brown Scapular is a sacramental of protection and devotion to Mary. It is Mary's gift and garment of love that she has given to her spiritual children. Mary gave the Scapular to St. Simon Stock (July 16, 1251) of the Carmelite Order promising that *"Whosoever dies wearing this Scapular shall not suffer eternal fire."* She promises to intercede for them to receive the grace of final perseverance. We should wear it the rest of our lives, as many of the Saints did. It is a sign of Mary's Immaculate Heart, a sign of salvation, protection, and peace, an external sign of commitment to Christian life and Marian devotion – just like how we treasure a gift someone has given us and appreciate when others treasure a gift we have given them.

Mary gave the Scapular to us from Heaven. By wearing the Scapular, we are telling Mary we venerate, love and trust her. We wear it to receive her special armor of protection against temptation, sin, and the devil. Included with the Scapular Promise is the Sabbatine privilege – those who die with the Scapular will be released from Purgatory the first Saturday after their death. This is not a *"get out of hell free"* card, but a true promise as part of the fruit of our true devotion to Mary.

There have been many amazing accounts of Mary's protection through the brown Scapular. In 1845 an English ship, King of the Ocean, was at sea in a wild storm and about to sink. One of the sailors, an Irish boy named John McAuliffe, threw his Scapular into the sea making the Sign of the Cross. At that very moment, the wind and seas calmed. A wave lapped the Scapular back onto the boat, all in the presence of an Anglican minister, Mr. Fisher, and his family, who soon became Catholics and had great devotion to the Scapular. Isidore Bakanja lived in Africa in the early 1900s. He wore his Scapular for all to see, telling others about the Rosary and Scapular of Our Lady. Isidore worked for a man who hated Jesus and who beat him for refusing to take off his Scapular. He was soon beaten so badly, he died. He is a martyr of the Scapular, and the Church has made him a Blessed. St. John Bosco's Scapular was found intact on his exhumed body. Thus, the great Marian prophecy is true!

The Rosary and the Brown Scapular are inseparable, as Our Lady prophesized to St. Dominic and Bl. Alan de La Roche: *"One day, through the Rosary and the Scapular, I will save the world."* As we will see in the next chapter, we are living in the times of the fulfillment of this prophecy!

The Image of Our Lady of Guadalupe

Mary appeared to St. Juan Diego in 1531 near Mexico City, where the Aztecs had been engaging in large numbers of human sacrifices to their serpent god. Mary asked him to ask the Bishop to build a basilica in her honor to combat the demonic activity and to convert the peoples. She asked him to gather some Castilian roses, which did not usually grow in that place or in that time of year, and which she then arranged in his tilma made of cactus fibers. Mary asked him to bring the roses to the Bishop as a proof of her heavenly appearance and request. When Juan did so, Our Lady's image miraculously appeared on his tilma.

Our Lady of Guadalupe spoke to St. Juan Diego with such tender love and motherly affection, as she speaks to each of us today, saying:

Know and understand well... that I am the ever virgin Holy Mary, Mother of the True God for whom we live, of the Creator of all things, Lord of heaven and the earth. I wish that a temple be erected here quickly, so I may therein exhibit and give all my love, compassion, help, and protection, because I am your merciful mother, to you, and to all the inhabitants on this land and all the rest who love me, invoke and confide in me; listen there to their lamentations, and remedy all their miseries, afflictions and sorrows...Hear me and understand well, my son the least, that nothing should frighten or grieve you. Let not your heart be disturbed. Do not fear that sickness, nor any other sickness or anguish. Am I not here, who is your Mother? Are you not under my protection? Am I not your health? Are you not happily within my fold? What else do you wish? Do not grieve nor be disturbed by anything.

The tilma of Guadalupe has maintained its structural integrity for 500 years. In addition to withstanding the elements, the tilma has also resisted a 1791 ammonia spill and a 1921 bomb blast. Photographers and ophthalmologists have located images reflected in the eyes of the Virgin. Images of Juan, the Bishop, and others, who were present during the unveiling of the Image before the Bishop in 1531, have been found in the Virgin's eyes, in the corneas of both eyes. Further, using an ophthalmoscope, doctors have observed that the Virgin's eyes have the distortion of actual normal human eyes. Noting the unique appearance of the eyes, ophthalmologist, Dr. Rafael Torrija Lavoignet, stated: *"They look strangely alive when examined."*[49] Miraculously, Our Lady sees! Our Heavenly Mother is with us. She sees us through the Holy Image of the tilma of Guadalupe!

Recently, on the day the Mexico City government passed a law approving abortion, the abdomen area of the pregnant Image of Our Lady of Guadalupe began to glow with a bright light in the shape of a fetus! Pictures were taken and circulated on the internet. What a powerful holy image from Heaven. We should keep Our Lady's heavenly image in our homes and look upon her with love as her eyes meet ours in mutual glances. John Paul II declared Our Lady of Guadalupe Patroness of the entire American continent. She is also patroness of the unborn. May she come to our aid once again in our times to convert those who are sacrificing human life through abortion.

The Miraculous Medal

Our Lady has given us another gift from Heaven. In 1830, the Blessed Mother appeared in a vision to St. Catherine Labouré, whose body is now incorrupt in Paris. Mary asked her to have a medal made of the vision, which showed Mary with rays of light coming forth from her hands encircled by the words: *"O Mary, conceived without sin, pray for us who have recourse to Thee."* On the back of the medal, there was to be an *"M"* and a cross, with the Two Hearts of Jesus and Mary, all encircled by twelve stars. Mary promised: *"All who wear it will receive great graces."* It was quickly approved by the Bishop and circulated. Immediately, there were so many miracles reported and attested to that the medal became known as the Miraculous Medal. What great devotion we can show Our Lady by wearing the Miraculous medal or another medal from her more recent apparitions, and what wonderful protection she gives us!

Secrets from Mary for Our Time

The Ten Secrets of Medjugorje

In our times, another heavenly apparition of major significance is *Medjugorje*. It is the greatest reported Marian apparition in history, and it will be the final of her apparitions given *in this way* until the end of time. Unprecedented in history, Our Lady Queen of Peace has been visiting with visionaries *daily* for over a quarter century, so as to form us in her School of Prayer and Holiness, just as she did her Son in His daily life in Nazareth. There have been many significant supporters of this still-ongoing apparition. John Paul II, Bl. Mother Teresa of Calcutta, Cardinal Ratzinger (Benedict XVI), Cardinal Schönborn, Cardinal Hans Urs Von Balthasar, the papal exorcist Fr. Gabriele Amorth, and Archbishop Frane Franic of the Split Archdiocese in Croatia have been among those who have spoken in personal support of Medjugorje. This is the first apparition that the Vatican has felt it necessary to remove the jurisdiction over the apparitions from the local Ordinary, the Bishop of Mostar.[50] The Vatican is handling the investigation themselves. We must remember that an apparition may be condemned at any time, of which Medjugorje has not been in its almost 30 years, while an apparition is never officially approved until after it ends. Hundreds of cardinals and bishops have visited Medjugorje as pilgrims (or have expressed their support for what is happening there), along with tens of thousands of priests and tens of millions of lay pilgrims. An interesting event happened concerning John Paul II to confirm his connection to Medjugorje – two hours after John Paul II's death on April 2, 2005, visionary Ivan Dragicevic reported that Our Lady brought John Paul, deceased and now in Heaven, with her when she appeared to Ivan.

Just as at Fatima in 1917 when Our Lady had given the visionaries three secrets, so too, at Medjugorje, Mary is reportedly giving the visionaries **ten secrets** of worldwide significance. The first three secrets of Medjugorje have to do with warnings. According to visionary, Mirjana, *"The first two secrets (the first of which is 'not good' and will 'shake us up') come as advance **warnings** for the whole world and as proof the Blessed Virgin Mary is here in Medjugorje,"* while **the third secret concerns a** *"permanent, indestructible and beautiful"* **Sign** that will appear in Medjugorje on the hill of the first apparitions, which will remain until the end of time. She has said that the eighth secret is worse than the other seven, but that it has been lessened due to our prayers and fasting. The ninth secret is even worse. The tenth secret is utterly dire and cannot be lessened whatsoever, she said. These last seven secrets may relate to the seven seals of the Book of Revelation. Visionary Mirjana says that Mary asks us to prepare spiritually and not to panic, but to convert now. Mirjana says that God is love, only love, and that cruelty and evil come from Satan. Those who freely choose Satan and disobey God's Commandments will perish. Punishments come for the sins of the world.

When all the secrets have been given to all six of the visionaries, then the apparitions will cease on a daily basis, and the secrets will begin to occur, some of which will be announced to the world (what, how, and where) three days before each occurs by the spiritual director of the visionaries (Mirjana has chosen Fr. Petar Ljubicic, O.F.M.). There is an invisible parchment that came from the Blessed Mother that has all the secrets written on them. The visionary can see it and will show it to the spiritual director at the proper time. As Aaron the priest announced each plague to Pharaoh in Egypt on behalf of Moses, so too the visionaries' spiritual director will announce to the world each warning three days before they occur, on behalf of each visionary, for the conversion of the world. When the secrets begin with the warning, then everyone will know the visionaries were telling the truth. Our Lady has promised to leave a supernatural, indestructible, and visible sign on the mountain where she first appeared. Our Lady said: *"This sign will be given for the atheists. You faithful already have signs and you have become the sign for the atheists. You faithful must not wait for the sign before you convert; convert soon. This time is a time of grace for you. You can never thank God enough for His grace. The time is for deepening your faith and for your conversion. When the sign comes, it will be too late for many."* The sign is to bring many to reconciliation and conversion.

The Sign that will appear in Medjugorje will bring great joy to many. But, pertaining to this Sign, Mirjana said: *"After the visible Sign those who are alive will have little time for conversion."* It seems that many will see the miracle and believe – there will be many conversions – but that others may at this point see the miracle and still not believe or convert. Mary speaks to us today, saying: ***"Hurry to be converted. I need your prayers and your penance."*** In this regard, she also said: *"Return to prayer! Nothing is more needed than prayer."* When the Sign comes, then we will know that the world's punishment is near. The ninth and tenth secrets are grave matters. They are a chastisement for the sins of the world. The punishment is inevitable because we can not expect the conversion of the entire world. The chastisement can be lessened by prayers and penance, but it can not be suppressed entirely. An evil which threatened the world as part of the seventh secret has been eliminated through prayer and fasting. For that reason the Blessed Virgin continues to ask for prayer and fasting. The invitation to prayer and penance is destined to ward off evil and war and above all to save souls. Our Lady says: *"You have forgotten that with prayer and fasting you can ward off wars, suspend natural laws."*[51]

Relating the messages and Miracle of the Sun that occurred at Fatima (1917) with the messages and great Miracle that will occur at Medjugorje (and also at Garabandal), Our Lady told locutionist Fr. Gobbi: *"You will see very soon the extraordinary signs which I will give, in order that you may* **prepare yourselves for the very great miracle** *which is at this time about to be accomplished. The miracle of the sun, which took place during my last apparition (at Fatima), was only a prophetic sign to indicate to you that you should all* **look at the Book which is still sealed** *(Revelation).* **Today I am being sent by God to open this Book,** *in order that the secrets may be revealed to you."*[52] **God is sending Mary to open the Book of the Apocalypse, and to reveal its mystery, in our times.** It is interesting to note that Our Lady gave the children of Fatima a century ago three secrets that would occur in the world if men did not convert. They were terrible predictions from Heaven. But, humanity did not convert. All three secrets then came about (WWII, Communism, and a spiritual crisis with an upcoming Church persecution). And it has been terrible. Now,

Our Lady is coming again in our time and she is giving the children of Medjugorje ten secrets that are to occur in the world to help us to convert. And, as these secrets too are reportedly from God, so shall they really occur. We are being called to convert while there is still time. And the sobering reality is that our world is much worse off than a century ago, and so we can conclude that the secrets to unfold in our time will be all the more serious than those of a century ago.

The Time of Mercy Has Been Prolonged

Our Lady has indicated that the events of the second Advent – the fulfillment of Marian prophesies (beginning with La Salette),[53] the worldwide purification, the great chastisement, the universal spread of apostasy (which will make the mystery of iniquity manifest), and the unfolding of the Marian secrets – have begun, as she tells Fr. Gobbi.[54] But, Our Lady also warns us about falsely over-speculating about what is to come and when, through Fr. Gobbi, saying:

> *Do not allow yourselves to be seduced by those who point to (specific) years and days, as though they wanted to impose a time-table on the infinite mercy of the divine Heart of my Son, Jesus (316c)...* **Everything can still be changed for you**, *my children (184g)... Live then in serenity of spirit and without fear, even in the midst of the anxieties and threats of your time (113q)... Don't be curious to know what is waiting for you, but*

at each moment live in perfect love (205g)... The more this motherly triumph comes about in the hearts and souls of my children in ever increasing numbers, the more the chastisement is put off by you and the more Jesus can pour out upon the world the torrents of His Divine Mercy (473k)... How many times have I intervened in order to set back further and further in time the beginning of the great trial, for the purification of this poor humanity, now possessed and dominated by the Spirits of Evil (553g)... **And thus I have again succeeded in postponing the time of the chastisement** *decreed by Divine Justice* **for a humanity which has become worse than at the time of the flood** *(576g)... [a world that] is a thousand times worse than at the time of the flood.*

Mary has warned us about the moment we are living in right now. Some have wondered in this regard why all these prophecies have not already come to pass, as Our Lady of Good Success mentions that some of these events will occur in *"the twentieth century,"* and similarly, the Marian messages to Fr. Gobbi *seemed* to warn that these events were to occur at the end of the twentieth century.[55] And while these prophetic events have in many ways begun already, **the time of iniquity and of the chastisement has been delayed[56] and shortened[57]** due to the prayers of Our Lady and of the sacrifices of the remnant faithful. To St. Faustina, Our Lord stated, *"I am **prolonging the time of mercy** for the sake of [sinners],"* while warning, *"But woe to them if they do not recognize this time of My visitation."*[58]

What Is to Come Is Conditional

It is important to make known that the prophesied catastrophes to come can in many cases be mitigated, delayed, lessened or even averted if those who hear the warnings will repent, pray and make sacrifices of reparation while there is still time. Much of what will happen depends upon us, as Mary indicates through Fr. Gobbi: *"**These evils can be avoided by you**, the dangers can be evaded. The plan of God's justice always can be changed by the force of His merciful love. Also, when I predict chastisements to you, remember that **everything, at any moment, may be changed by the force of your prayer and your reparative penance.**"*[59] Abraham had asked God to spare Sodom and Gomorrah if ten good persons could be found in the city. God responded by promising to spare the people if ten just persons were found. They were not found. Let us be among the just persons the Lord does find today!

Chapter One
The Secrets & Age of Prophecy

Jesus, Mary, I love you, save souls.
Let us eternally adore the Holy Sacrament through Mary.
To the Two Hearts of Jesus and Mary be honor and glory.
Let the Kingdom of the Divine Will (Fiat) come!

Efficacious Novena to the Sacred Heart of Jesus

I. O my Jesus, You have said: *"Truly I say to you, ask and you will receive, seek and you will find, knock and it will be opened to you."* Behold I knock, I seek and ask for the grace of...... *(here name your request)*
Our Father....Hail Mary....Glory Be....
Sacred Heart of Jesus, I place all my trust in You.

II. O my Jesus, You have said: *"Truly I say to you, if you ask anything of the Father in My Name, He will give it to you."* Behold, in Your Name, I ask the Father for the grace of....... *(here name your request)*
Our Father....Hail Mary....Glory Be....
Sacred Heart of Jesus, I place all my trust in You.

III. O my Jesus, You have said: *"Truly I say to you, heaven and earth will pass away but My words will not pass away."* Encouraged by Your infallible words I now ask for the grace of..... *(here name your request)*
Our Father....Hail Mary....Glory Be...
Sacred Heart of Jesus, I place all my trust in You.

O Sacred Heart of Jesus, for whom it is impossible not to have compassion on the afflicted, have pity on us miserable sinners and grant us the grace which we ask of You, through the Sorrowful and Immaculate Heart of Mary, Your tender Mother and ours.
(Then say the Hail, Holy Queen)
St. Joseph, foster father of Jesus, pray for us. Amen.
                                        -- St. Margaret Mary Alacoque
St. Pio recited this novena everyday for those who requested his prayers.

The Call of Conversion

I want YOU to comprehend that
God has chosen each one of you in order to use you
for the great plan of salvation of mankind.
YOU cannot comprehend
how great your role is in God's plan.
Our Lady of Medjugorje

The time has come when the small remnant (the Pope, bishops, priests,
and faithful), who will remain faithful and with whom Jesus will bring
about the realization of His reign,
must enter, in its entirety, into my Immaculate Heart.
Whoever does not enter into this refuge will be carried away by the
great tempest which has already begun to rage.
Our Lady to Fr. Gobbi

God is calling *all* the faithful through His Son and His Mother in our times to live lives of prayer and holiness. But, in reality, few are responding. God can however do a great deal of good through a small remnant of faithful people. In his book, *Jesus of Nazareth*, Pope

Benedict XVI mentions the power of the remnant faithful of God's people throughout salvation history. He mentions the prophets in Ezekiel who are sent to execute divine punishment on Jerusalem, which was full of wickedness (cf. Ezekiel 9:9). Before they do, however, one of them traces *"the Hebrew letter 'tau' (like the sign of the Cross) on the foreheads of all those 'who sigh and groan over all the abominations that are committed in the city' (Ezek 9:4). Those who bear this mark are exempted from punishment. They are people who do not run with the pack, who refuse to collide with the injustice that has become endemic, but who suffer under it instead."*[1]

God is calling us to be the faithful of today who do not conform to the world and its abominations, so that we too may be marked as exempted from the divine punishment, but also, so that we can offer our prayer and devotions to the Lord for the Church and the rest of humanity; so many are in need of God's mercy and thus in need of our prayers. Pope Benedict then compares the remnant faithful of Ezekiel to the remnant faithful who later stood at the foot of the Cross with Christ in the midst of the greatest crisis in history. We can, of course, further compare these generous souls to the remnant faithful of our day, to those of us who will not conform to evil, to those of us who will not compromise the doctrine and morality of the true Faith. Even though we may be only a small band of people who remain true in the midst of a modern world full of compromise, cruelty, and darkness, *we* can change the world, as *"the ones who open the windows of the world to let the light (of Christ) in."*[2]

Let us place ourselves on the side of Christ and remain true to Him until the end. Let us increase our devotions and pray more with our hearts – for God's people, *especially for the Pope, for priests, and for those in need of God's mercy*, and for a new day to dawn upon humanity – so that we too may be marked on our foreheads, not with the sign of the beast, but with the sign of the cross. Our Lord, through the apparitions of Our Lady of America, is encouraging us, saying: *"My little dove, do you know what I find most lacking in the world today? It is FAITH. There are so few souls who believe in Me and My love. They profess their belief and their love, but they do not live this belief. Their hearts are cold, for without faith there can be no love.* ***Pray and sacrifice yourself*** *my child, that faith may once again find entrance into the hearts of men."*[3] May the Lord send His Spirit to give us more theological faith so that we can help others to believe and to love.

The Sacred Heart Devotion
& Our Lord's Promises

Through St. Margaret Mary's visions, **Jesus asks us for** acts of reparation dedicated to His Sacred Heart, for **frequent Eucharistic Communion, and** the keeping of **a weekly Holy Hour, particularly on Thursday nights,** to soothe the heartache He felt when His apostles deserted Him in Gethsemane. He asks us to make up for others' ingratitude, by accepting any mortification or humiliation as a token of His love and by maintaining a spirit of obedience.

Jesus, Who knows the depths of His Father's love, has revealed to us the abyss of His mercy. Jesus requests that we consecrate ourselves and our families to His Sacred Heart. By consecrating ourselves to Him we are declaring our open and free acknowledgement and acceptance of His authority over us.

To encourage this Devotion, and so that we would know and understand the benefit of practicing it, **Our Lord gave the following twelve promises to those who venerate His Sacred Heart Image and adore His Heart in the Eucharist**:

1. I will give them all the graces necessary in their state of life.

2. I will give peace in their families and will unite families that are divided.

3. I will console them in all their troubles.

4. I will be their refuge during life and above all in death.

5. I will bestow the blessings of Heaven on all their enterprises.

6. Sinners shall find in My Heart the source and infinite ocean of mercy.

7. Tepid souls shall become fervent.

8. Fervent souls shall rise quickly to great perfection.

9. I will bless those places wherein the image of My Heart shall be exposed and honored and will imprint My love on the hearts of those who would wear this image on their person (like on the Scapular). I will also destroy in them all disordered movements.

10. I will give to priests who are animated by a tender devotion to My Divine Heart the gift of touching the most hardened hearts.

11. Those who promote this devotion shall have their names written in My Heart, never to be effaced.

12. First Friday Devotion: I promise you in the excessive mercy of My Heart, that My all-powerful love will grant to all those who (worthily) receive Holy Communion on the First Friday of *nine* consecutive months the grace of final repentance; they will not die in My disgrace, nor without receiving the Sacraments. My Divine Heart shall be their safe refuge in that last moment.

Jesus also asked St. Margaret Mary for the Feast of His Sacred Heart, which the Church approved for the Friday after the octave of

Corpus Christi in June. On that day, we are requested to consecrate ourselves to the Sacred Heart by receiving the Eucharist and making a solemn act of reparation for the indignities against the Eucharist that have taken place in the world. He promised to open His Heart to all who honor Him in this way and who get others to do the same.

Pope Pius XII stated that devotion to the Sacred Heart of Jesus is *"the foundation on which to build the kingdom of God in the hearts of individuals, families, and nations."*[4]

Authentic Witnesses of Eucharistic Devotion

The Martyr of the Eucharist

When she was eleven years old, Bl. Imelda was present with the rest of the community of nuns where she lived at the Ascension Day Mass. Since she was not yet twelve years old, Imelda had not received her first Holy Communion. After Mass, Imelda remained in her place in the choir. The sacristan busied herself putting out candles and removing the Mass vestments. A sound caused her to turn and look into the choir, and she saw a brilliant light shining above Imelda's head, and a Host suspended in the light. The sacristan hurried to get the priest. When the priest arrived, and saw the miracle, the priest felt that God had indicated that He wanted to give Himself to Imelda. So she received her First Holy Communion and then went into an ecstasy of joy. Later, she was found still kneeling. There was a smile on her face, but she had died. Bl. Imelda Lambertini died on May 12, 1333. Her relics are displayed in the Church of San Sigismondo in Bologna, Italy. She was made the patroness of First Holy Communicants by Pope St. Pius X in 1910. That same year, he decreed that children could receive their First Holy Communion at a much earlier age. Before her death, Blessed Imelda said: *"Tell me, can anyone receive Jesus into his heart and not die?"*

The Living Dead Saint

The Eucharistic Saint, St. Charbel Maklhouf, called the Great Wonder of our times, who was a Maronite Catholic priest ordained in 1859 in the Lebanese mountains, died on Christmas Eve, 1898, while saying Mass. He was known for levitating during prayer. He had a great devotion to the Blessed Virgin Mary and to the Holy Eucharist. Each day St. Charbel would prepare for Mass in the morning for many hours, and after Mass, he would spend the rest of the day in thanksgiving. He lived from one Eucharist to the next. This is how he lived his life. Months after he was buried, an extraordinary brightness surrounded his tomb. It was decided to exhume his body. His body was found floating in mud, perfectly incorrupt, and miraculously excreting water and blood. His tomb has been opened several times since, and each time it is the same, his body incorrupt, still flexible and still excreting blood and water. He is called *"the living dead saint."* Over the years, this miraculous liquid has been responsible for many cases of healing and miracles. The graces of his devoutly received Holy

Communions are still helping us through his holy incorrupt body even a century after his death. Such love for the Eucharist!

Saints like St. Charbel live for the Eucharist in a way that imitates the first and greatest Eucharistic adorer, Jesus' Mother. According to the mystics, Mary went to daily Mass, usually celebrated by St. John. She would receive Holy Communion, and afterwards remain in prayer for three hours. Mary was very fervent in both her preparation before and thanksgiving after Communion.[5] We too are invited to live from Eucharist to Eucharist, with a deeply Marian spirituality!

The Miracle Job

I remember several years ago when I first entered ministry, I moved my family to San Antonio to be closer to relatives. After researching where the perpetual adoration chapels were in town, we moved right across the street from one and settled into an apartment. I immediately went to the Lord in the Eucharist and told Him how I longed to serve Him as a high school Catholic formation teacher, if this was His will. So, I pledged to make a 9-day Eucharistic novena for this intention to get hired to teach the Faith. The next day I was called into an interview with the diocesan superintendent and a day or so later I interviewed at a local high school. Each day I crossed the street to spend my Holy Hour with the Lord for this intention. And it happened that on the ninth day I started my new job, on February 1, in the middle of a school year, and at the closest Catholic high school in the diocese to where we had moved. I gave great thanks to the Eucharist and have always since kept my daily time with the Eucharistic Lord. Time before the Eucharist is our happiest time on earth and our greatest good!

The Immaculate Heart Devotion
& Our Lady's Promises

Our Lady is calling us to convert– turn away from sin and return to God with repentant hearts – and to help save souls. This entails the usual demands of the Christian life – like prayer, reading Scripture, frequent participation in the Sacraments, obedience to the Commandments, having concern for others. The Fatima Message and the special requests of Our Lady are summarized as follows:

1. Daily Offering: *"**Offer up each day** whatever God requests of you... for the conversion of sinners and reparation for sin."*
2. Prayer and Sacrifices: *"Pray, **pray a great deal**, and make sacrifices for sinners, for many souls go to Hell because they have no one to make sacrifices and pray for them."*
3. Fasting: *"**Pray, fast, and make sacrifices** for your sins and for the sins of all sinners and unbelievers."*
4. Eucharistic Devotion: A renewed focus on the **Mass** and frequent **Adoration of the Blessed Sacrament** is requested and emphasized.

5. Daily Rosary: *"Say the Rosary every day to obtain peace for the world. And after each decade say the 'O My Jesus' [Prayer]."* *"**Each day recite the prayers of the Rosary**, five decades at least – meditating on the mysteries – to make reparation for sin."*

6. Devotion to the Immaculate Heart of Mary: *"God wishes to establish in the world **devotion to my Immaculate Heart**. If people do what I tell you, many souls will be saved and there will be peace."*

7. First Saturday Devotion: *"I promise to help at the hour of death with the graces needed for salvation those who, **on the first Saturday of five consecutive months**, go to confession, receive Holy Communion, say five decades of the Rosary and keep me company for fifteen minutes while meditating on the mysteries of the Rosary, with the intention of making reparation to my Immaculate Heart."* Jesus said to Sr. Lucia in December 1925: *"Have compassion on the heart of your Most Holy Mother, covered with thorns, with which ungrateful men pierce it at every moment, and there is no one to make reparation to remove them."* Our Lady then said: *"Look... at my Heart, surrounded with thorns with which ungrateful men pierce me at every moment by their blasphemies and ingratitude... Ask, ask again insistently for **the promulgation of the Communion of Reparation in honor of the Immaculate Heart of Mary on the first Saturdays.**"* Jesus continued later saying: *"Many souls begin the First Saturdays, but few finish*

them, and those who do complete them do so in order to receive the graces that are promised thereby. It would please Me more if they did Five with fervor and with the intention of making reparation to the Heart of your heavenly Mother, than if they did Fifteen, in a tepid and indifferent manner."

On March 19, 1939 Lucia wrote the message of Jesus as follows: *"**The time is coming when the rigor of My justice will punish the crimes of diverse nations.** Some of them will be annihilated. At last the severity of My justice will fall severely on those who want to destroy My reign in souls. **Whether the world has war or peace depends on the practice of this devotion**, along with the consecration to the Immaculate Heart of Mary. This is why I desire its propagation so ardently, especially because this is also the will of our dear Mother in Heaven."* On June 20, 1939 Lucia again wrote: *"Our Lady promised to delay the scourge of war, if this devotion was propagated and practiced. We see that She will obtain remission of this chastisement to the extent that efforts are made to propagate this devotion; but I fear that we cannot do any more than we are doing and that God, being displeased, will pull back the arm of His mercy and let the world be ravaged by this chastisement which will be unlike any other in the past, horrible, horrible."* Unfortunately, as people did not respond, WWII broke out two months later. We may wonder today: what is to come in our time, which is far worse off than in the last century, if we do not listen and heed these heavenly messages while there is still time?

8. Scapular Devotion: In the last apparition at Fatima with the Miracle of the Sun, Our Lady appeared as Our Lady of Mt. Carmel, holding the brown Scapular in her outstretched hand. The Scapular is the sign of our consecration to Mary's Immaculate Heart. As we wear it with devotion, it should daily remind us of the promise we have made to her. Lucia said: *"Our Lady wants all to wear the Scapular." "Yes, **the Rosary and the Scapular are inseparable!**"* To decide not to wear the Scapular or not to pray the Rosary daily is to say *"No"* to Our Mother, who has asked this of *you* with her loving Motherly Heart.

9. Consecration: Our Lady asks that we consecrate ourselves and our families to the Sacred Heart of Jesus and the Immaculate Heart of Mary. This means entrusting ourselves to their care and protection. Our Lord spoke with Lucia as follows: *"**I have need of souls** and of priests who serve Me by **sacrificing themselves for Me and for souls**." (6/12/41)* Lucia discusses this, saying: *"Jesus does not request great austerities, but a life of grace and fulfillment of the law: 'The penance that I request and require now is the sacrifice demanded of everybody by the accomplishment of his own duty and the observance of My law.'" (1943)* Jesus continues: *"I love, I am not loved; I manifest Myself, and I am not known; I give and nobody responds (to My advances)... I desire very ardently the propaga-*

tion of the cult and devotion to the Immaculate Heart of Mary, because this Heart is the magnet which draws souls to Me, the fire which makes the rays of My light and My love beam out over the earth, and the inexhaustible well causing the living water of [My Heart's] mercy to gush over the earth." (1943)

Our Lady is calling everyone who will listen and respond. But only a few will do so, she seems to acknowledge. However, even with a few she can do so much. Mary tells us through Fr. Gobbi: *"I reveal my secret only to the hearts of the little, the simple, and the poor because it is being accepted and believed by them... With a small number of these children, the Lord will soon restore on earth his glorious reign of love, of holiness, and of peace.*[6] Our *"yes"* to her motherly plea really will change the world for the good.

The Blessed Mother gave **fifteen promises** to St. Dominic and Bl. Alan de la Roche **for those who pray the Rosary regularly with devotion**, as follows:

1. Whoever shall faithfully serve me by the recitation of the Rosary, shall receive signal graces.

2. I promise my special protection and the greatest graces to all who shall recite the Rosary.

3. The Rosary shall be a powerful armor against hell, it will destroy vice, decrease sin, and defeat heresies.

4. It will cause virtue and good works to flourish; it will obtain for souls the abundant mercy of God; it will withdraw the hearts of men from the love of the world and its vanities, and will lift them to the desire of eternal things. Oh, that souls would sanctify themselves by this means.

5. The soul which recommends itself to me by the recitation of the Rosary, shall not perish.

6. Whoever shall recite the Rosary devoutly, applying himself to the consideration of its sacred mysteries, shall never be conquered by misfortune. God will not chastise him in His justice, he shall not perish by an unprovided death; if he be just he shall remain in the grace of God, and become worthy of eternal life.

7. Whoever shall have a true devotion for the Rosary shall not die without the Sacraments of the Church.

8. Those who are faithful in reciting the Rosary shall have during their life and at their death the light of God and the plenitude of His graces; at the moment of death they shall participate in the merits of the Saints in paradise.

9. I shall deliver from purgatory, those who have been devoted to the Rosary.

10. The faithful children of the Rosary shall merit a high degree of glory in Heaven.

11. You shall obtain all you ask of me by the recitation of the Rosary.

12. All those who propagate the holy Rosary shall be aided by me in their necessities.

13. I have obtained from my Divine Son, that all the advocates of the Rosary shall have for intercessors, the entire celestial court during their life and at the hour of death.

14. All who recite the Rosary are my sons (and daughters), and brothers (and sisters) of my only Son, Jesus Christ.

15. Devotion to my Rosary is a great sign of predestination.

St. Alphonsus Liguori said: *"Those who say the Rosary daily and wear the Brown Scapular and who do a little more, will go straight to Heaven."* This is precisely our goal, and not only this, but to get a million others to make this their goal as well, for then we would help to save the world, as Bl. Pope Pius IX said: *"If there were one million families praying the Rosary every day, the entire world would be saved,"* and as St. Pope Pius X repeated: *"Give me an army saying the Rosary and I will conquer the world."*

I remember when I first began to pray the Rosary daily. I had made a New Years' resolution on the solemnity of Mary, the Mother of God, on January 1, 1989. This was a pivotal moment in my life of conversion to Christ. For me, Mary was instrumental in my personal conversion from a life of sin. I remember praying the Rosary with great piety and love from the beginning, asking her each day for her assistance. I started by praying it each day and asking for the grace to pray it again the following day; and by God's grace, I have not stopped since. For the first year, I would especially offer my Rosary for the conversion of Russia and the fall of communism. I can attest to the power of prayer! I remember how humbled and awed I was to experience the fall of the Berlin Wall later that year, and the beginning of the fall of Communism in Europe. I really felt that my Rosary prayers had helped to bring this about. It has been wonderful to experience the power of the Rosary in so many ways. Many graces and supernatural blessings have occurred in my life and that of my family through the daily Rosary. To Jesus the glory and Mary the honor!

Authentic Witnesses of Marian Devotion

The Miraculous Cure

St. Thérèse has been called the greatest saint of modern times. Her family had a beautiful statue of Mary, which has become known as Our Lady of the Smile. She and her sisters loved this statue and would often smother their heavenly Mother with kisses and place flowers and candles in front of the statue in veneration of Mary. In May, they would go out and gather flowers in the country, and then decorate Our Lady's shrine with white hawthorn blossoms, and other flowers and green plants. Little Thérèse was delighted at this, and she would clap her hands for joy, as she looked at Our Lady with love. After her Mother died and her sister Pauline, her second mother, left home to become a Carmelite nun, nine year old Thérèse became very sick. She suffered greatly from severe headaches, nervousness and scary apparitions, obviously as attacks from the devil. During her illness, Thérèse stayed in the room with the statue of Our Lady, which was beside her bed. When her pains were less serious, she would weave garlands of daisies and forget-me-nots for Our Lady. She would often look at the statue and pray that Heaven would send her a cure.

One day in the month of May, when she was very much worse, her father came into her room. He was heartbroken over the condition of poor Thérèse. He gave his daughter Marie, some money, and told her to write to Paris for a novena of Masses, to be said at the shrine of Our Lady of Victories, to obtain the cure of his dear little girl. During the novena, on Sunday May 13, 1883, Thérèse became so ill that she did not recognize her sisters. Marie felt sure that little Thérèse was dying, and throwing herself on her knees before their beloved statue of Our Lady, she begged Our Lady to cure Thérèse. Leonie and Celine joined in with their prayers, as well, begging the Blessed Virgin Mary to have pity on their poor, sick, little sister. Then, when Thérèse was looking at the statue of Mary, it suddenly came to life. Our Lady's face glowed with a glorious beauty, and she smiled at Thérèse, which filled the girl with joy. Our Lady's smile was like a warm ray of sunshine and love. Two large tears of joy rolled down Thérèse's cheeks, and she thought, *"Ah! The Blessed Virgin smiled at me, how happy I am."*

During this time, Marie saw her sister Thérèse, as in an ecstasy of love, as she gazed at the Blessed Virgin Mary herself! The vision seemed to last about four or five minutes and during this time, little Thérèse was miraculously cured; all her pains and weariness had disappeared. Later, when Marie was alone with Thérèse, she asked her why she had just shed some tears. Thérèse didn't want to tell her secret of what happened, but when she saw that Marie had guessed that Our Lady had appeared to her, she said, *"I cried because Our Lady had disappeared."* Thérèse would never forget that special day when Mary smiled at her; she would recall it some years later and write about it in her autobiography, *The Story of a Soul*.

The Immaculata's Printing Press

St. Maximilian Kolbe was considered a rambunctious child until he completely changed his life in 1906 after he received a vision from Mary. St. Kolbe said, *"I asked the Mother of God what was to become of me. Then she came to me holding two crowns, one white, the other red. She asked if I was willing to accept either of these crowns. The white one meant that I should persevere in purity, and the red that I should become a martyr. I said that I would accept them both."*

St. Kolbe formed the *Militia of the Immaculata*, an organization of Marian consecration. Father Kolbe planned to start a printing house where information could be mass produced and sent to millions of people. However, he had only half of the necessary funds. He trusted the *Immaculata* to help, praying that she would supply them with the needed funds to complete the work and print their publications. During his prayer before a statue of the Blessed Mother, he noticed an envelope. On the envelope, it said, *"For you, Immaculata."* Inside, the exact amount needed to complete the project.

St. Kolbe and the other priests developed a monthly magazine with a circulation of over one million. The friars used the latest printing and administrative technologies to print and distribute their publications. When World War II started, the printing apostolate that Father Kolbe had started was a target of hatred from the Germans.

Father Kolbe was arrested by the Gestapo and was later transferred to the concentration camp at Auschwitz. One day, a man in St. Kolbe's block had escaped. All of the men from that block were brought out into the hot sun and made to stand all day with no food or drink. At the end of the day, the man that had escaped had not yet been found. Commandant Fritsch, the guard who was in charge of this group, told the men that ten would die in place of the one that had escaped. The guard called out the names. One man, Polish Sergeant Francis Gajowniczek, begged to be spared because he had a wife and children. Father Kolbe silently stepped forward and stood before Commandant Fritsch and said: *"I am a Catholic priest from Poland; I would like to take his place, because he has a wife and children."* The commandant stood silent for a moment, and then allowed St. Kolbe to take his place. He was then sent to the starvation chamber. St. Kolbe led the Rosary and sang hymns to the *Immaculata* with the other prisoners in the bunker. After two weeks, the cell had to be cleared out for more prisoners. Only four prisoners were left, Father Kolbe was one of them. They injected a lethal dose of carbolic acid into each prisoner. St. Kolbe, the last prisoner left to be killed, raised his arm to the guard. On August 14, 1941, the eve of the feast of the Assumption of Our Lady, St. Kolbe was martyred. The next day, his body was cremated. He had received both crowns promised by Our Lady.[7]

The Great Marian Pilgrimage

The most important aspect of Marian devotion and consecration is that it be personal and from the heart. No one exemplifies this better than Archbishop Fulton Sheen. While still a student, he made a pilgrimage to Our Lady of Lourdes. He had just enough money to get there, but then arrived broke. He thought: *"Well, if I have faith enough to go to Lourdes to celebrate the fifth anniversary of my Ordination, it is up to the Blessed Mother to get me out."* He decided that if Mary was going to pay his hotel bill, he would stay in a *good* hotel. He prayed a nine day novena, but on the ninth day nothing happened. It was serious. He finally decided to give the Blessed Mother another chance. He went to the Marian grotto late in the evening. An American tapped him on the shoulder and asked him to be an interpreter for him and his family in Paris for the rest of their trip. He agreed. As they were walking away, the man asked him: *"Have you paid your hotel bill yet?"* He then paid the bill in full. Fulton Sheen became friends with this couple, Mr. and Mrs. Thomas Farrell, who he said *"had become the agents of the Blessed Mother to save me from my creditors."* Mary loves her children, especially those who love her in return.[8]

The *Hail Mary Pass*

Roger Staubach, former Dallas Cowboys quarterback and member of the Pro Football Hall of Fame, allowed his Catholic faith to influence how he played. His most famous career moment was the *"Hail Mary Pass"* he threw in the 1975 playoff game against the Minnesota Vikings. With only seconds left and Dallas trailing 14-10, Staubach launched a 50-yard pass to Drew Pearson, who amazingly caught it and took the Cowboys to victory. After the game, Staubach confidently told reporters that he had prayed a *"Hail Mary"* prayer before throwing the pass, which indicated that he attributed the success of the *"miraculous"* play to the Virgin Mary. The term is now part of football vocabulary for passes made in desperation with very small chances of success.

Our Lady Consoles Her Son

When my family and I lived in Michigan a few years ago, we used to make a pilgrimage several times a year to Our Lady of Consolation, a Marian shrine that had a miraculous statue of Mary holding the

Christ Child, but which had otherwise fallen out of notoriety in recent years, which was located three hours south in Carey, Ohio. We would pray the full Rosary as we traveled, go to Confession and then to Mass at the shrine, venerate the relic of the true Cross and various other relics of Saints, and pray the Way of the Cross in the religious grotto and park nearby the basilica. We were amazed at all the pictures and crutches in the crypt that people had left as testimony of healings, attributed to Our Lady of Consolation's intercession. These pilgrimages were some of the best times our family had together. I took my Mariology students there on a class trip as well. Our Lady always consoled us and heard our prayers.

After four years living in Michigan, we moved to Atlanta, hundreds of miles and several states to the south, and into the middle of the Baptist Bible Belt – true missionary country for Catholics. I had taken a position working at a new Catholic college, but soon began to wonder if we had made the right decision, as things were difficult with selling the house, the kids' new schooling, and a new job, at least at first. So, as we went to daily Mass and gathered for our family Rosary each evening, we decided to add a novena prayer asking Our Lady to console us and to give us a signal grace to confirm the Lord's will concerning our life in Atlanta. Around nine days later, my wife Diana called me to tell me that she had bought some clothes for the children at a secular resale shop, and then stopped nearby at an antique store. While there, she came across an old small plastic statue of Mary that she thought I might like and so she had picked it up.

As I arrived home and saw the statue, I immediately realized it was the *signal grace* from our heavenly Mother. On the front of the statue was inscribed into the plastic, *Our Lady of Consolation*, and on the back it read, *Carey, Ohio*. It must have been several decades old, and we had never seen any statue for sale like it in all the times we had gone to the shrine. Mary had followed us to Atlanta to console us and to assure us that we were in her care and following her Son's will! We know that God is calling us to reach out to His Mother, to put our lives in her hands, and to trust in Him.

Chapter Two
The Call of Conversion

Jesus, Mary, I love you, save souls.
Let us eternally adore the Holy Sacrament through Mary.
To the Two Hearts of Jesus and Mary be honor and glory.
Let the Kingdom of the Divine Will (Fiat) come!

Prayer to the Sacred Heart
From the depth of my nothingness,
I prostrate myself before You,
O Most Sacred, Divine, and Adorable Heart of Jesus,
to pay You all the homage
of love, praise, and adoration in my power. Amen.
St. Margaret Mary

Prayers of Fatima
Pardon Prayer
My God, I believe, I adore, I hope, and I love You.
I implore pardon for those who do not believe,
do not adore, do not hope, and do not love You. Amen.

Angel of Peace Prayer
Most Holy Trinity - Father, Son, and Holy Spirit -
I adore You profoundly and I offer You
the most precious Body, Blood,
Soul, and Divinity of Jesus Christ,
present in all the tabernacles of the world,
in reparation for the outrages, sacrileges,
and indifferences by which He Himself is offended.
And by the infinite merits
of His Most Sacred Heart
and those of the Immaculate Heart of Mary,
I beg You for the conversion
of poor sinners. Amen.

Eucharistic Prayer
Most Holy Trinity, I adore you! My God,
my God, I love You in the Most Blessed Sacrament.

II

HOPE DURING

The vision awaits its time;
It hastens to the end – it will not lie.
If it seem slow, wait for it;
It will surely come, it will not delay.
Habakkuk 2: 2-3

And when you hear of wars and tumults,
do not be terrified;
for this must first take place,
but the end will not be at once…
Nation will rise against nation,
and kingdom against kingdom;
there will be great earthquakes,
and in various places famines and pestilences;
and there will be terrors and great signs from heaven…
And there will be signs in sun and moon and stars,
and upon the earth distress of nations in perplexity
at the roaring of the sea and the waves,
men fainting with fear
and with foreboding of what is coming on the world;
for the powers of the heavens will be shaken.
Luke 21:9-28

The chastisements are necessary;
they will serve to prepare the ground so that the Kingdom of the
Supreme Fiat may form in the midst of the human family…
The chastisements will serve to purify the face of the earth *so that*
the Divine Will may reign on it…
So, let Me do it, do not oppose My chastising the people.
Our Lord to Luisa Piccarreta

The Chastisement, Antichrist & Great Tribulation

છ

*Then the dragon was angry with the woman,
and went off to make war on the rest of her offspring,
on those who **keep the commandments** of God
and bear testimony to Jesus.*
Revelation 12:17

*The son of perdition,
who opposes and exults himself
against every so-called god or object of worship,
(will take) his seat in the temple of God,
proclaiming himself to be God...
and the Lord Jesus will slay him with the breath of his mouth and
destroy him by his appearing and his coming.
The coming of the lawless one by the activity of Satan will be with all
power and with pretended signs and wonders,
and with all wicked deception for those who are to perish,
because **they refused to love the truth** and so be saved.*
2 Thessalonians 2:3-10

The Book of Revelation is unfolding before us in our times. In various ways, God has allowed His Mother, the Prophetess of our times, to give us advanced warning, so that the children of the light may become spiritually prepared for the mystery of iniquity, which is coming through the ever increasing spread of apostasy. This is becoming more and more manifest and will do so until the time of the Antichrist and the great tribulation and persecution of the Church. Our Lady tells us through Fr. Gobbi that she desires us to become involved on her side of the great battle and that what is to come involves everyone: *"I have come from heaven to reveal to you my plan in this struggle which involves everyone, marshalled together at the orders of the two opposing leaders: the Woman clothed with the sun and the Red Dragon [that is, the Devil]. ... I am now announcing to you that **THIS is the time of the decisive battle**. During these years, I myself am intervening, as the Woman clothed with the sun, in order to bring to fulfillment the Triumph of my Immaculate Heart."* And so the divine battle plan unfolds.

Revelation 4-11

A Three-Fold Prophecy for Our Time

From 1961 to 1965, the Blessed Mother reportedly appeared to four visionaries (including a woman named Conchita) in Garabandal, Spain. The Archbishop Carlos Osoro Sierra of Oviedo, who is Apostolic Administrator of the region of Garabandal, said in May 2007: *"I respect the apparitions and have known of authentic conversions… I encourage you to continue maintaining this devotion to our Mother."*[1] Over the years, many holy persons have personally supported Garabandal. For example, Bl. Mother Teresa said: *"Garabandal is true."* John Paul II expressed support as well.[2] In these extraordinary apparitions which included visions, ecstatic marches, mystical Communions, and the reading of hearts, Our Lady is asking for the faithful to make many sacrifices, doing penance, and visiting the Blessed Sacrament frequently. She asks us to lead good lives. It seems that corresponding with the Great Tribulation, three great events of purification have been predicted at Garabandal: **a Warning** which will appear in the sky and then be felt interiorly to show every person in the world the state of their soul before God, and this miracle of souls will serve to correct the conscience of the world; **a Miracle Sign** in Garabandal that will leave a visible supernatural Sign to remain until the end of time; and, as the world still does not convert, after the Warning and Miracle, then may come **a worldwide Chastisement**.

This world is in need of cleansing and conversion more than ever, and it will come. Fear does not help. What is needed is a steady calm, which can only occur if we are grounded in a life of trust in Jesus, with a strong daily prayer life. Pray for safety and a swift coming of the Kingdom of God. Then, you will be assured of peace, even during the upheaval.

1. A Worldwide Warning of Purification and Mercy

"Seek the Lord while he may be found, call upon him while he is near; let the wicked forsake his way, and the unrighteous man his thoughts; let him return to the Lord, that he may have mercy on him."
Isaiah 55:6-7

The message of Garabandal speaks of a divine warning. Conchita wrote: *"The warning comes directly from God and will be visible to the whole world and from any place where anyone many happen to be. It will be like the revelation of our sins and **it will be seen and felt by everyone**, believer and unbeliever alike irrespective of whatever religion he may belong to. It will be seen and felt in all parts of the world and by every person."* She also said: *"Everyone in the whole world will see **a sign, a grace, or a punishment within themselves - in other words, a Warning**. They will find themselves all alone in the world no matter where they are at the time, alone with their conscience right before God. They will then see all their sins and what their sins have caused."* The Warning is further detailed as follows:

> ***First, a World-Wide Warning that will happen in the sky...like the collision of two stars that do not fall down...*** *it will frighten all humanity regardless of where one happens to be at the time... it will be a thousand times worse than earthquakes... like a fire that will not burn our flesh ... it will last a very short time, although to us it will seem to be a very long time ... no one can prevent it from happening ... **It will be recognized as coming from God...** it will resemble a punishment ... it is meant to be a purification ... like the revelation of our*

*sins and what we will feel in our hearts will be worse than sorrow. It will not kill us, if we die it will be caused by the emotion within us. The date was not revealed only that it will happen **before the announcement of the miracle.**[3]*

Our Lady of All Nations prophesied about **warning signs** to come as indication of the apocalyptic time, including **meteors** and natural disasters, along with political conflicts and economic disasters. She also promised that **if we seek her help, she will bestow Grace, Redemption, and Peace** to stave off degeneration, disaster, and war.[4] Further, Our Lady revealed to Fr. Gobbi concerning the Warning:

*A new **fire will come down from heaven and will purify all humanity**, which has again become pagan. It will be like a judgment in miniature and each one will see himself in the light of the very Truth of God. Thus sinners will come back to grace and holiness; the straying, to the road of righteousness; those far away, to the house of the Father...*[5]

It will be a *"correction"* of our conscience: the consciences of all will be illuminated by God so that we will see at once what sin really is and how we have offended God. We will see ourselves as we really are in the sight of God. This illumination of our minds will be *"the ultimate act of mercy"* before God's justice is sent upon the earth. The Warning will cause great fear (especially for the unprepared) and will make us reflect within ourselves on the consequences of our own personal sins. Even if it lasts only a moment, it will be very terrible and impressive. It will be a small judgment. Each person will know exactly where he or she stands with God. We will have *"something like an interior feeling of sorrow and pain for having offended God. He will help us to sense physically that deep sorrow."*

This prophecy did not originate with Garabandal. It has been prophesied by other mystics in recent times. Saint Edmund Campion, in the sixteenth century, spoke of *"a great day, not wherein any temporal potentate should minister, but wherein the Terrible Judge should reveal all men's consciences and try every man of each kind of religion."* Jesus revealed to St. Faustina that this great gift of His mercy He now plans to give humanity is *"a sign for the end times"*.

What makes **the Warning** prophesied at Garabandal completely unique is that it is promised to occur imminently – the visionary will be alive to experience it and to announce what will come afterwards. It **will occur in our lifetime, and soon!**

This divine miracle has been called the *"Warning," "Notification," "Illumination," "Enlightenment"* of conscience, *"Minor or Mini-Judgment,"* and the merciful divine *"Correction."*

2. A Miracle and Permanent Sign of Great Love

Then, very soon after this manifestation of the Lord's Mercy, the Lord will appear in Garabandal in a great Miracle. The message is summarized as follows:

A miracle is to occur in Garabandal within 12 months after the Warning... *It will be on a Thursday at 8:30 p.m. (lasting about 15 minutes) coinciding with a happy event in the Church, on a feast-day of a martyred Saint of the Eucharist ... (this martyr is not Jesus or Mary) ... it will happen in the month of March, April, or May... between the 7th and the 17th of the month but not the 7th or the 17th... it will be seen by looking up over the area of the Pines and will be visible from all the surrounding mountainside which will serve as a 'natural' amphitheater.* **The sick will be cured...the unbelievers will be converted...**

(Visionary) Conchita knows the nature of the great miracle as well as the exact date and she will announce the date eight days before it happens. The means of communicating the date to the world will be a miracle in itself. [The miracle] will be able to be filmed, photographed and televised. The Virgin told Conchita that before the Miracle, there will be only three popes (Paul VI, John Paul I and John Paul II), thus **it will occur during the papal reign of Benedict XVI.**

A Permanent Sign will remain at Garabandal in memory of the miracle as visible proof of our Blessed Mother's love for all humanity. It will be a 'thing' never before seen upon the earth, as something not of this world, but of God. It can be photographed but not touched.[6]

Our Lady seems to be promising that **a miraculous permanent Sign will be granted in several places** where she has been reportedly appearing in our times. Besides at **Garabandal**, at **Medjugorje**, the third of the ten secrets foretold there involves a similar prophecy concerning a Sign to appear in Medjugorje as well, on the original hill of apparitions, which will also remain until the end of the world. Our Lady has also reportedly appeared recently in Cuenca, Ecuador, to visionary Patricia "Pachi" Talbot, as *"Our Lady Guardian of the Faith"*, which has received initial diocesan recognition of support.[7] Our Lady reportedly prophesized that she will also leave a Sign at the apparition and shrine site of **El Cajas, near Cuenca**, to occur in the near future when all her apparitions in the world cease.

Our Lady is asking for prayer and penance to avert the coming chastisements while there is still time. Through the effects of the Sign, conversions will be vast and great. But, many will also harden their hearts. God will have to intervene again to bring His justice to humanity. Interestingly, Our Lady had also told Conchita that there would not be another world war.[8] So too said Our Lady at Medjugorje.[9]

Joey Lomangino, who has spent his life spreading the message of Garabandal, is totally and incurably blind. At the age of 16, he was blinded and his sense of smell was destroyed when a tire he was inflating blew up in his face. He went to visit St. Pio and asked him if Garabandal was true and whether he should go there. Padre Pio said, *"Yes"* to both questions. St. Pio touched Joey's face and his sense of smell was restored. Visionary Conchita of Garabandal told Joey that when the Miracle happens there, Joey will regain his sight. He is 79 years old in 2009.

The only other person to see Our Blessed Mother at Garabandal besides the visionaries was a 38-year old Spanish Jesuit Priest, **Father Luis Marie Andreu**. Father Luis witnessed the four visionaries of Garabandal in ecstasy in August 1961, and afterwards said: *"I feel myself truly full of joy and happiness. What a gift the Virgin has given me. How fortunate to have a mother like her in heaven! We shouldn't have any fear of the supernatural life. We should learn to act toward the Virgin as the children do. They have given us an example. I can't have the least doubt about the truth of their visions. Why has the most Holy Virgin chosen us? Today is the happiest day of my life!"* After saying this, he died that very moment in what seemed to have been a rapture of ecstasy and joy. Visionary Conchita revealed in 1964 that she had been told from a locution that Father Luis' body will be found incorrupt the day after the Great Miracle of Garabandal occurs.[10]

The purpose of the Great Miracle is **to show us the love God has for us and to convert the whole world**. And this is not the first time God has given such a great miracle through the Blessed Mother to bring conversion. God sent Our Lady to the New World in the sixteenth century to give His mercy to the Aztecs. Just as God gave the Aztecs of the New World the Great Miracle image of Our Lady of Guadalupe, which converted them almost overnight (10 million to Catholicism in the first 10 years); so too, through Our Lady, God is about to give the whole world in our day a new Great Miracle to bring all humanity to conversion. Just as the Aztecs were engaged in human sacrifice and Satanism, so too, today the whole world is engaging in the human sacrifice of the unborn through abortion and has handed itself over to the reign of Satan (remember Leo XIII's vision). And, just as it did the Aztecs, the new Great Miracle God is about to grant us *will* soon change the whole world forever. What a great day it will be! But, alas, some will still not listen; and so God's mercy and great miracle will be followed afterwards by His justice and chastisement.

A Great Sign in the Sky

The Great Sign prophesied in Garabandal, and as well in Medjugorje, may correspond to a prophecy that St. Faustina received from the Lord. **The Lord spoke to St. Faustina about a great darkness and a great sign**, explaining what would accompany it, saying:

> *Before I come as a just judge, I am coming first as 'King of Mercy!' Let all men now approach the throne of my mercy with absolute confidence! Some time before the last days of final justice arrive, there will be given to mankind a great sign in the heavens of this sort: all the light of the heavens will be totally extinguished... There will be **a great darkness** over the whole earth. Then **a great sign of the cross will appear** in the sky. From the openings from where the hands and feet of the savior were nailed will come forth great lights*

which will light up the earth for a period of time. This will happen before the very final days. It is the sign for the end of the world. **After it will come the days of justice!** *Let souls have recourse to the fount of my mercy while there is still time! Woe to him who does not recognize the time of my visitation…*

In the Old Covenant I sent prophets wielding thunderbolts to My people. **Today I am sending you with My mercy to the people of the whole world.** *I do not want to punish aching mankind, but I desire to heal it, pressing it to My merciful Heart. I use punishment when they themselves force Me to do so; My hand is reluctant to take hold of the sword of justice.* **Before the Day of Justice, I am sending the Day of Mercy.**[11]

3. A Terrible Divine Chastisement

The supernatural Sign given in Garabandal will be followed by a conditional Chastisement, a divine punishment. Conchita has written: *"I cannot reveal what kind of punishment it is except that it will be a result of the direct intervention of God, which makes it more terrible and fearful than anything we can imagine. It will be less painful for innocent babies to die a natural death than for those babies to die because of the punishment. All Catholics should go to confession before the punishment and the others should repent of their sins. When I saw IT (the punishment), I felt a great fear even though at the same time I was seeing Our Blessed Mother. The punishment, if it comes, will come after the miracle."* The final message of Garabandal is understood as follows:

> ***The final prophecy depends on whether or not mankind has heeded the message of Our Lady...*** *The vision of this 'conditional punishment' brought terror and tears to the children...* ***If it happens, it will be*** *more terrible than anything we can possibly imagine because it will be the result of* ***the direct intervention of God. It will have nothing to do with wars, revolutions or the hardness of men's hearts.*** *Conchita says, 'If the punishment comes, and I believe it will come, it will come after the promised miracle.'*[12]

Conchita also said: *"The Chastisement cannot be (altogether) avoided, because we have lost even the meaning of sin."*[13]

In a similar apparition, on October 13, 1973, which is the anniversary of the 1917 miracle of Fatima, Our Lady appeared to visionary and stigmatist, Sr. Agnes Sasagawa of Akita, in what has since been recognized as a Church-approved apparition,[14] stating as follows:

> *As I told you,* ***if*** *men do not repent and better themselves, the Father will inflict* ***a terrible punishment*** *on all humanity. It will be a punishment* ***greater than the deluge,*** *such as one will never have seen before.* ***Fire will fall from the sky and***

*will wipe out a great part of humanity, the good as well as the bad, sparing neither priests nor faithful. The survivors will find themselves so desolate that they will envy the dead. **The only arms which will remain for you will be the Rosary and the Sign** left by my Son. Each day, recite the prayers of the Rosary. **With the Rosary, pray for the Pope, the bishops and the priests.** The work of **the devil will infiltrate even into the Church** in such a way that one will see cardinals opposing cardinals, and bishops against other bishops. The priests who venerate me will be scorned and opposed by their Confreres. The churches and altars will be sacked. The Church will be full of those who accept compromises and the demon will press many priests and consecrated souls to leave the service of the Lord. The demon will rage especially against souls consecrated to God. The thought of the loss of so many souls is the cause of my sadness. If sins increase in number and gravity, there will no longer be pardon for them.*

While in Akita, Fr. Gobbi received this confirmation of the warning and chastisement that will soon purify the world, as had been foretold to Sr. Agnes:

*I now announce to you that the time of **the great trial** has come, because during these years all that I foretold to you will come to pass. **The apostasy** and **the great schism in the Church** is on the point of taking place **and the great chastisement,** about which I foretold you in this place (Akita), is* *now at the very doors. **Fire will come down from heaven and a great part of humanity will be destroyed.** Those who survive will envy the dead, because everywhere there will be desolation, death, and ruin... in order to be protected and saved, [you] must all enter right away into the safe refuge of my Immaculate Heart.*[15]

The messages to Fr. Gobbi include details of the chastisement, as follows:

*Because this humanity has not accepted my repeated call to conversion, to repentance, and to a return to God, there is about to fall upon it **the greatest chastisement which the history of mankind has ever known**. It is a chastisement much greater than that of the flood...*

In appearance everything remains calm and it seems that all is going well. In reality, [the Church] is being pervaded with an overwhelming lack of faith which is spreading the greatest apostasy everywhere. Many bishops, priests, religious and faithful no longer believe and have already lost the true faith in Jesus and in his Gospel. For this reason the Church must be purified with persecution and with blood...

These are the times foretold by me, when cardinals will be set against cardinals, bishops against bishops, and priests against priests and the flock of Christ will be torn to pieces by rapacious wolves who have found their way in under the clothing of defenseless and meek lambs. Among them there are even some who occupy posts of great responsibility and, by means of them, **Satan has succeeded in entering and in operating at the very summit of the Church... The activity of my Adversary to extend his reign over all humanity, will become stronger.** *Thus evil and sin, violence and hatred, perversion and unbelief will increase everywhere. Wars will spread...*

Even in the Church, the darkness will descend more densely yet, and will succeed in enveloping everything. Errors will spread much more and many will wander away from the true faith...

The contestation directed against the Pope will become stronger; theologians, bishops, priests and laity will openly oppose his Magisterium... *You have entered* **the conclusive period of the great tribulation, and the hour of the great trial... has now arrived for you. It is a trial so great and painful, that you cannot even imagine it, but it is necessary for the Church and for all humanity, in order that the new era, the new world, and the reconciliation of humanity with the Lord, may come upon you.**[16]

Archbishop Fulton Sheen once said that if the United States continued to kill life at its beginnings with **abortion**, at its mid-day with the **handicapped**, and at twilight with **euthanasia**, it would lead to the catastrophic midnight of nuclear war. Bl. Mother Teresa of Calcutta agreed, saying: *"Abortion leads to nuclear war!"* Remember that Our Lady of America warned: ***"Dear children, unless the United States accepts and carries out faithfully the mandate given to it by heaven to lead the world to peace, there will come upon it and all nations a great havoc of war and incredible suffering,"*** and she warned that this **may include nuclear warfare if we do not convert**. Our Lady also said through Fr. Gobbi: *"This crime (abortion) cries for vengeance in the sight of God."* It appears today to be well after eleven in the evening. But, there is still hope! And *we* know where, and from whom, our hope comes.

This Period of Mercy will include the Warning of Garabandal and the fulfilling of the first three secrets of Medjugorje (which are in the form of 3 warnings). Then the Miracle of Garabandal, which seems to correlate with the second part of the third secret of Medjugorje, will occur. At this point, the Book of Revelation discusses the "seven" seals events, which likely include Garabandal's Chastisement and the remaining "seven" of the Medjugorje secrets. The last two secrets are particularly "grave matters" in the form of a "chastisement." The last two seals of Revelation are also particularly grave. Then the great battle and God's justice! But, not until after the pivotal intervention of the "woman" of Revelation 12. God will send His Mother to help us, especially those who entrust themselves to her care. Our Lady said at Fatima: *"I am the only one who can help you!"*[17] The Our Lady of Akita statue (which is of Our Lady of All Nations) wept 101 times. In the end, Our Lady of Akita said: *"Whoever entrusts themselves to me will be saved."* What more do *you* need? Respond now, Our Lady is pleading!

Revelation 12
& the Triumph of the Immaculate Heart

The Great Pope and Monarch

Various prophecies, as summarized by Yves Dupont, author of *Catholic Prophecy*, warn that during these times, communism *and* democracy will collapse.[18] Concerning democracy, though a democratic form of government is legitimate and even preferred, when it cuts itself off from God, it necessarily disintegrates.[19] To remain legitimate, democracies must be guided by moral law – which is immutable, proper to human nature, and universal to all people, as established by reason.[20] When this is denied and replaced by ethical relativism, then *"the deepest meaning of democracy is lost and its stability is compromised."*[21] John Paul II warned, saying: *"It must be observed in this regard that if there is no ultimate truth to guide and direct political action, then ideas and convictions can easily be manipulated for reasons of power. As history demonstrates, a democracy without values easily turns into open or thinly disguised totalitarianism.*"[22] This is the state of democracy in the western de-Christianized world today, with its effects of practical atheism, relativism, and hedonism. Western society has today seen the establishment of *"structures of sin"* that include the cultural promotion of fornication, contraception, and pornography, just as Our Lady of Fatima prophesied that the greatest sins of our times would be sins of the flesh, and also the legalization of abortion. And these things have lead us to crisis on the verge of collapse.

After this takes place, a great Christian King, chosen by God through the Pope, will ascend the throne, and restore order. France and the world will be re-consecrated to the Sacred Heart. Confirming these events, Bl. Anna Maria Taigi prophesied, saying: *"France shall fall into a frightful anarchy. The French will have a desperate civil war... the Pope shall send to France a special legate... His Holiness himself shall nominate a most Christian King for the government of France."*[23] St. Bridget of Sweden thinks that he will be a monarch of Spanish origin who will be elected and who will in a wonderful manner be victorious *through the sign of the Cross*; he will restore the Church in *Santa Sophia* (in Constantinople/Istanbul), and all the earth shall enjoy a brief period of peace and prosperity. Bl. Anne Catherine Emmerick calls the Great Monarch by the name of *Henry*. She says he will be a close ally of the Holy Pontiff.

St. Francis Paola prophesied about the great king and the great
Pope who will together fight for peace, as follows:

> *He (the great king) shall be a first-born son; in his childhood
> he will be like a saint; in his youth, a great sinner; then he will
> be converted entirely to God and will do great penance; his
> sins will be forgiven him, and he will become a great saint.*

> *He shall be a great captain and prince of holy men, who shall
> be called 'the holy Cross-bearers of Jesus Christ,' with whom
> he shall destroy the Mahometan sect and the rest of the infidels
> (in a war of self-defense and with the Gospel of love). He shall
> annihilate all the heresies and tyrannies of the world. He shall
> reform the church of God by means of his followers, who shall
> be the best men upon earth in holiness, in arms, in science, and
> in every virtue, because such is the will of the Most High. They
> shall obtain the dominion of the whole world, both temporal
> and spiritual, and they shall support the Church of God until
> the end of time.*

> *... [Sinners should] be prepared for the greatest scourges to
> fall upon them. But from whom? First from heretics and infi-
> dels, then from the holy and most faithful Cross-bearers elected
> by the Most High, who, not succeeding in converting the here-
> tics with science, shall have to make vigorous use of their
> arms... The infidels also shall fight against Christians and
> heretics, sacking, destroying, and killing the largest portion of*

Christians. Lastly, the army styled 'of the Church,' namely, the holy Cross-bearers, shall move, not against Christians or Christianity, but against those infidels in pagan countries, and they shall conquer all those kingdoms with the death of a very great number of infidels. After this they shall turn their victorious arms against bad Christians, and destroy all the rebels against Jesus Christ. These holy Cross-bearers shall reign and dominate holily over the world until the end of time...

*But when shall this take place? When crosses with the stigmas shall be seen (Interestingly, Stigmatist **Fr. Zlatko Sudac**[24] in our day has the stigmata seal of the Cross on his forehead, as similar to what is mentioned in the Book of Revelation, Chapter 7), and the crucifix shall be carried as the standard... This standard will be admired by all good Catholics; but at the beginning it will be derided by bad Christians and by infidels. Their sneers shall, however, be changed into mourning when they shall witness the wonderful victories achieved through it against tyrants, heretics, and infidels...*

*That man (the leader of the Crucifers)... shall be the founder of a new religious order different from all the others. He shall divide it into three classes, namely: (1) military knights, (2) solitary priests, (3) most pious hospitallers. **This shall be the last religious order of the Church**, and it will do more good for our holy religion than all other religious institutes. By force of arms he shall take possession of a great kingdom. He shall de-*

stroy the sect of Mahomet, extirpate all tyrants and heresies. He shall bring the world to a more holy mode of life. There will be one fold and one Shepherd. He shall reign until the end of time. In the whole earth there shall be only twelve kings, one emperor, one pope. Rich gentlemen shall be few, but all saints.[25]

According to various prophesies, the great monarch will fight until he is about forty, when victory will be complete. Then, a period of peace and prosperity will follow, but it will not yet be the great era of peace. Toward the end of his reign, the great monarch will go to Jerusalem and lay down his crown on Mount Olivet. And the Antichrist will wage war against him.

An Interim of Peace for 25 Years

After the initial stage of the significant, historical purification of the Church and the world – which will occur with the Warning, Great Miracle, and Chastisement (with its seven seals and trumpets as described in Revelation 6-11) – Revelation Chapter 12 then speaks of a great red dragon that will make war on the "woman" who appears from Heaven. As this great war ensues, St. Michael and his angels will fight against the dragon and throw him down to the earth. The dragon will then pursue the woman. But, before he is able to defeat her, she will flee into the wilderness, for what Revelation 12:14 says is a period that will last *"for a time, and times, and half a time."* It is in this period of time that the great pope and monarch will reign. And after this period of relative peace and delay in the apocalyptic battle, according to the Book of Revelation, then there will come the time of the Antichrist who will *"make war on the rest of her offspring, on those who keep the commandments of God and bear testimony to Jesus"* (which will include the seven plagues from the seven bowls of the wrath of God as described in Revelation 16).

Revelation discusses how the Dragon will pursue the Woman into the desert (chapter 12). The Dragon then spews a flood of water after the Woman, hoping to drown her. Our Lady tells Fr. Gobbi the meaning of this, saying: *"What is this flood of water if not the ensemble of these **new theological theories**, by which an attempt is being made to bring your heavenly Mother down from the place where the Most Holy Trinity has put her? Thus it has been possible to obscure me in the souls, in the life, and in the piety of many of my (spiritual) children."*[26] But, Our Lady will shine in her radiant glory and usher in the springtime of the New Evangelization.

It is in this period of the interlude in the cosmic battle that the Triumph of the Blessed Virgin will occur and will in turn slow the work of the devil in these times. Many believe the Great Marian Triumph will occur through the proclamation of a new Marian Dogma to initiate the Triumph of the Immaculate Heart. And thus the Triumph of Mary will precede the Era of Peace and the Eucharistic Reign of the Jesus Christ, which will come after the Antichrist is destroyed. In all of this, Mary and her Son will crush the head of the serpent-dragon. And finally, the Two Hearts will triumph and reign together.

At the Church-approved apparition of **La Salette**, Our Lady speaks about this temporary period of peace, saying it will last 25 years, as an interim in the context of two series of events – first the intervention of Christ in a great manifestation of mercy (including the Warning and Great Miracle) and in various cataclysms (Rev. 4-11); then, the interim of **the great springtime of the Church for 25 years** (Rev. 12); and finally, the time of the Antichrist, the great tribulation, and the terrible chastisement (Rev. 13-20). Mary summarizes the three stages of the events of the Apocalypse, saying:

> *The righteous will suffer greatly. Their prayers, their penances and their tears will rise up to Heaven and all of God's people will beg for forgiveness and mercy and will plead for my help and intercession. And then Jesus Christ, in an act of His justice and His great mercy will command His angels to have all His enemies put to death.* ***Suddenly, the persecutors of the Church of Jesus Christ and all those given over to sin will perish and the earth will become desert-like. And then peace will be made, and man will be reconciled with God.*** *Jesus Christ will be served, worshipped, and glorified. Charity will flourish everywhere.* ***The new kings will be the right arm of the holy Church,*** *which will be strong, humble, pious, poor but fervent in the imitation of the virtues of Jesus Christ. The Gospel will be preached everywhere and mankind will make great progress*

in its faith, for there will be unity among the workers of Jesus Christ and man will live in fear of God.

This peace among men will be short-lived. Twenty-five years of plentiful harvests will make them forget that the sins of men are the cause of all the troubles on this earth. *A forerunner of the Antichrist, with his troops gathered from several nations, will fight against the true Christ, the only Savior of the world. He will shed much blood and will want to annihilate the worship of God to make himself be looked upon as a God.*

And so will unfold the apocalyptic battle that has already begun.

The New and Final Marian Dogma

We must wonder what will cause this period of 25 years of peace to interrupt the war between the "woman" and the dragon. What will cause the great springtime of renewal and evangelization after the divine warning, great miracle and chastisement? It will most assuredly be a great gift from God for the Church. Our Lady herself, just like described in the Third Secret of Fatima, will intervene to call on God's mercy for her children. It seems God will give us a great gift concerning Mary herself, to armor us for the final great battle of the Apocalypse. Could it be the fifth Marian dogma?

Our Lady of All Nations, the twentieth century, Church-approved apparitions of Our Lady and Our Lord to Ida Peerdeman of Amsterdam,[27] speaks of a victory and period of peace that will arrive after the final dogma of Mary is proclaimed by the Church – that of **Mary Coredemptrix, Mediatrix, and Advocate**. *When exactly this new Marian dogma will be proclaimed is unknown*, but that it will be proclaimed is assured by Our Lady of All Nations. Mary also stated that the new dogma will be proclaimed only after a period of struggle and upheaval for the Church. The final and greatest Marian dogma will come, that is assured, but only through a struggle that will arouse much controversy that will be hard and bitter, and the dogma will be much disputed. Giving us hope and commissioning us, Our Lady says: *"Let the following words sink in well: the Lady of All Nations can and will bestow on all peoples of the world who have recourse to her – **grace, redemption, and peace**. To you all, however, falls the task of introducing the Lady of All Nations to the whole world... Do **fight and ask for this Dogma**, it is the Crowning of your Lady!"*

Mary's heavenly role is already a doctrine of our Faith, but it has not yet been defined and declared a dogma by the Magisterium. This new dogma will usher in a period of peace for God's people in the midst of the battle with the dragon, as Revelation 12 indicates. Let's examine the three-fold title of the great and final Marian dogma as follows:

1. Co-Redemptrix

We should take a moment to discuss this climatic proposed-dogma of our time. It is important to understand that *"Co-redemptrix"* means *"Female (trix) with (co) the Redeemer,"* not *"equal to"* but *"with."* This doctrine has its foundation in the four great Marian biblical citations that speak of Mary as the *Woman* – Genesis 3:15 (*proto-evangelium*), John 2:1 (Cana), John 19:26 (Calvary), and Revelation 12.

There are already four dogmas of Mary that have been proclaimed and defined by the Church, as based upon Scripture and confirmed by Tradition: Mary's Immaculate Conception as being conceived without original sin; Mary, the Mother of God (*Theotokos*), as she is the Mother of the God-Man, Jesus Christ; Mary's Perpetual Virginity; and Mary's Assumption into Heaven full body and soul at the end of her earthly life.

While only Christ merited objective redemption for all; the fifth and final dogma will secure the truth that Mary shared in the redemption and mediation of Christ in an objective and unique way, though in a secondarily and subordinate way to Christ. As Co-redemptrix, Mary's cooperation in no way obscures or diminishes the one mediation of Christ for the human race. The Church teaches that, by God's Will, Mary, though innocent and without sin, freely cooperated in the work of man's salvation with her Son, associating herself with His Sacrifice, sharing in His sufferings, while cooperating in His work of restoring supernatural life to souls.[28] St. Irenaeus (193 AD) declared that **Mary** *"was obedient and became to herself and to the whole human race a cause of salvation."* Benedict XV (1918) confirmed: *"She immolated her Son in such a way that it can rightly be said that she redeemed the human race with Christ."*[29] The fifth dogma will define and definitively declare this truth for the joy of the faithful and the peace and unity of humanity. All to Jesus through Mary with Peter!

Mary has a two-fold heavenly role founded on her title of Co-redemptrix. This is exemplified by Jacob's ladder, which is an Old Testament type of Mary, where angels were *descending and ascending* the ladder from Heaven to earth. In an allegorical way, Mary not only distributes all graces (seen by Angels descending the ladder) as *Mediatrix*, but she also brings the needs of humanity back to Christ, all our prayers to her Son (seen by Angels ascending the ladder), as our *Advocate*.

2. Mediatrix of All Grace

The fifth dogma of Mary will also define more clearly what Vatican II has already stated concerning her role of **Mediatrix of all graces**. Mary is the Mother of intercession and reparation. She distributes all grace to the human race. Leo XIII stated that *"nothing of the vast treasure of all grace is given to us without Mary."*[30] St. Pius X said that *"she is the primary minister in the distribution of the divine* *graces.*"[31] Vatican II says she is *"united to all those who are to be saved."*[32]

Recent Marian private revelations point to this doctrine. The final vision of Sr. Lucia of Fatima (June 13, 1929) confirms this doctrine, when she saw God the Father, the Holy Spirit in the form of a dove, Christ on the Cross, the Eucharist, and Our Lady of Fatima (holding the Rosary). This private revelation confirms that all graces flow from the Father, in the Spirit, through Christ on the Cross, through the Eucharist – as the Source of all *graces and mercy* – which are then distributed through the hands of Mary who is Mediatrix. The apparition of the Miraculous Medal to St. Catherine also confirms that Mary is the distributor of all graces by showing the image of Our Lady of Grace, holding her hands out with rays of light (grace) pouring forth from them.

The Church teaches that from Heaven, **Mary *"continues to bring us the gifts of eternal salvation"*** (Vatican II). Mary is *"our Mother in the order of grace;"*[33] and the *Catechism* confirms that *"This motherhood of Mary in the order of grace continues uninterruptedly... until the eternal fulfillment of all the elect. Taken up to heaven she did not lay aside this saving office but by her manifold intercession continues to bring us the gifts of eternal salvation."*[34]

Our Lady instructs through Fr. Gobbi concerning her heavenly mediation as follows:

My task is that of distributing to my little children that grace which flows out from the bosom of the Father, is merited for you by the Son and is given to you by the Holy Spirit.

My task is that of distributing it to all my children, according to the particular needs of each one, which the Mother is very good at knowing.

*I am ever carrying out this duty of mine. However **I can carry it out fully only in the case of those children who entrust themselves to me with perfect abandonment... Entrust yourselves to me with confidence, and you will remain faithful, because I will be able to carry out fully my work as Mediatrix of Graces.** [35]*

Jesus consigns this key, which represents his divine power, into my hand because, as his Mother, Mediatrix between you and my Son, there is entrusted to me the task of conquering Satan and all his powerful army of evil. It is with this key that I am able to open and shut the door to the abyss.[36]

Mary states that she can only fulfill her heavenly mission as Mediatrix if we consecrate ourselves to her!

3. Advocate

As the Holy Spirit is our divine Advocate (Paraclete), so Mary, who is His spiritual spouse, is our motherly **Advocate** in Heaven. Mary consoles us, defends us, and calls upon God's mercy on our behalf. John Paul says that she is the *"mother who obtains for us divine mercy."[37]* St. Maximilian Kolbe called her *the incarnation of divine mercy.* She is the Queen Mother who intercedes for us and pleads our cause to her Son, the King of kings, as our Advocate, as the Mother of Mercy. As Christ is the Head, Mary is the Neck, and we are the Body! Everything passes through Mary from God to us and from us to God.

Mariologist, Mark Miravalle, S.T.D., explains Mary's role as Advocate, saying: *"The Marian title, 'Advocate' is one of her most ancient (second century) and captures her role of <u>intercession</u>, speaking to her Divine Son on behalf of the human family. An advocate is one who 'speaks on behalf of another' (Latin, advocare), and the greatest advocate the human family possesses is our Mother and Queen who, beyond any other intercessor, brings our petitioned needs to the throne of Christ the King on our behalf."[38]*

Our Lady speaks of the urgency of proclaiming the fifth Marian dogma and what fruits it will bring to humanity, through Fr. Gobbi, saying: *"I am the Woman clothed in the sun. I am in the heart of the Most Holy Trinity. Until I am acknowledged there where the Most Holy Trinity has willed me to be, I will not be able to exercise my power fully, in the maternal work of co-redemption and of the univer-sal mediation of graces.*[39] *... The task which the Most Holy Trinity has entrusted to me will be acknowledged by all; I will be able to exercise my great power fully, so that the victory of my Son Jesus may shine forth everywhere, when **He will restore, through you, his glorious reign of Love**.*"[40] Our Lady reminds us of the importance of our role in assisting her in the great victory, saying through Fr. Gobbi: *"**You are an important part of my plan** as Mediatrix and Coredemptrix... I want you thus to be associated in my motherly work of coredemption, and I am making you more and more a participant in my great sorrows."*[41]

Already in our time, the Popes, like Pius XI and Pius XII, have called Mary by the title of *Co-redemptrix.* **John Paul II used the title of *Co-redemptrix* for Mary at least six times during his pontificate**; and he told mariologist Mark Miravalle: *"The fifth dogma will be."*[42] The God-Man came to us by means of Mary in the Incarnation; He comes to us now in grace by means of Mary; and He will come again by means of her as well.

A special Prayer of Our Lady of All Nations was also given through this apparition, so *"that under this title and through this prayer, **she may deliver the world from a great world catastrophe... Through this prayer the Lady shall save the world**."* After giving this special prayer for the world, Our Lady said to Ida about **The Lady of All Nations Prayer**: *"You do not know how great and how important this prayer is before God! You cannot estimate the great value this will have. You do not know what the future has in store... This prayer is* *short and simple so that everyone in this quick and modern time can pray it. It is given in order to call down the True Spirit upon the world...* **This prayer has been given for the conversion of the world.**" "*I am the Lady of All Peoples... 'Who once was Mary.' Here is the meaning of this formula: Mary was known as Mary by a great number of men, but now,* **in the new era which is opening, I wish to be known as the Lady of All Peoples.** *And everyone will understand that.*" Mary is not relinquishing her name, but publicly expanding her office and heavenly role (Revelation 12) for the conversion and salvation of all souls.

The fifth dogma of Mary will bring a period of peace to the world and to humanity. Our Lady of All Nations prophesied to visionary Ida Peerdeman on May 31, 1954: "*The Lady of All Nations wishes for unity in the true Holy Spirit.* **The world is covered by a false spirit, by Satan. Once the dogma, the final dogma in Marian history, has been proclaimed, the Lady of All Nations will grant peace, true peace, to the world.** *The nations, however, must pray my prayer, together with the Church. They shall know that the Lady of All Nations has come as Coredemptrix, Mediatrix and Advocate.*" And twenty-five years later, to the day, Our Lord promised through visionary, Ida: "*The Holy Father will proclaim her Co-redemptrix, Mediatrix and Advocate.*"[43]

Mark Miravalle summarizes, saying: "***Mary's titles are her functions.*** *Her roles as the Co-redemptrix (or the 'Mother suffering,' cf. Second Vatican Council, Lumen Gentium, 58), the Mediatrix of all graces (or the 'Mother nourishing' in the order of grace, cf. LG 61,*

62) and the Advocate (or the 'Mother interceding,' cf. LG 62) are titles which refer to Mary's motherly spiritual functions of grace which she performs for humanity. If these roles are solemnly proclaimed by the Holy Father, the greatest spiritual authority on earth in the name of all humanity, then the Immaculate Virgin will be able to fully exercise these functions for the human family in a greater and more dynamic way than ever. [44]

Our Lady promises the nations of the world a new spring of *"grace, redemption, and peace"* that will save the world from *"degeneration, disaster, and war"*. As humanity's Queen Mother, she is and will soon become known to all as **the Co-Redemptrix of redemption, the Mediatrix of grace, and the Advocate of peace** for all nations and peoples. What a great hope we should place in Mary. She is our hope!

Revelation 13-19

St. Methodius explains why Satan will soon after this period of temporary peace regain control and seem to conquer all, saying:

In the last period Christians will not appreciate the great grace of God who provided a monarch, a long duration of peace, a splendid fertility of the earth. They will be very ungrateful, lead a sinful life, in pride, vanity, unchastely, frivolity, hatred, avarice, gluttony, and many other vices, [so] that the sins of men will stink more than a pestilence before God. Many will doubt whether the Catholic faith is the true and only saving one and whether the Jews are correct when they still expect the Messiah. Many will be the false teachings and resultant bewilderment. The just God will in consequence give Lucifer and all his devils power to come on earth and tempt his godless creatures...

Like the Israelites did when they were in the desert with Moses, humanity in this period will return to its evil ways.

The Antichrist & the Great Tribulation

St. Hildegard explains about the rise of the Antichrist after the great monarch, saying:

When the great ruler exterminates the Turks almost entirely, one of the remaining Mohammadans will be converted, become a priest, bishop and cardinal, and when the new pope is elected (immediately before Antichrist) this cardinal will kill the (newly elected) pope before he is crowned, through jealousy, wishing to be pope himself; then when the other cardinals elect the next pope this cardinal will proclaim himself

Anti-pope, and two-thirds of the Christians will go with him. He, as well as Antichrist, are descendants of the tribe of Dan.

The mark (of Antichrist) will be a hellish symbol of Baptism, because thereby a person will be stamped as an adherent of Antichrist and also of the Devil in that he thereby gives himself over to the influence of Satan. Whoever will not have this mark of Antichrist can neither buy nor sell anything and will be beheaded.

He will win over to himself the rulers, the mighty and the wealthy, will bring about the destruction of those who do not accept his faith and, finally, will subjugate the entire earth.

The Marian locution Messages to Fr. Gobbi of the Marian Movement of Priests unveil the details contained in the Book of Revelation, revealing the demonic events that will lead up to the person of the Antichrist in this period and the various spiritual meanings concerning *the struggle which is being fought out between the followers of the huge Red Dragon and the followers of the Woman Clothed with the Sun.*

The **Virgin of Revelation** says through Fr. Gobbi. *"I will bring you to the full understanding of Sacred Scripture. Above all, I will read to you the pages of its last book, which you are living. . . . I am opening for you the sealed book, that the secrets contained in it may be revealed."* Some of main detail and meaning of Revelation include:

The Red Dragon

*The huge Red Dragon is **atheistic communism** which has spread everywhere the error of the denial and obstinate rejection of God. The huge Red Dragon is **Marxist atheism**, which appears with **ten horns**, namely the power of its means of communication, in order to lead humanity to disobey the ten commandments of God, and with **seven heads**, upon each of which is a crown, signs of authority and royalty (see Revelation 17). The crowned heads indicate the nations in which atheistic communism is established and rules with the force of its ideological, political and military power. It is "red" because it uses wars and blood to gain conquests. (Gobbi)*

*The huge Red Dragon has succeeded during these years in conquering humanity with the error of its **theoretical and practical atheism, which has now seduced all nations of the earth**. It has thus succeeded in building up for itself **a new civilization without God**, materialistic, egoistic, hedonistic, arid and cold, which carries within itself the seeds of corruption and of death.[45] The Red Dragon works to bring all humanity to do without God, to **the denial of God**, and therefore spreads the error of atheism.[46] (Gobbi)*

About atheistic communism, Pius XI states: *"Today we see something that world history has never seen before: The waving of the flag of Satan in the battle against God and religion, against all peoples, and in all parts of the world; a phenomenon that outdoes all that happened before. **Atheistic Communism surpasses all*** *previous persecutions in the Church, even that of Nero and Dio-cletian, not only in its extent, but also in its violence."*

*Now you are living in that period of time when the Red Dragon, that is to say Marxist atheism, is spreading throughout the whole world and is increasingly bringing about the ruin of souls. **He is indeed succeeding in seducing and casting down a third of the stars of heaven. These stars, in the firmament of the Church, are the pastors (priests).*** [47] (Gobbi)

The Beast like a Leopard

Then two beasts come to aid the dragon (Revelation 13). The beast like a leopard is Freemasonry which comes up from the sea to aid the Dragon. *The black beast acts in the shadow, keeps out of sight and **hides himself in such a way as to enter in everywhere**. He has the claws of a bear and the mouth of a lion, because he works everywhere with cunning and **with the means of social communication, that is to say, through propaganda**. The **seven heads** indicate the various Masonic lodges, which act everywhere in a subtle and dangerous way.* [48] (Gobbi)

*This black beast has **ten horns** and, on the horns, ten crowns, which are the signs of dominion and royalty. Masonry rules and governs throughout the whole world by means of the ten horns. The horn, in the biblical world, has always been an instrument of amplifi-*

cation, a way of making one's voice better heard, a strong means of communication. (Gobbi)

*The aim of Masonry is not to deny God, but **to blaspheme him.** **The beast opens his mouth to utter blasphemies against God,** to blaspheme His name and His dwelling place, and against all those who dwell in heaven. The greatest blasphemy is that of **denying the worship due to God alone by giving it to creatures and to Satan** himself. (Gobbi)*

The Church recognizes the guise of the demonic beast in its *Compendium on the Social Doctrine of the Church,* which states: *"When human authority goes beyond the limits willed by God, it makes itself a deity and demands absolute submission – it becomes the Beast of the Apocalypse."*[49]

The Beast like a Lamb

*There comes out of the earth, by way of aid to the black beast which arises out of the sea, **a beast which has two horns like those of a lamb**... The beast has on its head two horns like those of a lamb. To the symbol of the sacrifice there is intimately connected that of the priesthood: the two horns. The high priest of the Old Testament wore a headpiece with two horns. The bishops of the Church wear the mitre - with two horns - to indicate the fullness of their priesthood. (Gobbi)*

The beast with the two horns like a lamb indicates Freemasonry infiltrated into the interior of the Church, that is to say, ecclesiastical Masonry, which has spread especially among the members of the hierarchy. This Masonic infiltration, in the interior of the Church, was already foretold to you by me at Fatima, when I announced to you that Satan would enter in even to the summit of the Church. (Gobbi)

*The task of ecclesiastical Masonry is that of destroying Christ and His Church, **building a new idol, namely a false christ and a false church**. [This is being attempted in **three ways** against Jesus as the Truth, the Life, and the Way.] (Gobbi)*

*1. **Jesus Christ is the Son of the Living God**, He is the Word Incarnate, He is true God and true Man because He unites in His divine Person human nature and divine nature. Jesus, in the Gospel, has given His most complete definition of Himself, saying that **He is the Truth**, the Way and the Life.*

*Jesus is the Truth because it is He - the living Word - who is the font and seal of all divine Revelation. And so **ecclesiastical Masonry works to obscure His divine Word, by means of natural and rational interpretations and, in the attempt to make it more understandable and acceptable, empties it of all its supernatural content.** Thus errors are spread in every part of the Catholic Church itself. Because of the spread of these errors, many are moving away today from the true faith, bringing to fulfillment the prophecy which was given to you by* *me at Fatima: 'The times will come when many will lose the true faith.' The loss of the faith is apostasy. Ecclesiastical Masonry works, in a subtle and diabolical way, **to lead all to apostasy**.*

*   **The Church is Truth**, because Jesus has entrusted to it alone the task of guarding, in its integrity, all the deposit of faith. He has entrusted to it the hierarchical Church, that is to say, to the Pope and to the bishops united with him. **Ecclesiastical Masonry seeks to destroy this reality through false ecumenism, which leads to the acceptance of all Christian Churches (and ecclesial communities), asserting that each one of them has some part of the truth.** It develops the plan of founding a universal ecumenical Church, formed by the fusion of the Christian confessions, among which, the Catholic Church. (Gobbi)*

*2. **Jesus is the Life**, because He gives us divine life itself, with the grace merited by Him through redemption, and He institutes the sacraments as efficacious means which communicate grace.*

*   **Jesus is the Life** because He gives grace. **The aim of ecclesiastical Masonry is that of justifying sin, of presenting it no longer as an evil but as something good and of value.** Thus one is advised to do this as a way of satisfying exigencies of one's own nature, destroying the root from which repentance could be born, and is told that it is no longer necessary to confess it. The pernicious fruit of this accursed cancer, which has spread throughout the whole Church, is the **disappearance everywhere of individual confession**. Souls are led to live in sin, rejecting the gift of life which Jesus has offered to us.*

The Church is Life, *because it gives grace and it alone possesses the efficacious means of grace, which are the seven sacraments. Especially it is life because* **to it alone is given the power to beget the Eucharist,** *by means of the hierarchical and ministerial priesthood. In the Eucharist, Jesus Christ is truly present with His glorified Body and His divinity. And so* **ecclesiastical Masonry, in many and subtle ways, seeks to attack the ecclesial devotion towards the sacrament of the Eucharist.** *It gives value only to the meal aspect, tends to minimize its sacrificial value,* **seeks to deny the real and personal presence of Jesus in the consecrated Host.** *In this way there are gradually suppressed all the external signs which are indicative of faith in the real presence of Jesus in the Eucharist, such as genuflections, hours of public adoration and the holy custom of surrounding the tabernacle with lights and flowers. (Gobbi)*

3. Jesus is the Way *which leads to the Father, by means of the Gospel which He has given us, as a way to follow to attain salvation.*

Jesus is the Way *which leads to the Father, by means of the Gospel.* **Ecclesiastical Masonry** *favors those forms of exegesis which gives it a rationalistic and natural interpretation, by means of the application of the various literary genres, in such a way that it becomes torn to pieces in all its parts. In the end, one* **arrives at denying the historical reality of the miracles and of the resurrection and places in doubt the very divinity of Jesus and His salvific mission.**

*The Church is the Way because it leads to the Father, through the Son, in the Holy Spirit, along the way of perfect unity. As the Father and the Son are one, so too must you be one among yourselves. Jesus has willed that His Church be a sign and an instrument of the unity of the whole human race. The Church succeeds in being united because it has been founded on the cornerstone of its unity: Peter, and the Pope who succeeds to the charism of Peter. And so **ecclesiastical Masonry seeks to destroy the foundation of the unity of the Church, through a subtle and insidious attack on the Pope.** It weaves plots of dissension and of contestation against the Pope; it supports and rewards those who vilify and disobey him; it disseminates the criticisms and the contentions of bishops and theologians. In this way the very foundation of its unity is demolished and thus the Church becomes more and more torn and divided.[50] (Gobbi)*

*Ecclesiastical Masonry goes as far as even **building a statue in honor of the beast and forces all to adore this statue...** they substitute for God a strong, powerful and dominating idol. **An idol so powerful that it puts to death all who do not adore the statue of the beast.** An idol so strong and dominating as to cause all, small and great, rich and poor, freeman and slaves, **to receive a mark** on the right hand and on the forehead, and that no one can buy or sell without having this mark, that is to say, the **name of the beast or the number of its name. This great idol,** built to be served by all, as I have already revealed to you in the preceding message, **is a false church and a false christ.**[51] (Gobbi)*

The Ten Horns

The red dragon has seven heads, symbolizing seven vices, and ten horns, symbolizing ten anti-commandments (Revelation 12). *The Lord has communicated His law with **the ten commandments**, Freemasonry spreads everywhere, through the power of its **ten horns**, a law which is **completely opposed to that of God**. (Gobbi)*

*TO THE FIRST COMMANDMENT: 'You shall not have any other God but me,' it builds other **false idols**, before which many today prostrate themselves in adoration.*

*TO THE SECOND COMMANDMENT: 'You shall not take the name of God in vain,' it sets itself up in opposition by **blaspheming God and His Christ**, in many subtle and diabolical ways, even to reducing His Name indecorously to the level of a brand-name of an object of sale and of producing sacrilegious films concerning His life and His Divine Person.*

*TO THE THIRD COMMANDMENT: 'Remember to keep holy the Sabbath Days,' it **transforms the Sunday into a weekend, into a day of sports, of competitions and of entertainments.***

*TO THE FOURTH COMMANDMENT: 'Honor your father and your mother,' it opposes **a new model of family based on co-habitation, even between homosexuals.***

*TO THE FIFTH COMMANDMENT: 'You shall not kill,' it has succeeded in **making abortion legal everywhere**, in **making euthanasia acceptable**, and in **causing respect due to the value of human life to all but disappear**.*

*TO THE SIXTH COMMANDMENT: 'You shall not commit impure acts,' it **justifies, exalts and propagates every form of impurity**, even to the justification of acts against nature.*

*TO THE SEVENTH COMMANDMENT: 'You shall not steal,' it works to the end that **theft, violence, kidnapping and robbery spread more and more**.*

*TO THE EIGHTH COMMANDMENT: 'You shall not bear false witness,' it acts in such a way that **the law of deceit, lying and duplicity becomes more and more propagated**.*

*TO THE NINTH AND TENTH COMMANDMENT: 'You shall not covet the goods and the wife of another,' it **works to corrupt in the depths of the conscience**, betraying the mind and the heart of man.*

*In this way souls become driven along **the perverse and wicked road of disobedience** to the laws of the Lord, become submerged in sin and are thus prevented from receiving the gift of grace and the life of God.[52] (Gobbi)*

The Seven Heads

*To the **seven theological and cardinal virtues**, which are the fruit of living in the grace of God, Freemasonry counters with the diffusion of **the seven capital vices**, which are the fruit of living habitually in the state of sin. To faith it opposes pride; to hope, lust; to charity, avarice; to prudence, anger; to fortitude, sloth; to justice, envy; to temperance, gluttony.*

***Whoever becomes a victim of the seven capital vices is gradually led to take away the worship that is due to God alone,** in order to give it to false divinities, who are the very personification of all these vices. **And in this consists the greatest and most horrible blasphemy.** This is why on **every head of the beast** there is written a blasphemous name. Each Masonic lodge has the task of making a different divinity adored. (Gobbi)*

The first three capital sins are of particular threat. We must combat against the first three capital sins by living the theological virtues (faith, hope, and love) and embracing the spirit of the evangelical counsels (poverty, chastity, and obedience) to help us fight the three temptations of the spiritual life (the world, the flesh, and the devil).

*1. PRIDE, OPPOSING FAITH (and obedience): leads one to offer worship to **the god of human reason and haughtiness, of technology and progress (demonic spirit)**.*

*2. LUST, OPPOSING HOPE (and chastity): brings one to offer worship to **the god of sexuality and impurity (fleshly spirit)**.*

*3. AVARICE (GREED), OPPOSING CHARITY (and poverty): spreads everywhere the worship of **the god of money (worldly spirit)**.*

*4. ANGER, OPPOSING PRUDENCE: leads one to offer worship to **the god of discord and division**.*

*5. SLOTH, OPPOSING FORTITUDE: disseminates the worship of **the idol of fear of public opinion and exploitation**.*

*6. ENVY, OPPOSING JUSTICE: leads one to offer worship to **the idol of violence and war**.*

*7. GLUTTONY, OPPOSING TEMPERANCE: leads one to offer worship to the so highly extolled **idol of hedonism, of materialism and of pleasure**.*

*The task of the Masonic lodges is that of working today, with great astuteness, **to bring humanity everywhere to disdain the holy law of God, to work in opposition to the ten commandments, and to take away the worship due to God alone in order to offer it to certain false idols which become extolled and adored by an ever increasing number of people: reason, flesh, money, discord, domination, violence, pleasure. Thus souls are precipitated into the dark slavery*** *of evil, of vice and of sin and, at the moment of death and of the judgment of God, into the pool of eternal fire which is hell...*

For this reason I am training all my children to observe the ten commandments of God; to live the Gospel to the letter; to make frequent use of the sacraments, especially those of penance and Eucharistic communion, as necessary helps in order to remain in the grace of God; to practice the virtues vigorously, to walk always along the path of goodness, of love, of purity and of holiness.[53] *(Gobbi)*

The Number of the Antichrist

The Antichrist is the person deciphered from the number, 666. Mary says through Fr. Gobbi: *"The Church will know the hour of its great apostasy. The man of iniquity will penetrate into its interior and will sit in the very Temple of God, while the remnant which will remain faithful will be subjected to the greatest trials and persecutions."*[54]

The great design of the Evil One will be to set up an idol to put in the place of Christ and of His Church: a false christ and a false church.[55] Fr. Gobbi relays Mary's message as follows:

666 indicated thrice, that is to say, for the third time, expresses the year 1998, nineteen hundred and ninety-eight. In this period of history (thus, not just in this particular year),

Freemasonry, assisted by its ecclesiastical form, will succeed in its great design: that of setting up an idol to put in the place of Christ and of his Church. **A false christ and a false church**. *Consequently,* **the statue built in honor of the first beast**, *to be adored by all the inhabitants of the earth and which* **will seal with its mark** *all those who want to buy or sell, is that of the Antichrist. You have thus arrived at the peak of the purification, of the great tribulation and of the apostasy. The apostasy will be, as of then, generalized because* **almost all will follow the false christ and the false church**. *Then the door will be open for the appearance of the man or of the very* **person of the Antichrist***!*

Mary explains **the mark of the beast** (six hundred and sixty-six) as the sign of the Antichrist that signifies those who belong completely to him who is opposed to Christ. His mark is imprinted on the forehead (the intellect) and the hand (the will):

On the Forehead: Such persons are led to accept the doctrine of the denial of God, of the rejection of His law, and of atheism.

On the Hand: Such persons act in an autonomous manner and independently of God, focused on material and worldly goods. He works for himself alone, to accumulate material goods, **to make money his god**, and **becomes a victim of materialism**. He works **solely for the gratification of his**

own senses, for the quest of his own well-being and pleasure, for the granting of full satisfaction to all his passions, **especially of impurity**, and **becomes a victim of hedonism**. He makes himself the center of his own actions, looks upon others as objects to be used and to be exploited for his own advantage, and **becomes a victim of unbridled egoism and of lovelessness**. (Gobbi)

On the other hand, Mary too marks those who have consecrated themselves to her Immaculate Heart with her motherly seal.[56] She says: *"I have now imprinted my sign on the forehead of each one of you. My Adversary is no longer able to do anything against those who have been signed by their Heavenly Mother."*[57] (Gobbi)[58]

Other Prophecies Concerning the Antichrist

The mystics have given us details of these times of the Antichrist. Bl. Joachim (12th century) warned: *"Toward the end of the world, Antichrist will overthrow the pope and usurp the See."* John of Vitiguerro (13th century) added: *"The pope will change his residence and the Church will not be defended for twenty-five months or more because, during all that time there will be no Pope in Rome... [But] after many tribulations, a Pope shall be elected out of those who survived the persecutions."* The Pope to be elected after the persecutions will be discussed later in this book.

Our Lady, in the apparitions of La Salette, warns what will happen in this time, saying: *"The earth will be struck by calamities of all kinds... the last war... will then be fought by* **the ten Kings of the Antichrist**, *all of whom will have one and the same plan and will be the only rulers of the world...* **Rome will lose faith and become the seat of the Antichrist**... *Now is the time."*[59] The Antichrist will set himself up in Rome with his false prophet acting *in the place of* the true Pope during the vacancy of the papal throne in Rome.

We must remember that we are fighting a battle that involves Satan himself. And Jesus tells us to take up a spiritual sword for this battle, and Paul says that we must fight the principalities and powers of wickedness.[60] We must remember that Mary intercedes for us and Jesus gives us His peace in the midst of this spiritual battle. With peace, we fight for peace.

Fulton Sheen wrote on the nature of the Antichrist and his counter-church, stating:

> *In the midst of all his seeming love for humanity and his glib talk of freedom and equality, he will have one great secret which he will tell to no one: he will not believe in God. Because his religion will be brotherhood without the fatherhood of God, he will deceive even the elect. He will set up a counterchurch which will be the ape of the Church, because he, the Devil, is the ape of God. It will have all the notes and characteristics of the Church, but in reverse and emptied of*

its divine content. It will be a mystical body of the Antichrist that will in all externals resemble the mystical body of Christ... Then will be verified a paradox – the very objections with which men in the last century (19th century) rejected the Church will be the reasons why they will now accept the counterchurch (it will claim to be infallible when its visible head speaks definitively).[61]

Sacred Scripture warns that there will be a falling away from faith before the Second Coming (2 Thessalonians 2:3f). The Bible also warns about the Antichrist who will deny Jesus has come in the flesh (2 John 7). **The *Catechism of the Catholic Church* confirms some details about the Antichrist,** saying he will be a pseudo-messiah glorifying *"himself in the place of God and of his Messiah come in the flesh;"* and it states that his deception will be *"a **religious deception** offering men an apparent solution to their problems at the price of apostasy from the truth."*[62] The *Catechism* also warns that this final trial will shake the faith of many believers; many believers will be misled. The Saints have also offered prophecy concerning the Antichrist, as exemplified by St. Cyril of Jerusalem (fourth century), who said: *"Antichrist will exceed in malice, perversity, lust, wickedness, impiety, and heartless cruelty and barbarity all men that have ever disgraced human nature... He shall through his great power, deceit and malice, succeed in decoying or forcing to his worship two-thirds of mankind; the remaining third part of men will most steadfastly continue true to the faith and worship of Jesus Christ."* Our Lady to

Fr. Gobbi confirms that *"in the land, **two-thirds of them will be cut off** **and perish**; and one-third shall be left. I will pass this third through fire; I will refine it as silver is refined, test it as gold is tested."*[63]

In the 1851 version of the secret of La Salette, Melanie spoke about the Antichrist and his mother, saying:

> *Lastly, hell will reign on earth. It will be then that **the Antichrist will be born of a Sister, but woe to her! Many will believe in him, because he will claim to have come from heaven**, woe to those who will believe in him!*

Later, in the 1879 written version of the secret of La Salette, Melanie elaborated, as follows:

> *It will be during this time that **the antichrist will be born of a Hebrew religious, of a false Virgin** who will have communication with the old serpent, the master of impurity; his father will be Bishop; at birth, he will vomit blasphemies, he will have teeth; in a word, this will be the devil incarnate; he will let out frightening cries, he will perform wonders, he will nourish himself only on impurities. He will have brothers who, although they will not be like him demons incarnate, will be children of evil; at 12 years, they will make themselves noticed by their brilliant victories which they will win; soon, **they will each be at the head of armies, assisted by the legions of hell**. [Melanie also commented on this point, as fol-*

lows: *It is said that the antichrist will be the devil incarnate, that is to say that he will be entirely possessed. I have seen that the good God does not permit the demon to personally incarnate himself in a human soul and body, but that the demon under a visible form will have familiar relations with the parents of the antichrist, and that they will consecrate him to his service from the first moment of his existence* (Le Secret De Melanie (1904), p. 55).]

The **seasons will be changed**, *the earth will produce only bad fruits, the stars will lose their regular movements, the moon will reflect only a feeble reddish light; water and fire will give to the globe of the earth convulsive movements and horrible earthquakes which will cause to be engulfed mountains, cities [etc.].* [The Blessed Virgin showed her other cataclysms that she does not name (Le Secret De Melanie, p.57).]

Rome will lose the faith and become the seat of the antichrist.

The demons of the air with the antichrist will perform great wonders on the earth and in the air, and men will corrupt themselves more and more. *God will have care of His faithful servants and men of good will; the Gospel will be preached everywhere, all peoples and all nations will have knowledge of the truth!*

The Church will be eclipsed, the world will be in con-sternation. But behold Enoch and Elie (Elijah) filled with the Spirit of God; they will preach with the strength of God, and good men will believe in God, and many souls will be con-soled; they will make great progress by the virtue of the Holy Spirit and will condemn the devilish errors of the anti-christ. [Abbé Combe, the editor of the 1904 edition, adds the following note after this paragraph: *I have from Melanie that the Church will be eclipsed in this sense, that 1) one will not know which is the true pope; 2) for a time: the holy Sacrifice will cease to be offered in churches, and also in houses: so there will be no more public worship. But she saw that yet the holy Sacrifice would not cease: it would be offered in caves, in tunnels, in barns and in alcoves.*]

Woe to the inhabitants of the earth! There will be **bloody wars and famines***; pestilences and contagious dis-eases; there will be rains of a dreadful hail of animals, thun-ders which will shake cities, earthquakes which will engulf countries; voices will be heard in the air, men will beat their head against the walls, they will call upon death, and on an-other side death will be their torture; blood will flow on all sides. Who will be able to overcome, if God does not shorten the time of the ordeal?* **By the blood, the tears and the prayers of the just, God will let Himself be swayed***, Enoch and Elie (Elijah) will be put to death; pagan Rome will dis-*

appear; fire from Heaven will fall and will consume three cities; **all the universe will be struck with terror, and many will let themselves be misled** *because they have not adored the true Christ living among them. It is time; the sun darkens; faith alone will live.*

Behold the time; the abyss opens. Behold the king of kings of darkness. Behold the beast with his subjects, calling himself the savior of the world. He will raise himself up with pride into the air in order to go even up to heaven.[64]

Maximin indicated that the Antichrist would appear in the apocalyptic image that he describes as like a *monster*, and Melanie states that he will be born of a religious, and his father will be a bishop, which she specifies in 1860. They prophesy a great famine to come. Scripture warns of such a famine, saying: *"Behold, the days are coming, says the Lord God, when I will send a famine on the land; not a famine of bread, nor a thirst for water, but of hearing the words of the Lord."*[65] Such a famine is already upon us. The spiritual war has begun.

Among those who have personally supported the Church-approved message of La Salette are Maritain, Claudel, St. Don Bosco, St. John Mary Vianney, St. Peter Julian Eymard, Popes Pius IX to Benedict XV, and recently, renowned Mariologist René Laurentin who published a book on the authenticity of La Salette (2002) and whose book has received the *imprimatur* of Bishop Zola of Lecce in Italy.

John Paul II also spoke of La Salette and its connection to other Marian prophecies, saying:

> *If victory comes it will be brought by Mary. Christ will conquer through her, because He wants the Church's victories now and in the future to be linked to her... I could see... that there was a certain continuity among La Salette, Lourdes, and Fatima... And thus we come to May 13, 1981, when I was wounded by gunshots fired in St. Peter's Square... the assassination attempt had occurred on the exact anniversary of the day Mary appeared to the three children at Fatima in Portugal and spoke to them the words that now, at the end of this century, seem to be close to their fulfillment... Andre Malraux was certainly right when he said that the twenty-first century would be the century of religion or it would not be at all.[66]*

The Abolishment of the Holy Mass & the Abomination

The prophecy of the abolishment of the Mass which is mentioned at La Salette is also confirmed in the messages of Fr. Gobbi. Giving us insights into the event of the Antichrist, who shall reign for seven years,[67] during which he will abolish the Mass, Mary reveals through Fr. Gobbi: *"Now from the moment the daily sacrifice is abolished and the horrible abomination is set up (the horrible sacrilege accomplished by the Antichrist), there shall be one thousand two hundred and ninety (1,290) days (about three-and-a-half years). Blessed is he who waits with patience and attains one thousand three hundred and thirty-five (1,335) days.* " (Daniel 12:9-12)[68]

The Sanctuary Light Will Go Out

The Church-approved apparitions of Our Lady of Good Success (17th century) gave five *"meanings"* concerning the sanctuary light that will go out in the Church during this period, as follows:

First Meaning: At the end of the Nineteenth Century and for duration of the Twentieth Century, various **heresies will flourish and the light of faith will go out in souls** because of almost total moral corruption.

Second Meaning: **Religious communities will be abandoned** and **many true vocations will be lost** for lack of prudent and skillful direction to form them.

Third Meaning: There will be **a spirit of impurity** which will flood the public places like a deluge of filth. The licentiousness will be such that there will be **no more virgin souls in the world.**

Fourth Meaning: The sects will **penetrate into the hearts of families and destroy even the children.** The innocence of childhood will almost disappear. Thus, priestly vocations will be lost. **Priests will abandon their sacred duties.** Then, the Church will go through a dark night for lack of a Pope to watch over it. Satan will take control of the earth through faithless men. There will be **all sorts of chastisements**: plagues, famines, war, apostasy, and the loss of souls. There will be **a terrible war** and it will seem as though wickedness will triumph.

Fifth Meaning: **Men possessing great wealth will look with indifference while the Church is oppressed, virtue is persecuted, and evil triumphs**. They will not use their wealth to fight evil or to reconstruct the faith. The people will be swept away by all vices and passions.

But, then will come the time of Our Lady and her Son. In astounding fashion, she will destroy Satan's pride, casting him beneath her feet, chaining him up in the depths of hell, leaving the Church freed from his cruel tyranny – so reports the messages of Our Lady of Good Success.

Our Lady has given us five general *"signs"* of the order of events that will bring upon humanity the Great Chastisement, before Christ comes to reign anew, through Fr. Gobbi, as follows:

> *First Sign:* ***Confusion*** *– The spread of errors which lead to the loss of faith and to apostasy. These errors are being propagated by false teachers, by renowned theologians who are no longer teaching the truths of the Gospel, but pernicious heresies based on errors and on human reasonings... It*

is because of these errors that the true faith is being lost and that the great apostasy is spreading everywhere. (See Matthew 24:4-5; 2 Thessalonians 2-3; 2 Peter 2:1-3)

Second Sign: **Wars and Catastrophes** *– The outbreak of wars and fratricidal struggles... while natural catastrophes, such as epidemics, famines, floods and earthquakes, become more and more frequent. (See Matthew 24:6-8, 12-13)*

Third Sign: **Persecution** *– The bloody persecution of those who remain faithful to Jesus and his Gospel and who stand fast in the true faith. (See Matthew 24:9-10, 14)*

Fourth Sign: **The Horrible Sacrilege** *– The horrible sacrilege, perpetrated by him who sets himself against Christ, that is, the Antichrist. He will enter into the holy temple of God and will sit on his throne, and have himself adored as God. In this abolition of the daily sacrifice consists the horrible sacrilege accomplished by the Antichrist. (See 2 Thessalonians 2:4, 9; Matthew 24:15)*

Fifth Sign: **Extraordinary Phenomena**, *which occur in the skies – The miracle of the sun, which took place at Fatima during my last apparition, is intended to point out to you that you are now entering into the times when those events will take place, events which prepare for the return of Jesus in glory.(See Matthew 24:29-33)*

*And then the sign of **the Son of Man will appear** in heaven. All the tribes of the earth will mourn, and men will see the Son of Man coming upon the clouds of heaven, with great power and splendor. (See Matthew 24:30)*

In the great tribulation, God will allow Satan to persecute the Church, and then God will exercise His just wrath as a punishment for our sins and finally overthrow Satan's dominion in the world with a divine intervention. In the midst of this, the remnant faithful will hold fast to the Tradition of the Faith and the faithful souls will glorify God with their lives as witnesses of hope. Our Lady of Fatima indicates that the Pope will have much to suffer, and so will his faithful children.

Prophecies Concerning the Pope

These prophecies of events to come upon the Church seem to also agree with various papal prophesies. **St. Malachy** was a twelfth century Saint who received a vision of future Popes, and in the account of it, he indicates over a hundred Popes from his day until now, and **writes concerning** the final Pope of our time, **the Pope who will reign after Pope Benedict XVI**, stating about him: *"In **the final persecution** of the Holy Roman Church there will reign **Peter the Roman**, who will feed his flock amid **many tribulations**, after which **the seven-hilled city (Rome) will be destroyed** and the dreadful Judge will judge the people."* Peter the Roman will reign for an extended period of time, but it seems that the Pope that will be elected after him will be killed before he is crowned. St. Pius X reveals some detail of this, saying: *"I saw one of my successors taking to flight over the bodies of his brethren. He will take refuge in disguise somewhere; and after a short retirement he will die a cruel death. The present wickedness of the world is only the beginning of the sorrows which must take place before the end of the world."*[69] John of the Cleft Rock (14th Century) prophesied: *"Towards the end of the world, tyrants and hostile mobs will rob the Church and the clergy of all their possessions and will afflict and martyr them. Those who heap the most abuse upon them will be held in high esteem... At that time, the Pope with his cardinals will have to flee Rome in tragic circumstances to a place where they will be unknown.* **The Pope will die a cruel death** *in his exile. The sufferings of the Church will be much greater than at any previous time in her history."*[70] He also said: *"It is said that twenty centuries after the Incarnation of the Word, the Beast in its turn shall become man. About the year 2000 A.D., Antichrist will reveal himself to the world."*[71] Our Lady of Fatima warned: *"If my requests are granted, Russia will be converted and there will be peace. If not, Russia will spread her errors in every country, raising up wars and persecution against the Church; many will be martyred.* **The Holy Father will have much to suffer**, *and many nations will be destroyed."*

We are approaching the times of the Great Tribulation. In the midst of the time of *purification*, the *Great Tribulation* will commence, and there will come a time when the Church will seem about to disappear. But, there will still be cause for hope against hope. The Great Tribulation will go on until the defeat of Satan and the terrible divine justice of the godless occurs.[72] Through this period, many will be brought to their knees and to repentance, and the faithful will be put to a hard test.

In the midst of the darkest times to come, God calls us to place all our trust in Him and to live in hope. Mary says through Fr. Gobbi: *"This is the hour of Calvary for my Church... [But] for her too, the Good Friday of her passion will certainly be followed by a joyous Easter and a new Pentecost of grace and life."*[73]

The Three Days of Darkness

Our times will see great spiritual and physical upheaval like never before in history. Scripture speaks of our times and offers hope: *"The sun will be turned into darkness, and the moon into blood before the great Day of the Lord. But whosoever calls upon the name of the Lord shall be saved"* (Joel 3:4; Matthew 24:29-31; Acts 2:20-21; Revelation 16:10). The current crisis will culminate in a great battle between good and evil in which it will seem as though Satan has won. But afterwards will come the Three Days of Darkness.

The Bible relates a unique event in the times of the Israelite captivity in Egypt, at the time of the redemption of Israel by Moses and the ten divine plagues. The ninth plague of Egypt was a plague of three days of darkness. The Book of Revelation and various mystics have prophesied that a similar event will occur again in our times. Jesus seems to be referring to the three days of darkness in the Gospel, when He says in Matthew: *"Immediately after the tribulation of those days the sun will be darkened, and the moon will not give its light, and the stars will fall from heaven, and the powers of the heavens will be shaken."*[74] Several Saints have prophesized about the three days of darkness.

Visionary **Bl. Anna Maria Taigi**, whose body is incorrupt, prophesied about the earthly scourge and the heavenly scourge of three days of darkness, saying:

> God will send **two punishments**: one will be in the form of **wars, revolutions and other evils**; it shall originate on earth. The other will be sent from Heaven. There shall come over the whole earth **an intense darkness lasting three days and three nights**. Nothing can be seen, and the air will be laden with pestilence which will claim mainly, but not only, the enemies of religion. It will be impossible to use any man-made lighting during this darkness, except blessed candles. He, who out of curiosity, opens his window to look out, or leaves his home, will fall dead on the spot. During these three

days, people should remain in their homes, pray the Rosary and beg God for mercy.

All the enemies of the Church, whether known or unknown, will perish over the whole earth during that universal darkness, with the exception of a few whom God will soon convert. The air shall be infected by demons who will appear under all sorts of hideous forms.[75]

Our Lady has prophesied about the three days of darkness[76] **at La Salette,** saying: *[The Antichrist]* **will be smothered by the breath of the holy Archangel Michael.** *He will fall, and the earth which for* **three days** *will be in continual evolutions will open its bosom full of fire; he will be plunged for ever with all his own into the eternal chasms of hell. Then* **water and fire will purify the earth** *and will consume all the works of the pride of men, and* **all will be renewed***: God will be served and glorified.*[77]

Christ has also revealed details about the three days of darkness and the great consummation, as described **to stigmatist and priest, St. Pio**, whose body is incorrupt, as follows:

The hour of My coming is near! But I will show mercy. A most dreadful punishment will bear witness to the times. My angels, who are to be the executioners of this work, are ready with their pointed swords! They will take special care to annihilate all those who mocked Me and would not believe in

*My revelations... **Hurricanes of fire** will pour forth from the clouds and spread over the entire earth! Storms, bad weather, thunderbolts and earthquakes will cover the earth for two days. An uninterrupted rain of fire will take place! It will begin during a very cold night. All this is to prove that God is the Master of Creation. **Those who hope in Me, and believe in My words, have nothing to fear** because I will not forsake them, nor those who spread My message. No harm will come to those who are in the state of grace and who seek My Mother's protection... The weight of the Divine balance has reached the earth! The wrath of My Father shall be poured out over the entire world!*

*The sins of men have multiplied beyond measure: irreverence in Church, sinful pride committed in sham religious activities, lack of true brotherly love, indecency in dress, especially at summer seasons...The world is filled with iniquity... The godless shall be annihilated, so that afterwards the just shall be able to stand afresh (one fourth of humanity will remain)... The **darkness shall last a day and a night, followed by another day and a night, and another day** – BUT on the night following, the stars will shine again, and on the next morning the sun shall rise again, and it will be **SPRINGTIME!!***

Be courageous soldiers of Christ! At the return of light, let everyone give thanks to the Holy Trinity for Their protec-

tion! The devastation shall be very great! But I, Your God, will have purified the earth. I am with you. Have confidence!

NOT the Rapture, a Doomsday Prediction, or Millenarianism

Interestingly, many non-Catholic Christians have a sense of the times we are in and of some great event to come, but not all Christians share a true understanding of what is to come. Some mainstream Protestants have come to believe in the notion of *"the rapture,"* a false belief that Jesus will come back soon to take true believers and innocent children to Heaven, while the Antichrist will then take control of the world. With this view, most Catholics will be left behind, since they are considered not to be true Christians.

In the 1840s, a British minister devised a new system that laid the foundation for many forms of modern apocalyptic expectations. His name was John Nelson Darby. Darby held that the coming of Christ was going to be soon, and then followed by a thousand-year kingdom. Darby named this moment of Christ's coming as *"the rapture."* He made up this term. It doesn't exist in the Bible at all and has no reputable record in Christian tradition. He made up his version what will happen the first time that Jesus returns.

In Darby's *"rapture,"* the Lord will snatch away *the elect* from the earth, while *the sinners*, many whom are Catholic, will have to remain behind to work out their salvation in a tribulation. *"The funda-*

mentalist authors of the current best-selling, rapture-promoting Left Behind novels, for example, have argued in nonfiction books that the Catholic Church is a creation of the Devil and will be a tool of the Antichrist."[78] But, in truth, this is the very opposite of the authentic prophesies concerning the three days of darkness, which speaks of a cleansing of the evils of the earth with the just commissioned to renew the earth with peace. This is how God has acted in the past, as exemplified by Noah and the Flood, by Lot in Sodom and Gomorrah, by Moses in Egypt with the tenth plague of the death of the first-born, and by the early Catholic Church which survives the collapse of the corrupted Roman Empire. Historically, God always punishes the wicked and blesses the innocent with prosperity. He is about to do the same again.

Many have misunderstood or misinterpreted our times. There have been several Doomsday cults that have sprung up in recent years, as exemplified by Hal Lindsey's *The Late Great Planet Earth*, John Hagee's *"The Rapture Hour,"* the *"Left Behind"* book and movie series, the Christian New Age group Heaven's Gate, whose members castrated and then killed themselves in preparation for what they called *"the next level,"* and by David Koresh with his Branch Davidians in Waco, Texas, in 1993, who were also waiting to be *"delivered"* by Christ, but who were burned up in a fire after many days of FBI interrogations. These related types of groups, often labeled together under the heresy of millenarianism and from whom some think Christ will come to reign *physically* for a thousand years, have been condemned by the Church.[79] It goes to show you can believe anything you want, and many people do, but that does not make it true. To remain in the truth concerning our times and those to come, we must trust the Bible, the authentic Church prophecies, and private revelations from above, with their overlapping consistencies that shed authentic light on our times.

Special Help from the Angels

The angels are playing an important role in the spiritual battle against the dragon. Through Fr. Gobbi, Our Lady has given us special insights into their mission in our times, saying:

In the struggle to which I am calling you… you are being especially helped and defended by the angels of light. I am the Queen of the Angels. At my orders, they are bringing together, from every part of the world, those who I am calling into my great victorious cohort… you must let yourself be guided docilely by them.

The angels, the archangels, and all the heavenly cohorts are united with you in the terrible battle against the Dragon and his followers. They are defending you against the terrible snares of Satan and the many demons who have now been unleashed with furious and destructive frenzy upon every part of the world.

*This is why I call upon you to entrust yourselves more and more to the angels of the Lord. Have an affectionate intimacy with them, because **they are closer to you than your friends and dear ones**. Walk in the light of their invisible, but certain and precious presence. They pray for you, walk at your side, sustain you in your weariness, console you in your sorrow, keep guard over your repose, take you by the hand and lead you gently along the road I have pointed out for you.*

Pray to your guardian angels and live out with trust and serenity the painful hours of the purification... *You have entered into the most painful and difficult phase of the battle between the Spirits of Good and the Spirits of Evil, between the angels and the demons. It is a terrible struggle which is taking place around you and above you. And so these are the times when the action of your guardian angels must become still stronger and more continuous.*[80]

So, let us pray often to our Guardian Angel.

Ven. Anne Catherine Emmerich had a vision of St. Michael fighting the dragon over St. Peter's Basilica in Rome. She relates as follows: *"In the most terrible moment of the battle there will descend, to the battlefield, to the side of the good, the angels who will multiply the forces of the combatants. A marvelous courage will inflame the ardor of everyone. St. Michael himself will wound the enemies, followed instantly by a general overthrow of these enemies. A sword of fire will then appear above the heads of the triumphant good."*

So, even though all will seem lost for a time, it will not be so. For, everything will change and then will come the new springtime and finally the universal restoration. It is important to note how all the various authentic prophecies concerning our times seem to coincide; and together, they comprise the prophetic pieces of a puzzle of the big picture of the cosmic apocalyptic battle plan, of what is to come. This does not mean there will be no more Popes after Peter the Roman. It means that these evil times that we are living through will come to an end amidst the persecution of the Church. But, when all seems lost, then, God will intervene and grant a new time of peace, a great renewal.

Chapter Three
The Chastisement, Antichrist & Great Tribulation

Jesus, Mary, I love you, save souls.
Let us eternally adore the Holy Sacrament through Mary.
To the Two Hearts of Jesus and Mary be honor and glory.
Let the Kingdom of the Divine Will (Fiat) come!

The Lady of All Nations Prayer
Lord Jesus Christ, Son of the Father,
send now Your Spirit over the earth.
Let the Holy Spirit live in the hearts of all nations,
that they may be preserved
from degeneration, disaster and war.
May the Lady of All Nations,
who once was Mary,
be our Advocate. Amen.

Prayer to the Immaculata
Immaculata, Queen of heaven and earth, refuge of sinners and
our most loving Mother, God has willed to entrust the entire
order of mercy to you. I, *(name),* a repentant sinner, cast myself
at your feet humbly imploring you to take me with all that I am
and have, wholly to yourself as your possession and property.
Please make of me, of all my powers of soul and body, of my
whole life, death and eternity, whatever most pleases you.
If it pleases you, use all that I am and have without reserve,
wholly to accomplish what was said of you: *"She will crush your
head,"* and, *"You alone have destroyed all heresies in the
world."* Let me be a fit instrument in your immaculate and
merciful hands for introducing and increasing your glory to the
maximum in all the many strayed and indifferent souls, and thus
help extend as far as possible the blessed kingdom of the most
Sacred Heart of Jesus. For wherever you enter you obtain the
grace of conversion and growth in holiness, since it is through
your hands that all graces come to us from the most Sacred Heart
of Jesus. Allow me to praise you, O sacred Virgin. Give me
strength against your enemies.   (St. Maximilian
Kolbe)

The Life of Consecration

 os

Totus tuus.
I am totally yours, Mary.
Bl. John Paul II's papal motto,
taken from St. Louis de Montfort

There are many plans that I cannot fulfill without YOU...
I cannot do anything without YOU...
I want to draw you closer to the Heart of Jesus.
Therefore, little children, I am inviting you today to the prayer of
consecration to Jesus, my dear Son, so that each of your hearts may be
His. And then, I am inviting you to consecration to my Immaculate
Heart. I want you to consecrate yourselves as persons, as families, and
as parishes so that all belongs to God through my hands.
Therefore, dear little children, pray that YOU may comprehend the
greatness of this message which I give YOU.
Our Lady of Medjugorje

God is calling His faithful to be especially consecrated to Him in
these times of the Apocalypse. St. Louis Marie de Montfort teaches
that Marian Consecration is perfect devotion, which is living always
devoted to Jesus through Mary. John Paul II was a great advocate of

this devotion, and he recommended *"the figure of Saint Louis Marie Grignion de Montfort, who proposes consecration to Christ through the hands of Mary, as an effective means for Christians to live faithfully their baptismal commitments."*[1] St. Louis de Montfort explains Marian consecration in his treatise, **True Devotion to Mary**. He says: *"This devotion is a smooth, short, perfect and sure way of attaining union with our Lord, in which Christian perfection consists."* He continues as follows:

> *As all perfection consists in our being conformed, united and consecrated to Jesus it naturally follows that **the most perfect of all devotions** is that which conforms, unites, and consecrates us most completely to Jesus. Now of all God's creatures Mary is the most conformed to Jesus. It therefore follows that, of all devotions, devotion to her makes for the most effective consecration and conformity to him. **The more one is consecrated to Mary, the more one is consecrated to Jesus.***

> *That is why perfect consecration to Jesus is but a perfect and complete consecration of oneself to the Blessed Virgin, which is the devotion I teach; or in other words, it is the perfect renewal of the vows and promises of holy baptism.*

> ***This devotion consists in giving oneself entirely to Mary in order to belong entirely to Jesus through her.*** *It requires us to give:*

1. Our body with its senses and members;

2. Our soul with its faculties;

3. Our present material possessions and all we shall acquire in the future;

4. Our interior and spiritual possessions, that is, our merits, virtues and good actions of the past, the present and the future.

*In other words, **we give her all that we possess** both in our natural life and in our spiritual life as well as everything we shall acquire in the future in the order of nature, of grace, and of glory in heaven. This we do **without any reservation**, not even of a penny, a hair, or the smallest good deed. And we give for all eternity without claiming or expecting, in return for our offering and our service, any other reward than the honor of belonging to our Lord through Mary and in Mary, even though our Mother were not - as in fact she always is - the most generous and appreciative of all God's creatures.[2]*

Both individuals and nations are called to be consecrated to Mary. In recent times, Marian consecration has produced great fruits. Cardinal Francis Bourne, Primate of England during WWI, claims the world war ended suddenly after consecrating England to the Sorrowful and Immaculate Heart of Mary. Portugal was consecrated to the Immaculate Heart before WWII and as a result remained protected from the war. At Our Lady's apparition at Fatima in 1917, Mary specifically asked for the consecration of Russia to stop the evil spread of communism. John Paul made the requested worldwide consecration in 1984. Soon, communism collapsed from within, without war or violence. The peaceful change came from changed hearts, from conversions due to the grace of God and the prayer of consecration. The Soviet Union finally dissolved in the early 1990s. Even though the consecrations are often made later than they are requested and after waiting longer than should be, every time these consecrations were made, the Two Hearts immediately intervened and brought divine peace, which came through no other attempted means.

Through this *perfect devotion,*[3] we offer our body and soul, and all our good actions past, present, and future, to Jesus through the hands of Mary. Mary then responds in love, guiding our life to our best good. She takes our good deeds and wraps them in her maternal heart before giving them to Jesus on our behalf. Mary also distributes the merits of our good deeds to those who need them most, maximizing our merits like a good spiritual stock broker. With her help, our lives become a great act of love par excellence.

I know many people who have made the 33-day preparation for Consecration to Jesus through Mary according to de Montfort's book, *True Devotion to Mary.* John Paul II took his papal motto, *Totus Tuus* (*I am totally yours Mary*) from St. Louis de Montfort, and he renewed his consecration daily. I know a man who was inspired by John Paul to begin the practice of renewing the Marian Consecration (Baptismal promises) each day, along with renewing his marriage vows. We should consecrate ourselves, our families, our schools, our nations, our world – to Jesus through Mary – and renew it often. This is a highly recommended practice for our times and the times to come! Through Fr. Gobbi, Our Lady said: *"**The times will be shortened**, because I am Mother of Mercy, and each day I offer, at the throne of Divine Justice, **my prayer united to that of the children who are** responding to me with a 'yes' and **consecrating themselves to my Immaculate Heart.**"*[4]

While the Marian consecration is a most powerful devotion in itself, it must be lived with a spirit of self-reform and renunciation to bear fruit that will last. Our Lady of America says, *"My children... think they have done enough in consecrating themselves to my Immaculate Heart. It is not enough. That which I ask for and is most important many have not given me. **What I ask, have asked, and will continue to ask is reformation of life.** There must be sanctification from within. **I will work my miracles of grace only in those who ask for them and empty their souls of the love and attachment to sin and all that is displeasing to my Son.** Souls who cling to sin cannot have their hands free to receive the treasures of grace that I hold out to them."*[5]

Mary Calls Us to Consecration at Medjugorje

At Medjugorje, Mary gives the secret recipe for holiness – a life of prayer and consecration. She calls the remnant faithful to live for holiness. For anyone who has an open heart, Mary is inviting each of us to her school of virtue and holiness, to join her army against the satanic foe, to consecrate our lives as part of God's salvation plan, as summarized in **five themes,** as similar to the five stones David gathered to triumph over Goliath:

1. Mary calls us to increased theological **faith** in God and in His Church's teachings, and to accept the messages of the apparitions. She says: *"Without faith, nothing is possible."* She is asking us to put our trust in Jesus and in her heavenly assistance. As the saints say, *"Have faith and all will be well."*

2. Mary calls us to **pray with the heart,** as she often says: *"Pray, pray, pray,"* especially for spiritual strength, conversions, and to disarm the efforts of Satan. She promises that *through prayer we can obtain everything.* Mary promises that prayer with the heart will be fruitful, that *"the ice cold hearts of your brothers will be melted and every barrier will disappear,"* and that *"In the power of love you [will be able to] do even those things that seem impossible to you."*

Mary asks us to pray everyday and to grow in prayer over time, just like friends spend more and more time together as their friendship grows. She asks her children to begin with the Apostles' Creed, and seven Our Father, Hail Mary and Glory Be prayers daily for peace and to pray before the Cross. As we grow in the habit of prayer, Mary requests that we add **daily Bible reading** (*lectio divina*) and begin going to **daily Mass** when possible. Our Lady says: *"Dear children! Today I ask you to read the Bible in your homes every day, and let it be in a visible place there, so that it always encourages you to read and pray... Every family must pray family prayer and read the Bible."* And about **daily Mass**, she says: *"Children, I want the Holy Mass to be the gift of the day for you. Go to it; long for it to begin, because Jesus Christ Himself gives Himself to you during Mass. So, live for this moment when you are purified. Pray much that the Holy Spirit will renew your parish. If people assist at Mass in a half-hearted fashion, they will return with cold, empty hearts."*

Mary calls us to **pray the (5-decade) Rosary every day**, especially the nightly family Rosary, saying that *"with Rosaries in your hand you will conquer."* She also asks that we should grow over time to pray the full Rosary each day, saying: *"Everyday to pray at least one (complete) Rosary: the joyful, (luminous,) sorrowful, and glorious mysteries."* Repeating the prayers of the Rosary helps us to slowly open ourselves to salvation just as we might open ourselves to evil by repeating harmful music lyrics or by regularly watching profane programs. At Lourdes, Mary came praying the Rosary; at Fatima, she came as Our Lady of the Rosary asking us to pray the Rosary every day; and at Medjugorje, she asks us to grow to pray the full Rosary daily. In his apostolic letter on the Most Holy Rosary, John Paul encouraged the same, saying: *"The Rosary can be recited in full every day, and there are those who most laudably do so,"* while he also acknowledges *"that many people will not be able to recite more than a part of the Rosary, according to a certain weekly pattern."* He calls the Rosary the *"sweet chain linking us to God."*[6]

Mary also calls us to regular (weekly) **Adoration of the Blessed Sacrament**. She says: *"Adore continually the Most Holy Sacrament. I am always present when the faithful are in adoration. Special graces are then being received."* The important thing is that we progress in prayer with God. Finally, after we grow proficient at prayer, Mary says we should grow to **pray three hours a day**, including daily Mass and the Rosary. She asks us to **pray until prayer becomes a great joy** for us, and as Paul says to pray unceasingly.

We should also pray with others and gather for prayer in groups. Mary suggests that we join a Rosary prayer group, or start one in our parish. Our Lady says: *"All people should be part of a prayer group... Every parish should have a prayer group."* Prayer groups can meet in homes. Our Lady asks for our homes to be domestic churches, with blessed objects present. Blessed objects have great importance. She says: *"I invite you to place more blessed objects in your homes and that each one wear some blessed object on himself. Let all the objects be blessed. For then, Satan will not tempt you so much, because you will be armed against him."*

3. Mary calls us to renewed **fasting**, as she says to us: *"Christians have forgotten they can prevent war and even natural calamities by prayer and fasting." "Only by prayer and fasting can war be stopped."* The authoritative book on the messages of Medjugorje, *Words From Heaven*, states: *"Through fasting, the whole plan of Our Lady, that God Himself planned for the world's salvation during this special time, will be achieved;"* and it also states, *"The whole world is affected by you individually fasting and is on the brink of being renewed. Fasting is specifically requested by Our Lady to be offered to Jesus for a new Pentecost, a new Springtime in the Church which will affect all creation.*[7] We should pray for the gift of fasting. Our Lady recommends the best way to fast is strictly on bread and water (which may include fruit) **on Wednesdays and Fridays** (except major feast days) as penance for the salvation of souls: *"I would like the people to pray... And to fast strictly on Wednesdays and Fridays."* Our Lady understands if we begin our spiritual journey with some daily prayers and then grow toward praying more over time, and that we fast weekly from a meal or two and then build up to a couple days a week. She also says we should go on occasional spiritual pilgrimages and focus more on heavenly things. A great way to fast is to give up something you like. Real fasting is forsaking sins. Mary says: *"Renounce that which hinders you from being closer to Jesus."*

Mary asks us to limit and at times fast from television and excessive (or profane) entertainments, for through the television and the Internet, a subtle and diabolical tactic of seduction and corruption has found its way into every family. One Lent, she said: *"Dear children... Start from this moment. Turn off the television and renounce other things that are useless. Dear children, I am calling you individually to convert. This time is for you. Thank you for your response to my call."* Our Blessed Mother also spoke about the evils promoted through television to Fr. Gobbi, saying: *"Never as today have immorality, impurity, and obscenity been so continually propagandized, through the press and all the means of social communication. Above all, television has become the perverse instrument of a daily bombardment with obscene images, directed to corrupt the purity of the mind and the heart of all. The places of entertainment – in particular the cinema and the [bars and night clubs] – have become places of public profanation of one's human and Christian dignity."*[8] And these warnings came from Our Lady before the Internet and the epidemic of pornography.

Fasting has a long tradition in religious practice and life. Christ fasted prior to His public life and calls us to fast in the Gospels. He indicates that when He the Bridegroom is gone, His followers will fast (Matthew 2:18-20). He spoke of the power of fasting, saying: *"Nothing will be impossible for you... by prayer and fasting"* (Matthew 2:20-21). The Apostles fasted (Acts 13:2-3, 14:21-3). Fasting is found in the Old Testament (Judith 4:9, 8:5-6; Tobit 12:8;

Esther 4:16; Jonah 3:5; 2 Maccabees 13:12) as well. Moses fasted before receiving the Ten Commandments. Elijah fasted while he traveled to Mount Horeb to commune with God. Daniel fasted for three weeks when he received a vision from God warning about a great war. The Bible shows us that fasting is for atonement, penance, and repentance. One fasts to show that one is determined to avoid committing evil, and one fasts when there is a threat of calamity to implore God's mercy and aid. Devout Jews fasted twice a week (Luke 18:12). The *Didache* (from the 1ˢᵗ century) recommends the Christian faithful to fast on Wednesdays and Fridays. According to tradition, Wednesday is the day Judas made the deal to betray Jesus and Friday is the day of the Passion. Mary is calling her children back to this most important biblical practice.

Fasting enables one to be chaste and pure. St. Benedict says to love two things in the spiritual life: *"To love fasting!"* and *"To love chastity!"* Cardinal Ratzinger (Benedict XVI) agrees, saying: *"Sexuality and nutrition belong to the fundamental elements of human corporality: a decreasing understanding of chastity is taking place simultaneously with a decreased understanding of fasting... [Whereas] Chastity and occasional renunciation of food witness [to a renewed focus on] eternal life."*[9] Besides, when one is skilled in the denial of food to satisfy the body, one will more easily be able to avoid un-chastity of the eyes or imagination to inordinately satisfy the flesh.

Fr. Slavko Barbaric of Medjugorje, who died after finishing the Way of the Cross on Mount Krizevac in November 2000, the day before he was going to be sent away from Medjugorje, wrote his final book on fasting, called *"Fast with the Heart."* A few days after he died, Our Lady told visionary Marija that he was with her in Heaven. He teaches that fasting as the way to holiness and perfection, as the way to grow in inner freedom to better receive God's graces and love. Fasting is needed to grow in the spiritual life, he taught. He made an acronym for the word FASTING: **F**orgiveness, **A**cceptance, **S**elf-control, **T**ruth, **I**ntegrity, **N**ourishment, and **G**race. He states that Mary is calling *everyone* to fast: *"We must not forget that the healthy and the sick, the young and the old, the rich and the poor, the holy and the sinful must all fast."*[10] Why diet when you can fast! And fasting leads to joy, Our Lady promises. She asks us to fast to prepare to meet Christ, especially in the Eucharist. Fr. Barbaric agrees saying: *"...fasting is connected to the Eucharist. While a person practices renunciation and lives for a period of time with bread, he prepares himself for a meeting with the Divine Bread."*[11]

Mary calls us to unite the two pillars of the spiritual life, saying: *"Fast and pray with the heart!"* and *"Renew fasting and prayer in your families."* Mary asks us to do so firmly and with seriousness. St. Bernard understood this relationship saying: *"fasting gives certainty to prayer and makes it fervent... By means of prayer strength is gained for fasting and through fasting the grace of prayer. Fasting strengthens prayer and prayer strengthens fasting and offers it to the Lord.*"[12] John Paul II wrote on the powerful effects of the union of prayer with fasting, admonishing: *"Let us therefore discover anew the humility and the courage to pray and fast so that the power from on high will break down the walls of lies and deceit... [and instead, build] resolutions and goals inspired by the civilization of life and love."*[13]

Our Lady is begging us to put these messages into practice in our lives now. Then, we will be an oasis of peace, love and goodness; and *"become apostles of love."*

4. Mary calls us to **total conversion** to God while there is still time. Mary calls us back to God. She says: *"Abandon yourselves totally to God. Renounce disordered passions. Reject fear and give yourself; those who know how to abandon themselves will no longer know either fear or obstacles."* She says: *"Be converted... turn away from the world and turn back to God. Decide for God against Satan."* Mary promises: *"Conversion will be easy for those who want it."*

Mary asks us to turn away from the glitter and noise of the world and of sin. Jesus will take account of every sin. Salvation is not available for those who walk the path of darkness and disobedience. Let nothing stand in the way of our full surrender to Christ. Our Lady strongly admonishes us to go to **monthly Confession** and not out of habit but with stirring contrition, saying, *"Monthly* *confession will be the remedy for the Church in the West."* We must participate in the Sacrament of Reconciliation to receive the *graces of peace* it brings to our soul. We must commit to go regularly, but not out of mere routine. Mary cautioned against going to Confession ritualistically and superficially, saying: *"Do not go to confession through habit, to remain the same after it. No, it is not good. Confession should give an impulse to your faith. It should stimulate you and bring you closer to Jesus. If confession does not mean anything for you, really you will be converted with great difficulty."* After a good confession, you will be happier, more content, and souls will be attracted to you in the apostolate.

Mary asks us to pray for our priests; that they would courageously call us to the life of prayer and to the Sacraments, while being faithful to their priestly duty and obedient to Christ's Vicar on earth, living in a spirit of commitment and renewal. We pray that priests will rededicate themselves to the Pope and reassert the authority of the Church. Some will and some will not; and we must pray for all priests. We all must spend more time in prayer.

Mary asks us to turn our life around with effort, her help, and God's grace. She says: *"Give up everything that goes against conversion."* Mary is calling us to the school of daily conversion, as she teaches us with her proven method: *"I would like for you to try to conquer some fault each day. If your fault is to get angry at everything, try each day, to get angry less. If your fault is not to be able to study, try to study. If your fault is not to be able to obey, or if you cannot stand those who do not please you, try on a given day, to speak with them. If your fault is not to be able to stand a proud person, you should try to approach that person. If you desire that person to be humble, be humble yourselves. Show that humility is worth more than pride. Thus, each day, try to go beyond, and to reject every vice from your heart."*

5. The Queen of Peace calls us to the **peace** of Christ. She says: *"Your responsibility is to accept divine peace; to live it." "Peace, peace, peace! Be reconciled... make peace with God and among yourselves. For that, it is necessary to believe, to pray and fast, and to go to confession."* Putting into practice the first four Medjugorje themes will lead to the fifth – to peace. The fruit of faith, prayer, fasting, and conversion is peace. Mary is calling you to choose to experience peace immediately. Live the Medjugorje messages now! Live in peace!

In the Medjugorje messages, Mary comes as our loving Mother and in every message *thanks us* for having responded to her call. She says: *"Dear children, if only you knew how great my love is for you, you would cry with joy."* She requests that we make the consecration to the Two Hearts, and she further requests her children to make reparation and atonement to her Son and to call on her protection. She warned that, in this day and age, most people go to Purgatory, the next greatest go to Hell, and only a few go directly to Heaven. She asks us to realize Hell is real and eternal and to then focus on Heaven and what God has in store for us if we choose love.

At Medjugorje, Mary warned that Satan is present and active in the world today, trying to thwart God's (and Mary's) plans. This corresponds to the vision of Leo XIII concerning the Hundred Years Reign of Satan. Mary said in Medjugorje: *"One day **(Satan) appeared before the throne of God** and asked permission to submit the Church to a period of trial. God gave him permission to try the Church for one century. **This century is under the power of the devil**, but when the secrets confided to you (the visionaries) come to pass, his power will be destroyed. Even now, **he is beginning to lose his power and has become aggressive.**"* Mary is calling you to offer your life for the souls of those who are not repenting on their own. Mary promises that your reward will be great!

In a message of *hope*, she calls us to give her our hearts so she can change them to be like hers and like her Son's, to begin to live a new life from today onwards. Then, we will be united with the Two Hearts in their mission to save souls. What more can God do to make us accept the love of the Two Hearts? Let us wake up and run to our Mother, while there is still time! She says to us: *"I want you to comprehend that God has chosen **each one of you** in order to use you for the great plan of salvation of mankind. You cannot comprehend **how great your role is** in God's plan... Thank you for having responded to my call."* She says: *"I want to save you and, through you, **to save the whole world.**"* Mary summarizes her call from Medjugorje for each of us, saying: *"Dear children, I am your Mother and, therefore, I want to lead you all to complete holiness. I want each one of you to be happy*

here on earth and to be with me in Heaven. That is, dear children, the
purpose of my coming here and it's my desire."[14]

Some years ago, just after my conversion from a worldly life to
my life in Christ and as I was beginning a renewed personal relationship with Jesus and Mary, I felt called to go to Medjugorje. But, I was
short on funds. I trusted that if Mary wanted me to come to see her,
she would provide a way. I looked into the trip and began making
reservations. The trip was drawing near and I had no money to pay for
the pilgrimage. So I prayed and trusted. Then, my brother called to ask
if he could buy my expensive stereo system, to which I agreed. I paid
for the trip and the tickets arrived the day before I was scheduled to
leave. On this first trip, I spent two weeks in Medjugorje. Our Lady
was wonderful. She provided for my every need. Having no money, I
was amazed how several times different people I did not know would
just come up to me and give me money for food. In Medjugorje, I
found a place where Heaven and earth meet; I felt the presence of
peace like nowhere else on earth. I experienced the presence of God,
and of Our Lady. I saw the Miracle of the Sun, where the sun dances
in the sky with radiant colors pulsating from behind it, on three
different days during the daily Marian apparition, and I saw the moon
turn red while spending the night on Mt. Krizavec. Medjugorje
changed my life. This pilgrimage provided me a foundation for my
new life in Jesus and Mary. I realized that God has sent His Mother,
who is my Mother, to speak to me from Heaven, and I want with all

my heart to listen to her and to do what she asks because she knows what is best for me.

You Are the Apostles of the Latter Times

In his *True Devotion to Mary*, St. Louis de Montfort prophesies about the great Marian Saints of the latter times, in our times, who will form a spiritual army consecrated to Mary acting as her instrument in defeating the Devil and his Antichrist, saying to us:

> *[The] great saints who shall surpass most of the other saints in sanctity... full of grace and zeal, [these holy persons] shall be chosen to match themselves against the enemies of God, who shall rage on all sides; and they shall be singularly devoted to our Blessed Lady, illuminated by her light, strengthened by her nourishment, led by her spirit, supported by her arm and sheltered under her protection... they shall fight, overthrow and crush the heretics with their heresies, the schismatics with their schisms, the idolaters with their idolatries and the sinners with their impieties... they shall draw the whole world to true devotion to Mary...*

> *It is through Mary that the salvation of the world was begun, and it is through Mary that it must be consummated... in order that, through her, Jesus Christ may be known, loved*

and served... God, then, wishes to reveal and make known Mary, the masterpiece of His hands, in these latter times...

[Satan] fears her not only more than all angels and men, but in a sense more than God Himself... because Satan, being proud, suffers infinitely more from being beaten and punished by a little and humble handmaid of God [and] because God has given Mary such great power against the devils... What Lucifer has lost by pride, Mary has gained by humility. What Eve has damned and lost by disobedience, Mary has saved by obedience... the power of Mary over the devils will especially shine forth in the latter times, when Satan will lay his snares against her heel: that is to say, her humble slaves and her poor (spiritual) children, whom she will raise up to make war against him. They shall be little and poor in the world's esteem [but] they shall be rich in the grace of God... in union with Mary, they shall crush the head of the devil and cause Jesus Christ to triumph...

[These holy persons] will consecrate themselves entirely to her service as subjects and slaves of love*... They will know that she is the surest, the easiest, the shortest and the most perfect means of going to Jesus Christ; and they will give themselves to Mary, body and soul, without reserve, that they may thus belong entirely to Jesus Christ... like burning fire [they] shall kindle the fire of divine love everywhere... [And] detaching themselves from everything and troubling them-*

selves about nothing, [they] shall shower forth the rain of the Word of God and of eternal life. They shall thunder against sin; they shall storm against the world; they shall strike the devil and his crew...

*They shall be the true **apostles of the latter times**... they shall be true disciples of Jesus Christ, walking in the footsteps of His poverty, humility, contempt of the world, charity; teaching the narrow way of God in pure truth, according to the holy Gospel... [and] **Mary is the one who, by order of the Most High, shall fashion them for the purpose of extending His empire over that of the impious, the idolaters and the Muslims.**[15]*

Are *you* listening? Do you hear your calling? Our Lady of La Salette is likewise asking you to take up *your mission*, to join *"**the Apostles of the Last Days**, the faithful disciples of Jesus Christ who have lived in scorn for the world and for themselves, in poverty and in humility, in scorn and in silence, in prayer and in mortification, in chastity and in union with God, in suffering and unknown to the world. It is time [you] came out and filled the world with light... (She says,) **Fight, children of light**, you, the few who can see. For now is the time of all times, the end of all ends."[16]*

With this in mind, we turn to Our Lady and invoke her, begging for the Lord's divine success in this war of wars – one that is both temporal and spiritual. And we recall that Our Lady of Good Success promises *"consolation and preservation to those faithful souls"* who foster this devotion, especially to her during this time, for it is her desire and that of her divine Son that she be known now under this invocation so filled with promise: *Our Lady of Good Success: Star of the stormy sea of my mortal life, may your light shine upon me so that I do not stray from the path that leads me (and others) to Heaven.*

This is the time of the great prophecy of the Book of Revelation (Chapter 12). As the Third Secret of Fatima and the prophesies of St. John Bosco, St. Louis de Montfort, and Our Lady of Good Success foretold, in this time, *we are the offspring of Mary* who will fight and attain the Lord's victory against the evil one! The time of crisis has commenced and the upheaval is upon us, just as Our Lady of Good Success had prophesied, and as Paul VI understood, saying: *"It is as if from some mysterious crack, no, it is not mysterious, from some crack the smoke of Satan has entered the temple of God."*[17] But, as Paul VI also knew, we must fight the spiritual battle with spiritual weapons: *"[As] evils increase, the devotion of the People of God should also increase."*[18] Giving us hope, *"Where sin abounds, grace abounds all the more,"*[19] Scripture promises.

Living Consecrated to the Two Hearts

Dear reader, *your* participation is needed. If you will simply let Jesus and Mary lead you, you will see your life bear fruit a hundred fold and even more. Think of what is at stake and how many are dependent upon you for help! If you will be willing to live a quiet, peaceful, prayerful, life with suffering, offered to God, then you are a victim soul and *God thanks you.*

We are living in the days described in the Book of Revelation – the beginning of the last days. All around us the final secret of Fatima is unfolding. The prophecy of victim souls echoed by the Third Secret of Fatima mentions the Pope and other victim souls who do penance and offer their lives, united to the Two Hearts, as spiritual children of the *Woman*, for the salvation of the world in our times. We must recall that this coming time of upheaval is permitted by God to wake us up from our darkness and sin and to *liberate* us. The faithful must *rejoice* that this time is upon us. Our Lady, our Liberatrix, says that it is our sacrifices that will usher in the era of peace, and bring about the triumph and reign of the Two Hearts.

Today, these prophecies are being fulfilled, and *this book* has been *your* guide to participation in the divine restoration that will bring about the era of peace. You are part of those who, even if only a remnant, will offer their lives for the world. We recall in 64 AD, when Emperor Nero was burning Rome and St. Peter was fleeing, the words which he addressed to Christ Who appeared running toward Rome in a vision, saying: *"Quo vadis?"* – *"Where are you going?"* Jesus responded to Peter, saying, *"I am going to Rome to be crucified again,"* and Peter too regained his courage to return to Rome and offer his life for Christ. And now, you too are being invited to take up anew your mission of selfless love, to suffer for the Truth and for others as Christ suffered for you, to accept the two crowns of *purity* (chastity and modesty) and *sacrifice* (witness and martyrdom), as St. Peter, who was crucified in Rome up-side-down, and more recently St. Maximilian Kolbe, who was martyred under Hitler with starvation, both did – though not within the first century Rome under Nero or the twentieth century under Hitler, but *now* within the world today which is under Satan's influence, to live your vocation and state of life with Christian fervor, to live with an authentic witness of the true Faith and to lay down your life for the salvation of souls and for the ultimate glory of Christ.

Just as in playing sports, you must consider that if you have anything left at the end of a sporting event, you have failed to give enough. So too, you must not just venerate the Saints; you must imitate them and do so until the end. YOU are called to be a Saint, and right now! Like Peter and Kolbe, St. Paul offered his life and his all for the glory of God until his sacrifice was complete through the martyrdom of his beheading, as he knowingly witnessed, saying: *"For I am already on the point of being sacrificed... I have fought the good fight, I have finished the race, I have kept the faith."*[20] We must be able to do and say the same! And then Christ too will award us *"the (eternal) crown of righteousness."* Dear reader, consecrate your life to Jesus through Mary anew right now and again everyday, determine to be pure and holy, and join the greatest Saints of all time!

Chapter Four
The Life of Consecration

Jesus, Mary, I love you, save souls.
Let us eternally adore the Holy Sacrament through Mary.
To the Two Hearts of Jesus and Mary be honor and glory.
Let the Kingdom of the Divine Will (Fiat) come!

Marian Consecration – *Totus Tuus*

I, (*name*), a faithless sinner,
renew and ratify today in your hands, O Immaculate Mother,
the vows of my Baptism;
I renounce forever Satan, his pomps and works;
and I give myself entirely to Jesus Christ, the Incarnate
Wisdom, to carry my cross after Him all the days of my life,
and to be more faithful to Him than I have ever been before.
In the presence of all the heavenly court,
I choose you this day for my Mother and Queen.
I deliver and consecrate to you, as your slave, my body and
soul, my goods, both interior and exterior,
and even the value of all my good actions,
past, present, and future;
leaving to you the entire and full right of disposing of me, and
all that belongs to me, without exception, according to your
good pleasure, for the greater glory of God,
in time and eternity. Amen.

(St. Louis Marie de Montfort)

Prayer Given By Our Lord Jesus Christ

O my Jesus,
May our feet journey together,
May our hands gather in unity,
May our hearts beat to the same rhythm,
May our souls be in harmony,
May our thoughts be in unison,
May our ears listen to the silence together,
May our glances melt in one another,
And may our lips beg Our Heavenly Father,
together, to obtain Mercy.

(To Elizabeth Kindelmann, 1962, with 2009 Imprimatur)

III

LOVE FOREVER AFTER

God is love,
and he who abides in love abides in God,
and God abides in him.
1 John 4:16

For behold, I create new heavens and a new earth;
and the former things shall not be remembered or come into mind. But
be glad and rejoice forever in that which I create;
behold, I create Jerusalem a rejoicing, and her people a joy. I will
rejoice in Jerusalem, and be glad in my people;
no more shall be heard in it the sound of weeping and the cry of
distress.
Isaiah 65:17-19

Salvation belongs to our God Who sits upon the throne,
and to the Lamb!...
Amen!
Blessing and glory and wisdom and thanksgiving and honor and
power and might be to our God for ever and ever! Amen...
Revelation 7:10, 12

The Triumph
of the Two Hearts
&
Era of Peace

☙

The Heart of Jesus and Mary is one heart.
St. John Eudes

Then I saw an angel coming down from heaven…
And he seized the dragon, that ancient serpent, who is the Devil and
Satan, and bound him for a thousand years.
Revelation 20:1-2

The great renewal of peace will come through the purification of humanity and the manifestation and ultimate defeat of the Antichrist. Our Lady confirms through Fr. Gobbi: *"The new era, which I am preparing for you, coincides with the defeat of Satan and of his universal reign. All his power is destroyed. He is bound, with all the wicked spirits, and shut up in hell. Herein, Christ reigns in the splendor of His glorified body, and the Immaculate Heart of your heavenly Mother triumphs in the light of her body, assumed into the glory of paradise.*"[1] Mystic Ven. Mary of Agreda (17th Century) spoke about Mary's role **concerning the great renewal to come**, saying: *"It was revealed to me that through the intercession of the Mother of God,* **all heresies will disappear.** *This victory over heresies has been reserved by Christ for His Blessed Mother... Before the Second Coming of Christ, Mary must, more than ever, shine in mercy, might, and grace in order to bring unbelievers into the Catholic Faith. The powers of Mary in the last times over the demons will be very conspicuous.* **Mary will extend the Reign of Christ over the heathens and Mohammedans (Muslims), and it will be a time of great joy when Mary, as Mistress and Queen of Hearts, is enthroned.** *"*[2] Our Lady adds through Fr. Gobbi concerning these times saying that *"the reunion of all Christians in the Catholic Church will coincide with the Triumph of my Immaculate Heart in the world."*[3] Through Mary the Church will enter the new Age of Obedience and Love. **Jesus will reign in hearts, in souls, in individuals, in families, and in all society! It will be a universal reign of grace, of beauty, of harmony, of communion, of holiness, of justice, and of peace! It will be the time of the renewed and more beautiful earthly paradise!**[4]

Our Lady of La Salette promised likewise that when the earth will have been in *"a continuous series of evolutions for three days,"* St. Michael will smother the Beast and his followers who will then be plunged into hell, *"the Antichrist will be defeated, fire (and water) will purge the earth and consume all the work of men's pride, and all will be renewed. God will be served and glorified."* The water will cleanse, the fire will purify, and God will reign again on earth among His faithful ones!

Melanie, visionary of La Salette, in about 1900, entrusted to Abbot Combe the basic principles of the times to come. She presented the broad outline of them to Miss Vernet as follows:

> ***There will only be true peace on earth after the death of the Antichrist****... After the Antichrist, who will fall body and soul into hell, the ground opening in the presence of the thousands of spectators coming from all the parts of the world to be witness to his exaltation (as he had announced) and (claimed) entrance to heaven, all will convert, glorifying the single God of heaven and earth; the Gospel of Jesus-Christ will be preached in all his purity on all the earth. **The churches will be re-established (réouvertes); the kings will be the right hand of the Holy See; there will be one Shepherd and only one herd; charity will reign in all peoples' hearts. The world will still last (for) centuries.**[5]*

The Chain That Binds Satan

What shall cause the downfall of the devil? How shall the Red Dragon be destroyed? The two-fold remedy that will destroy Satan is told by Mary to Fr. Gobbi: *"**Satan's pride will again be conquered by the humility of little ones**, and **the Red Dragon will find himself**"* *decisively humiliated and defeated when I bind him not by a great chain but by a very frail cord: the holy rosary.*"[6] Giving us details of the chain that Our Lady will use to bind the great dragon, Satan, and to throw him into the abyss, Our Lady explains through Fr. Gobbi as follows:

> **The chain,** *with which the great Dragon is to be bound, is made up of prayer made by me and by means of me. This prayer* **is that of the holy rosary.** *A chain has in fact* **three functions** *of first of all limiting action, then of imprisoning, and finally of making ineffective every activity of the one who has been bound by it.*

> *The chain of the holy rosary has first of all the function of* **limiting the action of my Adversary.** *Every rosary which you recite with me has the effect of restricting the action of the Evil One, of drawing souls away from his pernicious influence, and of giving greater impetus to the expansion of goodness in the life of many of my children.*

> *The chain of the holy rosary has also the effect of* **imprisoning Satan, that is, of making his action impotent, and of diminishing and weakening more and more the force of his diabolical power.** *And so, each rosary which is recited well deals a mighty blow to the power of evil, and it represents one part of his reign which is destroyed.*

*The chain of the holy rosary brings about, in the end, the result of **making Satan completely harmless**. His great power is destroyed. All the evil spirits are cast into the pool of fire and sulphur, the door is shut by me with the key of the power of Christ, and thus they will no longer be able to go out into the world to do harm to souls.*[7]

Just as Our Lady had promised through St. Dominic, **Mary really will save the world through the Rosary and the Scapular.**

A New Pope and a Great Renewal

Then there will be a new Pope. John of the Cleft Rock prophesied in the fourteenth century of what would occur after the great upheaval, persecution of the Church, and the death of the Pope in exile, saying: ***"But [then] God will raise a holy Pope**, and the Angels will rejoice. Enlightened by God, this man will rebuild almost the whole world through his holiness. He will lead everyone to the true Faith… He will lead all erring sheep back to the fold."*[8] The prophecy of Bl. Anna Maria Taigi indicates what will happen after Rome falls, and after the Antichrist is dethroned and the three days of darkness has occurred:

*After the three days of darkness, St. Peter and St. Paul, having come down from Heaven, will preach in the whole world and designate **a new Pope**. A great light will flash from their bodies and will settle upon the cardinal who is to be-*

*come Pope. Christianity, then, will spread throughout the world. He is the Holy Pontiff, chosen by God to withstand the storm. At the end, he will have the gift of miracles, and his name shall be praised over the whole earth. Whole nations will come back to the Church and **the face of the earth will be renewed. Russia, England, and China will come into the Church.***

The Two Pillars and the Perfect Calm after the Storm

It is in this context that the famous dream of St. John Bosco becomes clearer than ever. St. Bosco had a famous dream (1862), one that he described as a parable, an allegory or simile that teaches a moral. As reported by witnesses who heard him tell it, it is as follows:

On the whole surface of the sea you see an infinity of ships, each ending in a beak of sharp iron that pierces whatever it hits. Some of these ships have arms, cannons, guns; others have books and incendiary materials, and others have hands, fists, blasphemies, and curses. All of them are thronging after a ship that is considerably bigger, trying to ram it, set fire to it, and do it every possible sort of damage. There is a great storm.

Imagine that in the middle of the sea you also see two very tall columns. On one is the statue of the Blessed Virgin

Immaculate, with the inscription underneath: "Help of Chris-
tians." On the other one, which is even bigger and taller,
there is a Eucharistic Host of proportionately large size in re-
lation to the column, and under it the words: "Salvation of
believers." From the base of the column hang many chains
with anchors to which ships can be attached.

The bigger ship of the allied fleet that is under attack is
captained by the Pope, and all his efforts are bent to steer this
ship of the Holy See in between those two columns. But, as I
said, the other ships try in every way to block it and destroy it,
some with arms, with the beaks of their prows, with fire from
books and journals. But all their weapons are in vain. Every
weapon and substance only splinters the larger ship and then
sinks. Now and then the cannons make a deep hole some-
where in the ship's sides. There is indescribable rejoicing on
the enemy ships at the damage they do the Pope's ship. But a
breeze blowing from the two columns is enough to heal every
wound and close up the holes.

The ship again continues on its way. There are during
this time two papally summoned conferences of the captains
of the allied ships.

On the way the Pope falls once because he had been
gravely wounded, then rises again, is wounded again, falls a
second time and dies. When he falls the second time, dead, a

shout of joy goes up among the remaining enemies. As soon as he is dead, there is a conclave of the allied captains to elect a new Pope, and another Pope immediately replaces him. He guides the ship to the two columns.

Once there, he attaches the ship with one anchor to the column with the consecrated Host, with another anchor to the column with the Immaculate Conception.

Then total disorder breaks out *over the whole surface of the sea. **All the ships that so far had been battling the Pope's ship scatter, flee, and collide** with one another, some foundering and trying to sink the others.*

*Those at a distance keep prudently back until the remains of all the demolished ships have sunk into the depths of the sea, and then they vigorously make their way to the side of the bigger ship. Having joined it, they too attach themselves to the anchors hanging from the two columns and remain there in **perfect calm**, all safe and secure.*[9]

The ship of the Pope and his allied fleet is the Church, of which he is the head. The enemy ships are the persecutions in store for the Church, and the sea is this world. Those who were defending the Church are the good people, attached to the Holy See; the others are its enemies, who try to destroy it with every sort of weapon. And the two columns of safety are devotion to Mary Most Holy and to the Most

Blessed Sacrament of the Eucharist. The Marian title *"Help of Christians"* originated from the Christian naval victory over the invading Muslim Turks at Lepanto, on October 7, 1571. Later, the Pope called this feast: Our Lady of the Most Holy Rosary. The Church now and then will suffer damages, symbolized by the holes made in the big ship by the weapons, but a *"breeze"* from the Almighty and the Blessed Virgin is enough to repair those damages, though with the loss of some souls. The moral, then, is that **we have only two means to stand firm in this confusion: devotion to the Virgin Mary and** frequent reception and adoration of **the Most Holy Eucharist.**

Many people have interpreted this dream to be referring to our times. And I think, in the context of this book that they are right. Some also thought the first Pope in the dream was John Paul II, who was wounded by an assassin on May 13, 1981, on the anniversary of Fatima. Many wondered if, as the dream seemed to them to indicate, whether he would die as a martyr. But, in hind-sight, this is not exactly how things worked out.

What now appears more the case, considering the prophesies related in this book, is that there are more than two popes involved in Bosco's dream. This was already thought to be so by one of Bosco's students who retold the story some years after 1862 in Bosco's presence, but this important point was not picked up in the popular retellings of the dream that have come down to us.[10] It may prove to be a significant detail.

John Paul II was the spark that prepared for and began the divine renewal; this is true, as the Lord did indeed foretell to St. Faustina, saying, *"From [Poland] will come forth the spark that will prepare the world for My final coming."* But, the purifying fire that will bring world peace has yet to be fully ignited. This seems evident also in light of the revelations of La Salette and of those to Bl. Anna Maria Taigi. Our Lady warns through Fr. Gobbi: *"You must defend [the Pope], because he will have to carry the Cross in the midst of **the greatest storm in history**... more than ever this world is in the power of the Evil One."*[11] The Popes of this period are enduring the great disorder; and as all fall into chaos, he will secure the bark of Peter to the Eucharist and to Mary. Toward the end of the vision, Bosco's dream mentions ***"another Pope who will immediately replace [the previous one], who guides the ship [of the Church] to the two columns"* of Mary and the Eucharist and to "perfect calm."** Might this be the Pope of the Great Renewal and Era of Peace?

The Three Ages of the World

At the monastery in Casamari, south of Rome, the twelfth century Italian monk, Bl. Joachim of Fiore, contributed greatly to Christian prophetic thinking. He has been called the most important prophetic thinker of the whole medieval period and maybe, after the Apostle John, the most important in the history of Christianity. Joachim saw human history as aligned in three ages with the Holy Trinity. The first age of the Father had been the age of ancient Israel. The second age of the Son has been the age of the Church. The third age of the Spirit, brought about by a great purification, will usher in a time of peace, and the whole world will look like and live like a monastery and people will believe like in ancient times. St. Bernard of Clairvaux explains: *"We know that there are three comings of the Lord. [The first has occurred; the Second Coming will occur at the end of time.] The third lies between the other two. It is invisible, while the other two are visible... The intermediate coming is a hidden one; in it only the elect will see the Lord within their own selves... in this middle coming, He is our rest and consolation."*[12] St. Justin Martyr said: *"There will be a resurrection of the flesh, followed by a thousand years in the rebuilt, embellished, and enlarged city of Jerusalem."*[13] I think it will be a time when the whole world will experience the peace of Medjugorje as many experience there where Our Lady is reportedly appearing.

As the third stage begins, **the Latins (Catholics) and Greeks (Orthodox) will be united** in the new spiritual kingdom, freed alike from the fetters of the letter; **the Jews will be converted**, and the *"Eternal Gospel"* will abide until the end of the world. In this third age, that of the Kingdom of the Holy Spirit, there will be a new dispensation of universal love, which will proceed from the Gospel of Christ, but transcend the letter of it, and in which there will be no need for disciplinary institutions.

Prophesizing about the upheaval that would occur before the era of peace, Joachim of Fiore held that the third epoch would begin after some great cataclysm. And he prophesied about this, saying: *"To-wards the end of the world, **Antichrist will overthrow the pope and usurp his see.**"[14]*

The Three Renewals of the World

Similarly, in the twentieth century, the Lord revealed to Servant of God Luisa Piccarreta about **the three renewals**, saying:

> *I renewed the world every two thousand years. In the first two thousand years I renewed it with the Deluge (Flood of Noah); in the second two thousand I renewed it with My coming upon earth... Now we are almost at the end of the third two thousand years, and there will be **a third renewal**. This is the reason for the general confusion: it is nothing other than the preparation of the third renewal... now, in this third renewal, **after the earth will be purged and a great part of the current generation destroyed**, I will be even more generous with creatures, accomplishing **the renewal**... and I await the creatures to come to live in My Volition ("My Will in action"), and repeat in My Will all that I did... **I will have the army of the souls who (not just resigned and submitted, but who) will live in My Will, and in them will I have My Creation restored** - all beautiful and striking, just as It came out from My hands.*[15]

The renewal of our times will come about as an army of souls dedicates their lives to living *in* the Divine Will, as Our Lord prophesized through Luisa Piccarreta. God revealed to her that in these latter-times, **"the Church will be renewed and the face of the earth transformed"**, **through a universal abandonment to the Divine Will**. Thus, each of us is called to say with St. Rose Venerini, who always strove to follow God's will: *"I find myself so bound to the Divine Will that neither death nor life is important: I want to live as He wishes and I want to serve Him as He likes, and nothing more."*[16] God will lead His faithful to the restoration of His creation, and then He will lead His people to live in His Divine Will (*Fiat*) in the great renewal to come!

The *Catechism* discusses this Age of the Spirit, saying: *"In these 'end times,' ushered in by the Son's redeeming Incarnation, the Spirit is revealed and given, recognized and welcomed as a person. Now can this divine plan, accomplished in Christ, the firstborn and head of the new creation, be embodied in mankind by* **the outpouring of the Spirit**.*"*[17] Fr. Joseph Iannuzzi reflects on such a time, remarking: *"If before that final end there is to be a period, more or less prolonged, of triumphant sanctity, such a result will be brought about not by the apparition of the person of Christ in Majesty but by the operation of those powers of sanctification which are now at work, the Holy [Spirit] and the Sacraments of the Church."*[18]

The Era of Peace Begins

These coming days of darkness shall be overcome with the help of God's Light, and with His angel, as the Book of Revelation seems to allude, stating: *"Then I saw an angel coming down from heaven, holding in his hand the key of the bottomless pit and a great chain. And* **he seized the dragon, that ancient serpent, who is the Devil and Satan, and bound him for a thousand years**, *and threw him into the pit, and shut it and sealed it over him, that he should deceive the nations no more... [and the holy ones shall reign] with Christ a thousand years."*[19]

The message of Our Lady of Good Success ends with a similar note of great hope: just when everything will seem lost and paralyzed, Our Lady said, then will come *"the happy beginning of the complete restoration. This will mark the arrival of my hour, when I, in a marvelous way, will dethrone the proud and cursed Satan, trampling him under my feet and fetter him in the infernal abyss."*

The world is about to enter a new age, the age of the Spirit and of peace, but only through a divine chastisement and the great tribulation. This will be the Age of the Two Hearts, of the Triumph of the Immaculate Heart and the Reign of the Sacred Heart together. This echoes the promise of Our Lady at Fatima, when she said: *"**In the end, My Immaculate Heart will triumph.**"* Our Lord also told Lucia of Fatima: **"Put the devotion of the Immaculate Heart besides the** *devotion of My Sacred Heart."* Mankind will love God and God's people will dwell in unity, under the reign of the Two Hearts.

The Thousand Years of Peace

The Kingdom of God will soon be manifest in a great way. And thus will begin the celebration of the building of the *New Jerusalem*. And *you* are helping to bring about this great Plan of God. Our Lady said to Fr. Gobbi: *"Thus **you are already contributing to the forming of the new Jerusalem**, the holy city, which must come down from heaven, as a bride adorned for her husband."*[20]

During this new era of peace, Jesus will come in glory in His Spirit. Jesus will not be present in the flesh, but will reign in our hearts and, in a most powerful way, by means of the Eucharist. This will be a mighty triumph of Christ here on earth before the final consummation of all things. This is not related to the heresy of Millenarianism (Latin, *mille*, 1000), which is the condemned position that Jesus Christ would come down to earth in the flesh (in His glorified human form) and reign as an earthly king with His Saints for a literal one thousand years before the end of time. Instead, the new era of peace will be a *"spiritual," "temporal," "second"* (but not final), *"intermediate"* or *"middle"* coming of Christ to take place before the end of the world. This renewed coming of Christ in the Spirit upon the earth for a significant period or *"age"* has been taught in different degrees and expressions by the Church Fathers, among them Papias, St. Justin Martyr, St. Irenaeus, Tertullian, St. Hippolytus, Lactantius, St. Bernard of Clairvaux, St. Augustine and others, and is based on Revelation 20.[21]

This period of *"a thousand years"* is symbolic, biblical language for a long period of time, but not necessarily a literal thousand year period of time. Christ's intermediate coming is a *"returning"* insofar as He will manifest Himself to this world in a glorious way and will bring His Kingdom to this world. Christ will not descend bodily in His resurrected glory until the end of time, but He will come by way of his glorified Spirit who will purge, illuminate and unify all creation in the intermediate coming. He will reign within His Church and within His people. Evidently, we will still have our weakened human nature, but without the great influence of Satan and with the special presence of the Spirit of Christ. Our Lady spoke about this to Fr. Gobbi: *"And then the Holy Spirit will work **the new miracle of universal transformation** in the heart and the life of all: sinners will be converted; the weak will find support; the sick will receive healing; those far away will return to the house of the Father; those separated and divided will attain full unity. In this way, the miracle of the Second Pentecost will take place. It will come with **the triumph of my Immaculate Heart** in the world,"*[22] together with a new Eucharistic Reign of Christ.

The universe will be renewed in a form of universal restoration. God will bring forth a renewed creation where *both* the material world and humanity will be transformed. Eventually, He will restore the world to its original state.[23] And at some point, God will begin to establish the new heavens and the new earth,[24] and make all things new. St. Bernadette spoke a prophecy of our time, saying: *"The Virgin has told me that when the Twentieth Century passes away... **A new Age of Faith will dawn around the world**... There will follow a century of peace and joy as all the nations of the earth lay down their swords and shields. Great prosperity will follow... Millions will return to Christ ...The Twenty-First Century will come to be known as **the Second Golden Age of Mankind**."* Our Lady tells Fr. Gobbi:

> And **then Jesus Christ will bring his glorious reign in the world**... *the triumph of my Immaculate Heart in the glorious coming of my Son Jesus."*[25] Our Lady also revealed that **"The glorious reign of Christ will be established after the complete defeat of Satan and all the spirits of evil, and the destruction of Satan's diabolical power.** *Thus he will be bound and cast into hell, and the gate of the abyss will be shut so that he can no longer get out to harm the world. And Christ will reign in the world."*[26] **"The glorious reign of Christ [will] bring all humanity... back to the state of his terrestrial paradise...** *and all creation will become again that marvelous garden, created for man to reflect in a perfect manner the greatest glory of God... That which is being prepared is so great that its equal has never existed since the creation of the world.*[27]

After the fire of Justice and the defeat of Satan, which is soon to occur, the Church shall revive, the earth shall be set aflame with love, and all creation shall be restored in Christ.

Revelation 20
& the Glorious Eucharistic Reign of Christ

Our Lady's messages to Fr. Gobbi give us a glimpse of the great period of Christ's new reign after the defeat of the Evil One, (as also proclaimed in Revelation 20):

> *And so, my beloved ones and children consecrated to my Heart, it is **you who must be today a clarion call for the full return of the whole Church Militant to Jesus present in the Eucharist**. Because there alone is to be found the spring of living water which will purify its aridity and renew the desert to which it has been reduced; there alone is to be found the secret of life which will open up for it a second Pentecost of grace and of light; there alone is to be found the fount of its renewed holiness: Jesus in the Eucharist!*[28]

> *It is not your pastoral plans and your discussions; it is not the human means on which you put reliance and so much assurance, but **it is only Jesus in the Eucharist which will give to the whole Church the strength of a complete re-***

newal, which will lead it to be poor, evangelical, chaste, stripped of all those supports on which it relies, holy, beautiful and without spot or wrinkle, in imitation of your heavenly Mother.[29]

In the end my Immaculate Heart will triumph.

This will come about in the greatest triumph of Jesus, who will bring into the world his glorious reign of love, of justice and of peace, and will make all things new.

Open your hearts to hope. *Throw open the doors to Christ who comes to you in glory. Live the trembling hour of this second Advent.*[30]

Then, the prophetic words of John Paul the Great will come to pass, as he said at the 45th International Eucharistic Congress in Seville, Spain (June 1993): *"I hope that ... perpetual adoration, with permanent exposition of the Blessed Sacrament, will continue into the future. Specifically, I hope that the fruit of this Congress results in **the establishment of perpetual Eucharistic Adoration in all parishes and Christian communities throughout the world**."* As Our Lady confirms through Fr. Gobbi: *"This **New Era will coincide with the greatest Triumph of the Eucharistic Jesus**... The New Era, which I announce to you, coincides with the complete fulfillment of the Divine Will."*[31] Be serene and joyful, knowing what is to come!

Living in an Alliance with the Two Hearts in Love

In the age to come, and already now for some of us, we will live united to the Two Hearts of Jesus and Mary in an alliance of love. This is based on sound doctrine and is in union with God's will. St. John Eudes, who St. Pius X calls the father, doctor, and apostle of the Hearts of Jesus and Mary Devotion, enunciates this doctrine saying: *"I shall only tell you that you must never separate what God has so perfectly united. So closely are Jesus and Mary bound up with each other that whoever beholds Jesus sees Mary; whoever loves Jesus, loves Mary; whoever has devotion to Jesus, has devotion to Mary."[32]* He continues elsewhere, saying: *"Although the Heart of Jesus is distinct from that of Mary... and infinitely surpasses it in excellence and holiness nevertheless, God has so closely united these two Hearts that we may say with truth that They are but one, because They have always been animated with the same spirit and filled with the same sentiments and affections... Jesus is enshrined in the Heart of Mary so completely that in honoring and glorifying her Heart, we honor and glorify Jesus Christ Himself."[33]* Focusing now on *our* union with the Two Hearts to make a single united Heart of love, we pray: *"O Jesus living in the heart of Mary! Be the life of my heart. Mary, Mother of Jesus, obtain by your intercession, I beseech you, that I may have but one heart with your beloved Son and yourself."[34]*

John Paul spoke profoundly concerning the alliance (covenant) of the Two Hearts, *and* concerning our insertion into that alliance:

When the side of Christ was pierced with the centurion's lance, Simeon's prophecy was fulfilled in her: 'And a sword will pierce through your own soul, also' (Lk. 2:35).

The words of the prophet are a foretelling of the definitive alliance of these hearts: of the Son and of the Mother; of the Mother and of the Son. 'Heart of Jesus, in whom dwells all the fullness of the divinity.' Heart of Mary – Heart of the sorrowful Virgin – heart of the Mother of God!

*May our prayer... **unite us today with that admirable alliance of hearts**.*[35]

John Paul also spoke of what would happen when we unite ourselves with the Two Hearts, saying:

This spiritual bond always leads to a great awakening of apostolic zeal. Adorers of the Divine Heart become men with a sensitive conscience. And when it is granted to them to have relations with the Heart of our Lord and Master, in them also there then springs up the need of atonement for the sins of the world, for the indifference of so many hearts and their negligences.

*How necessary this host of watchful hearts is in the Church in order that the Love of the Divine Heart may not remain isolated and unrequited! Among this host special mention deserves to go to all those who offer their sufferings as **living*** *victims in union with the Heart of Christ, pierced on the cross. Thus transformed with love, human suffering becomes a particular leaven of Christ's work of salvation in the Church.*[36]

Through Mary's heart, we experience Jesus' Heart. Mary helps us to do whatever He tells us, to follow His will with trust. **Benedict XVI observes the relation between the Eucharist and Mary**, saying: *"Obedient faith in response to God's work shapes [Mary's] life at every moment. A virgin attentive to God's word, she lives in complete harmony with his will... Mary is the great Believer who places herself confidently in God's hands, abandoning herself to his will... Consequently, **every time we approach the Body and Blood of Christ in the eucharistic liturgy, we also turn to her** who, by her complete fidelity, received Christ's sacrifice for the whole Church."*[37] We welcome Jesus' Mother into our home, into our heart. We are a child of God and of Mary, with Jesus our Brother. We hope to love her as much as Jesus does. We know she loves us as much as she loves Jesus. We want to thank her for spending her life and her *"time"* in Heaven praying for us, looking after us, consoling us, loving us. She guides us to the Eucharist with perfect love. United to the Two Hearts, together with the Church, we have a Petrine-Marian-Eucharistic spirituality: All to Jesus through Mary with the Pope, together with St. Joseph.

Fr. Manelli, Founder and Minister General of the Franciscan Friars of the Immaculate, is internationally known for his distinguished preaching and biblical, Mariological scholarship. He speaks with profound insight on the relation between Mary and the Eucharist:

The Eucharist is the Bread of the Mother of God, our Mother. It is Bread made by Mary from the flour of her immaculate flesh, kneaded with her virginal milk. St. Augustine wrote, "Jesus took His Flesh from the flesh of Mary"...Therefore, at every Holy Communion we receive, it would be quite correct, and a very beautiful thing, to take notice of our holy Mother's sweet and mysterious presence, inseparably and totally united with Jesus in the Host.

... when we receive Him we cannot but receive her as well, who, by bonds of highest love, and by bonds of flesh and blood, forms with Jesus a single alliance of love, one whole, as she is always and inseparably "leaning upon her Beloved" (Cant. 8:5). Is it not true that love, and above all divine love, unites and unifies? And after the unity of Persons in the Blessed Trinity, can we conceive a unity more intimate and absorbing than that between Jesus and the Virgin Mary?

...It is in the Eucharist, and especially in Holy Communion, that our union with Our Lady becomes a full and loving conformity with her. With the Host which is Jesus, she, too, enters in us and becomes entirely one with each of us, her children, pouring out her motherly love upon our souls and bodies.[38]

Mary unites us to the Eucharistic Christ by first uniting herself to us. St. Augustine further illustrates how Mary unites herself to each one of us in Holy Communion, saying: *"The Word is the Food of the angels. Men have not the strength to nourish themselves with this Heavenly Food; yet, they have need for it. What is needed is a mother who may eat this super-substantial Bread, transform it into her milk, and in this way feed her poor children. This mother is Mary. She nourishes herself with the Word and transforms Him into the Sacred Humanity. She transforms Him into Flesh and Blood, i.e., into this most sweet milk which is called the Eucharist."* *"Imagine,"* St. John Bosco says to us, *"that it is no longer the priest but the most holy Madonna herself who comes to give you the Holy Host."* With this in mind, we are called to ask Mary to cover us with the mantle of her pure Immaculate Heart as we receive the Eucharist, the Sacred Heart of Jesus. Our Lady of the Most Holy Eucharist is the Mother of the Eucharist. At the Annunciation, at Cana, at Calvary, and *in the Eucharist*, the Hearts of Jesus and Mary are united as one Heart. Our Lady revealed to St. Bridget, saying: *"Jesus and I loved each other so tenderly on earth that we were one Heart."* We must recognize that when we receive the Eucharist, our heart is conjoined to their Two Hearts. Christ tells us from the Cross to come to Him (in the Eucharist) through Mary. Here is the wellspring of all graces and mercy. In this way, receiving the Eucharist makes us three hearts in one!

Not to misunderstand – the Eucharist is the Heart of Christ, but Mary's heart is always united to His, and when we receive Him, we always receive them both. And as we find ourselves united to the Two Hearts, we also find, therein, the hearts of the whole Communion of

Saints in the unity of the Triune God. We are one in union and love, in this life continually through the Rosary and Holy Communion and in the next life through the beatific vision, forever. God intends this to be the fulfillment and joy of *every* human being, of *your life redeemed!* What a profound mystery! When the Two Hearts triumph, and they will, then they will usher in the era of peace for the world. Then, the reign of the Two Hearts will begin!

Practically speaking, it is recommended as well to have your family consecrated to the Two Hearts, and to hang a picture of the Two Hearts in your home and to even keep one in your wallet (as you do the pictures of your other loved ones). Honor the Two Hearts always!

Now it is time to pray and give thanks with all your heart, saying:

Jesus, I want to always give You shelter in my heart, to experience Your Love's fire ever anew and to live to set the world ablaze with It. Help me to always believe in Your love for me, and make my love for You total and whole-hearted. Jesus and Mary, pray for me to live... all for the Triune God, all for the Eucharistic and Sacred Heart of Jesus, all for the Sorrowful and Immaculate Heart of Mary, in union with St. Joseph, the Saints and Angels, faithful to holy Mother Church and the Vicar of Christ, forever! Glory be to the Father, Glory be to the Son, Glory be to the Holy Spirit, as it was in the beginning, is now, and ever shall be. I offer you my life as a sacrifice of love. Jesus, Mary, I love you, save souls.

We become a handmaid/servant of the Handmaid of the Lord, as the Pope is the servant of the servants of God. We want to be *"like a weaned child on its mother's lap"* (Ps 131:2b, NAB); while at prayer, cleaning the stalls in the grotto at Bethlehem, washing the floor at the Holy House of Nazareth now in Loreto, or cleaning Our Lady's clothes after the Lord's Passion while at Mass. We may even hope to be a servant to the servants of Mary, and a servant of Joseph her beloved spouse.

New Devotion to St. Joseph

St. Joseph too will come with the Holy Child
to bring peace to the world.
Our Lady of Fatima

St. Joseph revealed:
God wishes me to be honored in union with Jesus and Mary
to obtain peace among men and nations…
The Divine Trinity has placed into our keeping
the peace of the world.
Our Lady of America apparitions

St. Joseph: Protector of the Two Hearts

St. Joseph is, after all, revered above all Saints, second to Mary. He was the first to contemplate the Face of Jesus, the first to adore

Him, to touch and caress Him, the first to listen to Him teach, the first to suffer for Him. Joseph was given the highest office in the history of humanity, that of father of God's Son, and thus he was given all the graces necessary to succeed with dignity and perfection in the office confided in Him by Providence.[39] He had the abundance of heavenly graces. He was firm in faith, angelic in purity, profound in humility, perfect in obedience, admirable in patience, most ardent in charity, and greatest in his devotion. Joseph is patron of a happy death because he died with Jesus and Mary by his side. Some holy writers have proposed that Joseph is already in Heaven body and soul, like Mary and Jesus.[40]

After Mary, St. Joseph is the nearest to Jesus in Heaven and the greatest Saint. St. Thomas Aquinas explains his greatness in relation to Jesus, Mary, and the Saints, saying: *"There are three things God cannot make greater than He has made them: the Humanity of Our Lord, the glory of the elect (Saints), and the incomparable Mother of God, of whom it is said that God can make no mother greater than the Mother of God. You may add a fourth in honor of Saint Joseph. God cannot make a greater father than the father of God."*

As the head of the Holy Family, Joseph now has authority, in certain regard, even over Jesus and Mary in Heaven. After all, *"Joseph is the father of our Judge."*[41] He is the patron of virgins, married people, fathers, workers, education, repentant souls, the afflicted, interior souls, religious, priests, prelates, of a happy death, and of the Universal Church. He can help us in all circumstances. Oh how we need to reawaken devotion to St. Joseph in the Church! Let everyone say with St. Catherine of Siena: *"This is **my irrevocable resolution – for all eternity to belong entirely to Jesus, to Mary, and to Joseph**, and I renounce, as far as it is possible for me to do so, all power of ever revoking this promise."*[42]

St. Joseph: Coredemptor of the Human Race

Through the apparitions of Our Lady of America to Sr. Mildred, St. Joseph spoke the following words:

*It is true my daughter, that **immediately after my conception**, I was, through the future merits of Jesus and because of my exceptional role of future Virgin-Father, cleansed from the stain of original sin.*

__I was from that moment confirmed in grace and never had the slightest stain on my soul.__ This is my unique privilege among men.

*My pure heart also was from the first moment of existence inflamed with love for God. Immediately, at the moment when my soul was cleansed from original sin, grace was infused into it in such abundance that, excluding my holy spouse, **I surpassed the holiness of the highest angel in the angelic choir.***

My heart suffered with the Hearts of Jesus and Mary. Mine was a silent suffering, for it was my special vocation to hide and shield as long as God willed, the Virgin Mother and Son from the malice and hatred of men.

The most painful of my sorrows was that I knew beforehand of their passion, yet would not be there to console them.

*Their future suffering was ever present to me and became my daily cross. **I became, in union with my holy spouse, coredemptor of the human race.** Through compassion for the sufferings of Jesus and Mary I co-operated, as no other, in the salvation of the world.*

St. Joseph: Spiritual Father of All God's Children

St. Joseph spoke to visionary Sr. Mildred, giving great insights to bring countless souls to a new way of life, saying:

I bring to souls the purity of my life and the obedience that crowned it.

***All fatherhood is blest in me** whom the Eternal Father chose as His representative on earth, the Virgin-Father of His own Divine Son. Through me, the Heavenly Father has blessed all fatherhood, and through me He continues and will continue to do so till the end of time.*

My spiritual fatherhood extends to all God's children, and together with my Virgin spouse, I watch over them with great love and solicitude.

*Fathers must come to me, small one, to learn **obedience** to authority: to the Church always, as the mouthpiece of God, to the laws of the country in which they live, insofar as these do not go against God and their neighbor.*

Mine was perfect obedience to the Divine Will, and it was shown and made known to me by the Jewish law and religion. To be careless in this is most displeasing to God and will be severely punished in the next world.

*Let fathers also imitate my great **purity** of life and the deep respect I held for my Immaculate Spouse. Let them be an example to their children and fellowmen, never willfully doing anything that would cause scandal among God's people.*

Fatherhood is from God, *and it must take once again its rightful place among men.*

Visionary Sr. Mildred describes what she saw next: *As St. Joseph ceased speaking, I saw his most pure heart. It seemed to be lying on a cross which was of brown color. It appeared to me that at the top of the heart, in the midst of the flames pouring out, was a pure white lily. Then I heard these words:*

Behold this pure heart so pleasing to Him Who made it.

The cross, my little one, upon which my heart rests is the cross of the Passion, which was ever present before me, causing me intense suffering.

I desire souls to come to my heart *that they may learn true union with the Divine Will.*

Stating that he desired a day set aside to honor his fatherhood, St. Joseph continued, saying:

The privilege of being chosen by God to be the Virgin-Father of His Son was mine alone, and no honor, excluding that bestowed upon my Holy Spouse, was ever, or will ever, be as sublime or as high as this.

The Holy Trinity desires thus to honor me *that in my unique fatherhood all fatherhood might be blessed.*

Dear child, I was king in the little home of Nazareth, for I sheltered within it the Prince of Peace and the Queen of Heaven. To me they looked for protection and sustenance, and I did not fail them.

I received from them the deepest love and reverence, for in me they saw Him Whose place I took over them.

*So **the head of the family must be loved, obeyed, and respected, and in return be a true father and protector to those under his care.***

Receive my blessing. May Jesus and Mary through my hands bestow upon you eternal peace.

Devotion to the Heart of St. Joseph

Calling for **a new devotion dedicated to the heart of St. Joseph to be celebrated on First Wednesdays**, placed together with the First Friday Sacred Heart Devotion and the First Saturday Immaculate Heart Devotion, St. Joseph states:

***I am the protector of the Church and the home**, as I was the protector of Christ and His Mother while I lived upon earth. Jesus and Mary desire that my pure heart, so long hidden and unknown, be now honored in a special way. Let my children honor my most pure heart in a special manner on **the First Wednesday of the month** by reciting the Joyful Mysteries of the rosary in memory of my life with Jesus and Mary and the love I bore them, the sorrow I suffered with them. Let them receive Holy Communion in union with the love with which I received the Savior for the first time and each time I held Him in my arms.*

Those who honor me in this way will be consoled by my presence at their death, and I myself will conduct them safely into the presence of Jesus and Mary.[43]

What a beautiful life of peace-on-earth Heaven is calling each of us to live within the family – founded, renewed and continually blessed by the Two Hearts of Jesus and Mary, together with the heart of Joseph – our family in the Holy Family and in the Trinity! Peace on earth!

Chapter Five
The Triumph of the Two Hearts & Era of Peace

Jesus, Mary, I love you, save souls.
Let us eternally adore the Holy Sacrament through Mary.
To the Two Hearts of Jesus and Mary be honor and glory.
Let the Kingdom of the Divine Will (Fiat) come!

PRAYER TO THE ALLIANCE OF THE TWO HEARTS

Hail, most loving Hearts of Jesus and Mary! We venerate You. We love and honor you. We give and consecrate ourselves to You forever. Receive us and possess us entirely. Purify, enlighten, and sanctify us so that we may love You, Jesus with the heart of Mary, and love you, Mary, with the Heart of Jesus.

O Heart of Jesus, living in Mary and by Mary! O heart of Mary, living in Jesus and for Jesus! O Heart of Jesus pierced for our sins and giving us Your Mother on Calvary! O heart of Mary pierced by sorrow and sharing in the sufferings of your Divine Son for our redemption! O sacred union of these Two Hearts.

Praise be God, the Father, the Son, and the Holy Spirit. Praise be the Holy Spirit of God Who united these Two Hearts together! May He unite our hearts and every heart so that all hearts may live in unity, in imitation of that sacred unity which exists in these Two Hearts.

Triumph, O Sorrowful and Immaculate Heart of Mary! Reign, O (Eucharistic and) Most Sacred Heart of Jesus! In our hearts, in our homes and families, in Your Church, in the lives of the faithful, and in the hearts of those who as yet know You not, and in all the nations of the world. Establish in the hearts of all mankind the sovereign triumph and reign of Your Two Hearts so that the earth may resound from pole to pole with one cry: *"Blessed forever be the (Eucharistic and) Most Sacred Heart of Jesus and the Sorrowful and Immaculate Heart of Mary!"*

O dearest St. Joseph, I entrust myself to your honor and give myself to you that you may always be my father, my protector and my guide on the way to salvation. Obtain for me a greater purity of heart and a fervent love of the interior life. After your example, may I do all my actions for the greater glory of the Triune God in union with the (Sacred) Heart of Jesus and the Immaculate Heart of Mary. O Blessed St. Joseph, pray for me that I may share in the peace and joy of your holy death. Amen.

(Two Hearts Media)

The Fruit of Reparation

*There is a lack of victim souls
to offset this Great Chastisement which threatens us.*
St. Gemma

*I have need of souls and of priests who serve Me
by sacrificing themselves for Me and for souls.*
Our Lady of Fatima

*The two means to save the world are prayer and sacrifice
in these last times in which we live.*
Lucia of Fatima

*The small number of souls, who hidden,
will preserve the treasures of the Faith and practice virtue
will suffer a cruel, unspeakable and prolonged martyrdom.*
Our Lady of Good Success

*This will be the hour of the martyrs who, in great numbers,
will shed their blood, and of the remnant who will envy those they see
persecuted and slain.*
Mary to Fr. Gobbi

Have you truly decided to become the rejected stone?
Our Lady of Akita

This book has contained three sections that correspond to the three phases of the divine renewal and of spiritual growth – the warning, chastisement, and triumph – and the correlating responses: as the remnant faithful who convert, the consecrated who live lives of hope, and now the perfect who sacrifice their lives in love. While each of these approaches corresponded well to a particular phase of renewal, still it is important to note that we are called to live all three responses even now and throughout all three phases of the renewal. We should not wait until the next phase begins to consider growing in our spiritual life and living each of the theological virtues of faith, hope, and love as part of the life of being a Catholic who wants to become a Saint. As beginners, we should become proficient, and as proficient, we should become perfect.

We must wonder what will finally cause the upheaval to cease and the Faith to be restored. Our Lady provides the answer: a group of victim souls will offer their lives and bring about a turning of the tide. Mary is calling together an army of victim souls, all of whom are Her handmaids with spiritual littleness – ready to serve Her in any way possible. Our Lady is asking us to offer our lives in reparation not only for our own sins, but also for the sins of others, **to suffer without complaint as victims of love**. As victim souls, we die to our own free will and give to the Lord everything – great and small, joy and suffering alike – for the conversion of sinners. In this, we become **martyrs of love**. As Paul states: *"Now I rejoice in my sufferings for your sake, and in my flesh I complete what is lacking in Christ's afflictions for the* *sake of his body, the church.*"[1] Our sufferings and sacrifices help other souls to go to Heaven. This is rooted in *hope*.

It is not easy to *sacrifice*, and people typically try to avoid pain when they can, but to ask for grace to suffer with a higher purpose, for love of others, is of great value to Christ in His mission to save souls. John Paul spoke about redemptive suffering in relation to Christ, saying: *"Suffering in Christ created the good of the world's Redemption. This good in itself is inexhaustible and infinite. No man can add anything to it. But at the same time, in the mystery of the Church in His body, Christ has in a sense opened His own Redemptive mystery to all human suffering... Redemption, accomplished through satisfactory love, remains always open to all love expressed in human suffering."*[2] Christ invites us to unite our suffering with His to bring about the salvation of humanity, as Vatican II confirms, saying: *"The unique mediation of the Redeemer does not exclude but rather gives rise to a manifold cooperation which is but a sharing in this one source."*[3] In this, suffering gains a positive meaning; united with Christ, it becomes truly redemptive.

We must set our spiritual bar very high, and remain recollected in times of panic, and then our initial revulsion at the idea of suffering will pass quickly. We must learn from the Saints to reject the desire for too much affection and adulation, to seek lowliness, and to serve the poor, unloved, and forsaken people the Lord puts in our life; and He will reward us greatly forever. Jesus said to all: *"If any man would come after me, let him deny himself and take up his cross daily and follow me. For whoever would save his life will lose it; and whoever loses his life for my sake, he will save it."*[4]

The Church teaches that Mary is the perfect model of redemptive suffering. Pius XII states: *"By the willing of God, the most Blessed Virgin Mary was inseparably joined with Christ in accomplishing the work of man's Redemption, so that our salvation flows from the love of Jesus Christ and his suffering intimately united with the love and sorrows of his mother."*[5] Benedict XV in his 1918 apostolic letter states: *"To such extent did she (Mary) suffer and almost die with her suffering and dying Son, and to such extent did she surrender her maternal rights over her Son for man's salvation...that we may rightly say that **she together with Christ redeemed the human race.**"*[6] John Paul II clarifies that Mary's role is subordinate to the one mediation of Christ, saying: *"And [Mary's] cooperation is precisely this mediation subordinated to the mediation of Christ."*[7] On the other hand, John Paul goes so far as to say that Mary was *"crucified spiritually with her crucified Son."* Vatican II thus declares: *"Therefore the Blessed Virgin is invoked in the Church under the titles of Advocate, Helper, Benefactress, and Mediatrix. This, however, is so understood that it neither takes away anything from nor adds anything to the dignity and efficacy of Christ the one Mediator."*[8] Let us go to Mary and ask her to teach us to love and to offer our lives and our sufferings for the glory of God and the salvation of souls. Let us go to Mary to learn the path of holiness and of peace.

LIVE The Messages! SPREAD The Messages!

This book has sought to discuss the Good News of the revelations of God to His people for the times we live in today, of the Apocalypse. We now have the mission to share this good news with others and to share our hope. Like the Apostles, we should say: *"We cannot but speak of what we have seen and heard."*[9] If we proclaim this heavenly message to others, the Bible promises that we will **become joyful**, as St. John writes: *"That which we have seen and heard we proclaim also to you… And we are writing this **that our joy may be complete**."*[10]

The more people we can get to listen to this message and respond to it, the more the forces of darkness and of God's just wrath will be averted. The heavenly prophesies discussed in this book are not absolutely predetermined. The Bible shows us that conditional prophesies may be altered before being fulfilled and that this is dependent upon our response to prophetic warnings. In the case of Jonah, for example, the Ninevites repented and God relented on His warning of punishment.

Recent history also demonstrates that unheeded divine warnings bring about the forewarned calamity. In the case of Fatima, the conditional secrets came to pass because humanity did not heed the heavenly warnings. The future is always in the Hands of God. Prayer and fasting, with repentance, and atonement for the sins of humanity, are what is called for here and now. And while prayer and penance can diminish the divine punishment, revelations have stated that a divine chastisement cannot be totally eliminated at this late of a time. These heavenly secrets and warnings are meant to give us a wakeup call from God, to motivate us and not to cause fear or hysteria. They show us that God is in control and He desires to bring us through purification to renewal. He has planned each step of the purification for our good. Our duty is to *accept divine peace now and then to spread it, and to spread the heavenly messages of hope.* Our Lady of Medjugorje reminds us of how important our cooperation is, as she says: *"My dear children, I want to collaborate with you, for I need your collaboration... I need you, dear children, to cooperate with me, because* **there are many plans that I cannot fulfill without you... I cannot do anything without you.** *"*[11]

Each of us can hear Jesus speaking to us about our new mission in the Two Hearts, as He says:

"Tell the whole world"![12]

Thus, dear reader, <u>Our Lady is calling *you* to do two things</u>: to fully live and urgently spread this heavenly Message! Listen, our heavenly Mother, who is being sent by God to us today, says: *"Today I am calling on you to decide whether or not you wish to* **live the messages** *which I am giving you. I wish you to* **be active in living and spreading the messages.** *"*[13] Our Lady reminds us that they are *the* Message from Heaven in our times, saying: ***"Live my messages** and put into life every word that I am giving you. May they be precious to you because they come from Heaven.*"[14] She also says: ***"Today I invite***

YOU to become <u>missionaries of my messages</u>... to transmit them to the whole world... to be my joyful carriers of peace... Through YOU, I wish to renew the world."[15] Will *YOU* respond now? You can use *this book* as The Guide to living the heavenly messages, and give copies of it to everyone you meet to spread this Message!

Peace the World Has Never Known

This time of preparation is soon giving way to the period of increasing upheaval, to the time of the Great Conversion, caused by the love, mercy, *and* justice of God, and to the time of the Tribulation and the Antichrist, a time which will afterwards see the ushering in of the Restoration, and the era of love and peace. Peace is God's gift to man; it is the result also of the human project in conformity with the divine plan.[16] Scripture reveals that peace is an attribute of God Himself: *"the Lord is peace."*[17] When the resurrected Jesus meets His disciples, and every time He meets us in the Mass, He says: *"Peace be with you."* He is inviting us to join Him and His Mother in *"the battle for peace!"*[18] Let us share *the good news of peace*; let us build the culture of peace and love! Our Lady of Fatima promised that in the end there would be peace. And so it will be as Mary had prophesied: *"In the end, my Immaculate Heart will triumph"* **and there will be a great era of peace.**

Now is a time of peace, of mercy, of forgiveness and conversion, and of reconciliation. For soon comes justice, which will also bring us peace as well, but with greater difficulty, because peace is the fruit of justice and love. Now is the time for victim souls to offer their lives as a sacrifice of love to save humanity. It is time for the whole Church and all the faithful to acknowledge that the Devotion to the Two Hearts, which are united as one Heart, is a single true Devotion of greatest importance for our world today, and for the Renewal of our world in what will be the greatest Renewal in the history of the world since Christ and the Church's first Pentecost.

We are being called to help usher in the Age of the Two Hearts! We are united to Jesus through the Heart of Mary. Let us pray that the Two Hearts triumph and reign to bring upon humanity a new dawn and the new era of peace!

Divine Mercy in My Soul

The Great Heavenly Resource for Reparation

Jesus spoke to St. Faustina about His plan to renew humanity in our time and to prepare the world for His coming, through a remnant faithful who will day and night call upon His mercy for themselves and for humanity in our times. Jesus is asking us to live lives of reparation. Through her, He is asking us to celebrate *daily* the Holy Hour of Great Mercy (3-4 pm) if even for just a moment, which is the Hour He died on the Cross for our Redemption. Jesus promises tremendous graces, both for us and those of others, if we will implore His grace and mercy during this Holy Hour. He says:

> *At three o'clock, implore My mercy, especially for sinners; and, if only for a brief moment, immerse yourself in My Passion, particularly in My abandonment at the moment of agony.* ***This is the hour of great mercy... In this hour I will refuse nothing to the soul that makes a request of Me in virtue of My Passion...*** *As often as you hear the clock strike the third hour immerse yourself completely in My mercy, adoring and glorifying it, invoke it's omnipotence for the whole world, and particularly for poor sinners, for at that moment mercy was opened wide for every soul.* ***In this hour you can obtain everything for yourself and for others*** *for the asking; it was the hour of grace for the whole world - mercy triumphed over justice. Try your best to make the Stations of the Cross in this hour, provided that your duties permit it; and if you are not able to make the Stations of the Cross, then at least step into the chapel for a moment and adore, in the Most Blessed Sacrament, My Heart, which is full of mercy; and should you be unable to step into chapel, immerse yourself in prayer there where you happen to be, if only for a very brief instant.*[19]

Jesus is also calling the faithful to be co-redeemers – to implore God's mercy upon all of humanity in these times of crisis through a new prayer of mercy and reparation that He gave to us called the Chaplet of Divine Mercy. Our Lord has given us a most special prayer for these times of great crisis and for the latter times. Jesus said to Sister Faustina about praying the Chaplet of Divine Mercy: *"**Say unceasingly this (Divine Mercy) chaplet** that I have taught you. Anyone who says it will receive great Mercy at the hour of death. Priests will recommend it to sinners as the last hope. Even the most hardened sinner, if he recites this Chaplet even once, will receive grace from My Infinite Mercy. I want the whole world to know My Infinite Mercy. **I want to give unimaginable graces to those who trust in My Mercy**... When they say this Chaplet in the presence of the dying, I will stand between My Father and the dying person not as the just judge but as the Merciful Savior."*

Testimony of God's Mercy for a Soul

The Lord wishes us to offer reparation, and **Jesus has given us the Chaplet of Divine Mercy as the great prayer of reparation**. I have known the great power and grace that comes from this prayer and devotion both in my life and for those I have prayed for. I remember one remarkable example. Some years ago, when I was living in Ohio studying theology, I made plans to visit with my family in Texas over Christmas. I had been concerned about my family, and for their lives of faith particularly, for some time. Growing up, we had been a somewhat nominal Catholic family in many ways. I was at this time most concerned about my father. I loved my family and my father (and I know they loved me), and so I decided to pray each day the Chaplet for them, until I went home a few months later to visit. During my visit, I asked my family and relatives to gather together after Christmas Day Mass to spend a few minutes in prayer, to pray a prayer called the Chaplet of Divine Mercy. You see, I was familiar with the promises of Jesus for those who prayed the Chaplet: *"Let no soul fear to draw near to Me, even though its sins be as scarlet,"*[20] and *"Sooner would heaven and earth turn into nothingness than would My mercy not embrace a trusting soul."*[21] Knowing my family, I understood this was a great request. Amazingly though, all agreed. I introduced them to the Chaplet prayer and we prayed it together. After we finished, something wonderful spontaneously happened. There was a great spirit of love and tears of peace within our family that day. It was a wonderful day!

But, the greatest graces were yet to come. A couple months later, my father called me to tell me that he had just been diagnosed with terminal cancer and had only a short time to live. He insisted that I finish my studies and come to see him in the summer. He then asked me a simple question, *"Kelly, will you help me to prepare my soul for death?"* He wanted me to give him spiritual direction and prepare his soul to meet Jesus after he died. I agreed, and we spoke often that spring about the things of God and how to prepare to meet Christ after death. My father was very responsive, and we exchanged sentiments of filial love every conversation we had. Little did I know at the time – that Christmas was the last time I would ever see my father alive again. Tears come to my eyes even now when I recall the mercy of God. My dad died before I could get home again, but I am so glad for God's mercy and the gift He gave to us both that last Christmas I was blessed to spend with my dad. My family asked me to give his eulogy, and we said good-by to our dad with joy and peace, in awe at the mercy of God. Our family has prayed the Chaplet daily ever since. I would highly recommend: Pray the Chaplet daily, and during the 3pm Hour of Mercy when you can. At least invoke His graces and mercy during this holy hour of mercy every day. And engage in the works of mercy; make reparation for sinners!

Mary Calls Her Children to Reparation

Penance, Penance, Penance

Mary is calling the faithful to lives of conversion, consecration, *and* reparation – especially to sacrifice for sinners and souls in Purgatory in these times of great crisis. During the third apparition of Lourdes to St. Bernadette, Our Lady spoke for the first time. She spoke of a call to reparation, saying: *"I do not promise to make you happy in this world but in the other."* Our Lady asks Bernadette to live out the Incarnation, Passion and Death, and then the Resurrection of Christ in her own life. She is asking the same of us. Our Lady asks us to live for souls, saying: ***"Penance, penance, penance, pray for sinners."***

The Third Secret and the Fruit of Reparation

At Fatima, Portugal, in 1917, Jesus' Mother warned of the impending events of WWII and Communism. At Fatima, the Virgin Mary came with the title of Our Lady of the Rosary to three children, asking us to pray very much, especially the daily Rosary, and to make sacrifices for the conversion of sinners and the souls in Purgatory. Before Our Lady appeared, an angel of the Lord appeared three times to the children. He gave them prayers to recite and called them to lives of reparation, saying: *"Pray, pray a great deal. The Hearts of Jesus and Mary have merciful designs on you. Offer prayers and sacrifices continually to the Most High. **Make everything you do a sacrifice, and offer it as an act of reparation for the sins by which God is offended**, and as a petition for the conversion of sinners... Accept and bear with submission all the sufferings the Lord will send you."*

As background, Portugal had been taken over by freemasons and the royal family murdered; Lisbon had been declared the atheistic capital of the world in 1915. Deliberate plans were under way to destroy the Catholic Church within two generations. But, Mary came with the heavenly remedy to this diabolical poison. She asked *her children* to offer little sacrifices, saying as we offer them: *"O my*

Jesus, it is for love of You, in reparation for the offenses committed against the Immaculate Heart of Mary, and for the conversion of poor sinners. "

At the very first apparition of Our Lady at Fatima, Our Lady continued the theme of heavenly request that the angel had requested from the children, and now from us, saying: *"Do you want to **offer yourselves to God to endure all the sufferings He may choose to send you, as an act of reparation for the sins** by which He is offended and as a supplication for the conversion of sinners?"*

And now today, through the message of Fatima, Mary is asking *us* to cooperate in the divine Plan for our times. As the children responded, so should we. Our Lady promises and reassures us, saying: *"Then **you are going to suffer a great deal**, but the grace of God will be your comfort."* The Lord's love and grace is enough for us. Mary later continued: *"Pray, pray a great deal and **make many sacrifices** for many souls go to Hell because they have no one to make sacrifices and to pray for them."* We must make reparation for sin – for our sins and for the sins of others. We offer Christ reparation in the Eucharist. We offer Our Lady reparation as well, especially through the Five First Saturdays devotion of reparation to her Immaculate Heart and with Communions of Reparation. Reparation is the foundation of the Fatima messages.

We should not be troubled by suffering with love. There is great joy in redemptive suffering. This is a mystery that can be seen in the case of St. Peter, for example: *"It is a greater happiness for St. Peter"* writes St. John Chrysostom, *"to be imprisoned for Jesus Christ than to be with Him in His glory on Mt. Tabor; it is a greater glory for him to wear his prisoner's chains than to bear in his hands the keys to Paradise."* Suffering that is offered to God gains purpose and brings joy. The purpose of reparation is explained by Pope Pius XI, who called the faithful to the frequent practice of acts of reparation, saying that the goal of reparation is ***"to make amends for the insults offered to the Divine Love by oblivion and neglect, and by the sins and offences of mankind."***[22]

There are two ways to understand the work of reparation. First, only Jesus could have repaired the damage done due to our sins and make full repair to the Father in justice, in what is called redemption, reparation, reconciliation, atonement, expiation and satisfaction.[23] Jesus won our redemption in the great act of reparation on the Cross, which is renewed daily on our altars at Mass; and He continues this work of reparation even after His Ascension, as John Paul II states: *"Risen from the dead and glorified at the right hand of the Father, [Jesus] preserves in his immortal body the marks of the wounds of his nailed hands and feet, of his pierced heart (cf. Jn 20:27; Lk 24:39-40) and presents them to the Father in his incessant prayer of intercession on our behalf (cf. Heb 7:25; Rom 8:34)."*[24] Second, along with His superabundant work of Redemption, Jesus is inviting us to participate by consoling Him with our own acts of reparation, united to His to the Father, to be offered both for our own sins and for the sins of others.

Christ still suffers in His Mystical Body, the Church, and in this, He desires the faithful of His Church to partake in His expiation.[25] This is called redemptive suffering.

Two Similar Visions to Avert God's Wrath

From a vision St. Faustina received, she writes about how powerful the Chaplet of Divine Mercy prayer is for saving sinners: *"I saw a great light, with God the Father in the midst of it. Between this light and the earth I saw Jesus nailed to the Cross and in such a way that God, wanting to look upon the earth, had to look through Our Lord's wounds and I understood that God blessed the earth for the sake of Jesus… **I saw an Angel, the executor of God's wrath… about to strike the earth**… I began to beg God earnestly for the world with words which I heard interiorly (the Chaplet of Divine Mercy). As I prayed in this way, I saw the Angel's helplessness, and he could not carry out the just punishment."* This vision is similar to the Third Secret of Fatima, especially concerning the warning of God's just wrath for the sins of humanity, and of Our Lady's intervention together with victim souls.

The Third Secret of Fatima, given by Our Lady in 1917 to the visionaries of Fatima, and revealed publically by John Paul II in 2000 (the first two secrets having already been revealed and fulfilled), reveals Heaven's plan to call us to penance and sacrifice for the salvation of humanity, as follows:

*At the left of Our Lady and a little above, we saw **an Angel with a flaming sword** in his left hand; flashing, it gave out flames that looked as though they would set the world on fire; **but** they died out in contact with the splendor that **Our Lady radiated towards him** from her right hand: pointing to the earth with his right hand, the Angel cried out in a loud voice: '**Penance, Penance, Penance!**' And we saw in an immense light that is God: 'something similar to how people appear in a mirror when they pass in front of it' **a Bishop dressed in White** 'we had the impression that it was the Holy Father'. Other Bishops, Priests, men and women Religious going up a steep mountain, at the top of which there was a big Cross of rough-hewn trunks as of a cork-tree with the bark; before reaching there **the Holy Father passed through a big city half in ruins and half trembling with halting step, afflicted with pain and sorrow, he prayed for the souls of the corpses he met on his way; having reached the top of the mountain, on his knees at the foot of the big Cross he was killed** by a group of soldiers who fired bullets and arrows at him, and in the same way there died one after another the other Bishops, Priests, men and women Religious, and various lay people of different ranks and positions. Beneath the two arms of the Cross there were **two Angels** each with a crystal aspersorium* *in his hand, in which they **gathered up the blood of the Martyrs and with it sprinkled the souls** that were making their way to God.*[26]

In the vision of Fatima, an Angel above the earth is attempting to set it afire with a flaming sword of God's just wrath and judgment. But, then the Virgin **Mary intervenes**, holding out her right hand to stop him. The Angel cries: *Penance, Penance, Penance!* Then the vision moves to the earth itself, showing the Pope and the faithful passing through the city, where the people around them have lost faith; they are as corpses. They are on a journey through a time of violence, destruction and persecution. In a related way, to St. Faustina, Jesus revealed that lukewarm souls caused Him the most revulsion in His sufferings during His Passion. He expressed loathing such persons and referred to them as like living 'corpses.' But, He also promised through Faustina that they too would receive His unfathomable mercy.

In the Fatima vision, while many of those all around the Pope have lost faith, he and his companions hold fast to the Lord and His Church in faith; and they are strengthened. The Pope prays for the lost ones to be restored to faith. As they leave the city, they travel up a steep mountain; and there the Pope and the others with him do penance and lay down their lives for the rest who are like corpses. Then, two Angels gather the fruits of their sacrifices to sprinkle on the other souls. In the end, by the Blessed Mother's intervention and by their sacrifices, humanity is restored to life. Then, all is well again, as faith is restored, even better than ever before, and then Our Lady of Fatima promises that in the end, there will be the era of peace. On May 13, 2000, when John Paul first made public this final secret of Fatima and when he beatified two of the visionaries of Fatima, he revealed that this Fatima secret had to do with *our world today* that is in such a spiritual crisis. In doing so, he called the faithful to acts of penance for ourselves and for souls in need of God's mercy, and he seemed to hint of Church persecutions to come. We must intercede for humanity with Mary and beg God for His mercy.

The Congregation for the Doctrine of the Faith (CDF) then commented on Fatima's Third Secret, saying: *"The angel with the flaming sword on the left of the Mother of God recalls similar images in the Book of Revelation. This represents the threat of judgment which looms over the world."* The CDF cautioned that we should understand that the third secret is conditional, stating: *"The importance of human freedom [must be] underlined: the future is not in fact unchangeably set, and the image which the children saw is in no way a film preview of a future in which nothing can be changed... The purpose of the vision is not to show a film of an irrevocably fixed future. Its meaning is exactly the opposite: it is meant to mobilize the forces of change in the right direction...* ***the vision speaks of dangers and how we might be saved from them.***" While indicating that the third secret had to do in part with John Paul II, the CDF also clarified that, in the secret, *"In his arduous ascent of the mountain we can undoubtedly see a convergence of different Popes."*

In a similar fashion, the prophet Ezekiel related a prophecy of death and new life in the Old Testament. While receiving a vision from God, he was brought by God to a distant valley that was filled with dry human bones. All of a sudden, he saw God intervene to bring these bones back to life and to make them living persons again.

These two visions, old and new, are for *us*; they address our age of lust for power and pleasure, an age that has caused so many to become like living corpses, with some living like spiritual zombies, living faithless and lifeless, haven chosen to embrace the culture of death. Both visions speak of our world today, where so many have lost faith or never had it to begin with and where so many live in mortal sin without repenting, and some leading others into sin. Both visions have a similar ending as well: when all seems lost, there is still reason to *hope*. At the end of the first vision, a remnant of faithful believers, together with Our Lady and the Pope, brings humanity back to life by their sacrifices; and then a new era of peace begins. In Ezekiel's vision, God intervenes and the corpses come back to life as well. Such is the time we are living in and such concerns the time to come. The third secret of Fatima reveals a great crisis of spiritual matters that will assuredly carry over more and more into great physical upheavals as well, greater than has ever been known, as Our Lady of Akita attests.

We must remember that at the last major Apparition of Fatima, on October 13, 1917, **the Miracle of the Sun** occurred. After a long rainstorm, the skies suddenly cleared and the sun came out. The sun began to move around in the sky, as if dancing, and then it began to crash toward the earth. The people responded with fear, and many thought they were going to die and that the world was coming to an end. But, then the sun stopped and returned to its original place and all were blessed. Immediately afterwards, the ground and the people's clothes were completely dry. Images of Jesus, Mary, and Joseph then appeared in the sun and were seen by all, believers and unbelievers alike. It is interesting to note that only 3 people witnessed the Transfiguration, and an amazing 500 people witnessed Jesus Christ after His Resurrection before His Ascension into Heaven. We believe in their testimony, we rest our faith upon it. We should believe as well in our times when a staggering 70,000 people witnessed the Miracle of the Sun at Fatima in 1917. What a marvelous sight! Yet only a prelude to what will occur in our times!

Some years later, after visionary Lucia of Fatima had entered a convent, in 1929, she received another great supernatural vision. It showed the Heavenly Father at the top, the Holy Spirit in the form of a dove of light below Him, Christ on the Cross with His Blood flowing from His Sacred Heart to the Eucharistic Host and into the Cup suspended in the air, and beneath Him was Our Lady of Fatima holding her Immaculate Heart with a crown of thorns and flames in her hand. She is depicted all in white, wearing a Scapular-like medallion of a ball of light, with a yellow star on her tunic near her feet, often holding the Rosary in one hand. In this vision, the words, *"Grace and Mercy"* flowed from the Hand of Christ crucified like water onto the altar. And Sr. Lucia was present at the foot of the vision, representing the heavenly call to each of us to participate in the work of reparation. This wonderful vision confirmed the doctrinal truth that all grace and mercy flow from the Father, in the Spirit, through Christ on the Cross, through the Eucharist, and through the hands of Mary, through the Two Hearts, and through victim souls, to the whole world, and that we are called to participate in the distribution of grace as well. *Now* is the time of grace and mercy! Jesus also said to Lucia: *"Have compassion on the Heart of your Most Holy Mother, covered with thorns, with which ungrateful men pierce it at every moment, and **there is no one to make an act of reparation** to remove them"* (12/10/25). Is there no one to make reparation? What about *you*?

During World War II, when **atomic bombs** were dropped on two Japanese cities, an extraordinary thing occurred. At Hiroshima, a small community of Jesuits was in their house eight blocks from the center of the bomb blast. They had just finished Mass. While hundreds of thousands of people around them in a radius of a mile had died, they were unscathed. The surrounding buildings were destroyed, yet their house untouched. Expert Dr. Stephen Rinehart said that the temperature around the blast was in excess of 20,000 to 30,000 degrees F and that the blast wave hit at sonic velocity with pressures (at one kilometer) greater than 600 psi. Persons cannot survive 350° F and 30 psi. Most people died at ten times the distance of the priests from the blast's epicenter, and the few survivors at that distance were all dead from radiation soon afterwards. But, these eight priests survived and were later examined by 200 scientists and doctors.

Thirty-three years later, survivor, Jesuit Fr. Hubert Schiffer, explained that in their house there was just one thing that was different from their neighbors: *"We believe that we survived because we were living the Message of Fatima... In that house, the Holy Rosary was recited together everyday."* Just as eight people had survived the deluge in the Flood of Noah, so too, now eight people survived the atomic bomb blast inside the new *"ark"* of Our Lady, holding on to the protection of the Rosary. Popular Catholic writer, Dr. Peter Kreeft, recently wrote that today *"We are living in a spiritual Hiroshima;"* and he further suggests that what John Paul II called the Culture of Death is today quickly progressing into the Culture of Murder.[27] We must enter into the protection of Our Lady, and bring others with us, while there is still time.

Similarly, at the community center called Marytown, or the City of the Immaculata, located in Nagasaki, another group of priests was unscathed by the atomic blast from the atomic bomb that was dropped there. St. Maximilian Kolbe had founded this community a decade before the war. The heavenly message for us is clear – through the Rosary, as we open our hearts to Mary, she is able to help us, to save us from the *"bombs and blasts"* that threaten us in our daily life especially in these times. *You* must live the Message of Fatima; and *you* must share this Good News to save others in today's spiritual wasteland of corpses and dry bones. Pray the Rosary every day!

Our Lady Thanks Us for Responding to Her Call

Our Lady of Medjugorje calls her children to embrace the cross and unite with the Lord Jesus, saying: *"Dear children! I wish to tell you to put the Cross at the center of your life. Pray, especially before the Cross from which great graces are coming. Now, in your homes, make a special consecration to the Cross of the Lord. Promise that you will not offend Jesus and that you will not insult Him... Dear children! Without prayer, there is no peace. Therefore, I say to you, pray at the foot of the Cross for peace.*

Our Lady reminds us of the times of grace we are living in now, before the times of justice. She calls us to respond with confession and reparation in this time. She says: *"Dear children! In this time of renunciation, prayer and penance, I call you anew: go and confess your sins so that grace may open your hearts, and permit it to change you."* She calls us to grow in love through giving ourselves to others: *"I am with you and I desire to help you to grow in renunciation and mortification, that you may be able to understand the beauty of the life of people who go on giving themselves to me in special way. Dear children, God blesses you day after day and desires a change of your life"* because *"Through prayer and your acts of renunciation you will become more open to the gift of faith, to love for the Church, and to those around you."* Through acts of reparation, Our heavenly Mother is leading us to the true joy that comes only from God; and **Our Lady's plan is for us to experience God's joy and then bring God's joy to the world**: *"Be strong in God. I desire that, through you, the* *whole world may get to know the God of joy. By your life, bear witness for God's joy.*" Our Lady, Queen of Peace, always ends her Medjugorje messages saying: *"Thank you for having responded to my call."*

A Model of Reparation in Our Time

There is a great gift that has been given by God to America, which is related to Medjugorje. And it has come through an unlikely heroine. Audrey Santo, mystic and victim soul, wandered into the swimming pool in her back yard on August 9, 1987, at her home in Worcester, Massachusetts, when she was three years old. She was resuscitated and suffered massive hypoxia – the oxygen supply to her brain was cut off for several minutes, killing off blocks of brain cells. Doctors informed her parents she would spend the rest of her days on life-support, in a coma. Sometime after the accident, her mother, Linda Santo, flew with Audrey to Medjugorje. It was there, her mother says, that Audrey communicated directly with the Virgin Mary and agreed to take on the status of **a *"victim soul"* – a pious person who willingly takes on the suffering, pain and sickness of other people, sometimes to the extent of manifesting symptoms.** A *"victim soul"* may take on the disease or the punishment of sins of other persons or the souls in purgatory. A victim soul is one who suffers, physical, spiritual, or emotional pain, without complaint and without fanfare as a victim of love, accepting all suffering for the salvation of others with as much hiddeness as possible.

Audrey willingly offered herself for others. Jesus redeemed humankind by suffering and dying for our sins. Christ crucified is *the* Scapegoat of our sins. This goes back to the ancient Jewish custom of letting a goat loose in the wilderness on Yom Kippur, the Jewish Day of Atonement when the high priest entered the Holy of Holies in the Temple and symbolically laid upon the goat all the sins of the people: *"But the goat, on which the lot fell to be the scapegoat, shall be presented alive before the LORD, to make an atonement with him, and to let him go for a scapegoat into the wilderness."*[28] Audrey's mother believed that Audrey committed herself and her sufferings to God by her own free will. *"Suffering is not useless,"* she says. *"By offering trials, one becomes a co-redeemer with Christ."* Linda quotes Blessed Mother Teresa for saying that: *"Man's most beautiful gift is that he can share in the passion of Christ."*[29] Audrey, like all victim souls, had allowed herself to become a scapegoat.

The miracles started soon after Audrey's return to Worcester – the scent of roses; oil exuding from images of Jesus, Mary and some Saints; a crucifix, statues, and icons weeping tears of oil and blood; statues moving of their own accord; miraculous healings of persons with diseases which seem to occur after Audrey's body begins to show forth new unexplainable ailments; and most remarkably, on five occasions during Mass, which was said in her home chapel, consecrated Communion Hosts miraculously bled (one Mass being celebrated by Bishop Flanagan, and the others by Fr. George Joyce), and the Hosts have been preserved for Adoration; Blood also appeared spontaneously inside the Tabernacle that had been located near Audrey's bed on Good Friday (April 5,1996). As a victim soul, Audrey also developed the stigmata, in which the five wounds of the crucified Christ spontaneously appeared on her body. She is a testimony of the miraculous presence of God and the fruit of sacrifice for others so needed in these difficult times. Audrey died on April 14, 2007, on the vigil of Divine Mercy Sunday (two years after John Paul II's death on the same vigil). Bishop McManus of Worcester, in a supportive way, wrote after she died: *"We may never fully understand the causes of various paranormal events which have been reported... God works in mysterious ways."* I visited her home just a day and a half after her death, as a privileged first pilgrim praying for Audrey's soul and seeking Audrey's intercession. I adored the Blood-stained Host and saw the weeping images. It was a marvelous experience I will not forget! I wondered how never in the history of the Church has there been so much supernatural phenomenon occurring in one place to one person. I thought how desperate God must be to get our attention right now, to prepare us for what is to come, *and* how valuable a victim soul is to Him in these times!

Become Victim Souls of Love:
This is *the Mission of Missions - the Apostolate of Apostolates*!

Our Lady is also calling us to be authentic living witnesses of faith, hope, and love – to offer our lives motivated by love. She is asking us to be witnesses (martyrs) of love. Some may be called to a white martyrdom of internal suffering and faithful witness of Christ and to the Faith, while others may be called to a red martyrdom of physical suffering and possibly death for the truth of Christ. The grace of the Lord will be sufficient for us and the Lord will never give us more than we can handle. Our merits will be in the intention of love, for the glory of God and the salvation and sanctification of souls, and we shall be filled with the joy of the Spirit!

Our Lord wants to begin the restoration of His Peace *now*, in this initial phase *through us*, through *your* life of holiness and self-giving, through your faithful vocation and fruitful apostolate, through your life bound to the Immaculate Heart and linked to souls in need of her maternal help, by unbroken chains of Rosaries and continuous acts of mercy and love, all united with the Eucharistic Lord. Our Lady is asking us to offer our lives to delay and possibly even prevent some of the prevailing evil and divine justice that is to come and to help save souls who cannot save themselves. Our Lady of Akita said: *"I have prevented the coming of calamities by offering to the Father, together with all the **victim souls** who console Him, the sufferings endured by the Son on the Cross, by His Blood and by His very loving Soul. Prayer, penance, and courageous sacrifices can appease the anger of* *the Father."* Mary is asking for *your* prayer, penance, and courageous sacrifices to save the world!

This army of victims of love is needed to combat the apostasy, heresy, and compromises, which are currently challenging the Faith. These souls offer their crosses with *joy and love* to Jesus through Mary. These victims are the power of this age. About these victim souls, Our Lady of Good Success says:

*The **small number of souls, who hidden, will preserve the treasures of the Faith and practice virtue** will suffer a cruel, unspeakable and prolonged martyrdom. Many will succumb to death from the violence of their sufferings and those who sacrifice themselves for the Church and their country will be counted as martyrs. In order to free men from the bondage to these heresies, those whom the merciful love of my most Holy Son has designated **to effect the restoration**, will need great strength of will, constancy, valor, and confidence in God. There will be occasions when all will seem lost and paralyzed. This then will be **the happy beginning of the complete restoration**.*

Jesus speaks to us through "Anne", who reportedly receives messages from Heaven by way of interior locution, saying: *"My beloved apostles, please know that **you obtain a constant stream of grace for the world**. You do this by serving so generously. Your generosity obtains for others sublime graces of calm and peace, sublime graces of charity and truth, and sublime graces of conversion and perseverance.*

When you see how heaven has used your service, you will rejoice that you gave so willingly and consistently… **If I did not wish you to serve, I would not have called you into service.** *I need My chosen ones to remain closely tied to their decision to bring My light to others. Only in this way will the renewal push further into the world… Please be loyal to your decision for heavenly service as you live your time on earth. If you remain faithful, I can do many things. I am with you. I am directing all that occurs in your life. We walk together and together we will triumph over all temptations.”[30]*

Living *in* the Divine Will, *the Sanctity of Sanctities*!

One of the greatest ways to live the call of reparation is to live according to God's will, to embrace His will in everything. Through mystic Luisa Piccarreta, the Little Daughter of the Divine Will, God is asking us not only to seek and obey His Divine Will, but to live in the Divine Will, which is *"the most beautiful and the brightest among all other sanctities."* Jesus promises: *"If you put yourself at the mercy of my Will, you will no longer have concerns for anything."[31]* Living constantly in this way, we will have nothing on our own, but everything will be in common with Jesus. In this, Our Lady's *FIAT ("Let it be done to me according to Your Word")* becomes our constant motto. Our passion is the Divine Will, to *live in* God's Will. This is the fruit of living united to the Two Hearts. As we commit to living our consecrated lives in Jesus and Mary, let us pray to do so by living in the

Divine Will. Our Lord tells Luisa that this will become common in the era to come; we can begin now.

It's a Matter of Love

Finally, as St. Thomas More had said, *"It's a matter of love."* The truth is that *"we have come from love, that we have been redeemed by an infinite love, and that* ***we are destined for an eternity of love with Love*** *itself... the Love that became incarnate in the world in Jesus of Nazareth, especially in his suffering, death, and resurrection."*[32] As in all things that come to an end, I am left with the simple question of eternal consequences: *"Have I loved as much as I could have?"* Ultimately, this is the only question worth asking until the end. And when we feel the reality that we have not loved as we could have, there is still hope. The Two Hearts are calling us to live lives of **repentance, penance, and good works of mercy**. So, go to the House of Nazareth and spend time with the Holy Family – greeting Joseph, placing your head on the Heart of Christ, sitting with Mother Mary, being in their company, listening to their Hearts and offering them your heart in an exchange of heartfelt love – *Wow*! This is Heaven on earth, literally.

Catholic writer Michael D. O'Brien speaks powerfully about the intimacy of being united with Jesus and Mary as the greatest blessing of our lives, that each of us should take advantage of more often, and with ever greater devotion and appreciation. He shares about his rest periods in prayer, saying:

> *During these brief – sometimes all too brief – inner rest periods, I find it helpful to see myself as a very small child, a toddler...* **climbing onto Our Lady's lap (where the Child Jesus is) and resting in her motherly embrace***... It only takes a few seconds – just enough to take a deep breath, exhale, feel the tension subside, "hear" the thump-thump-thump of the great Hearts. I try to rest there as long as I can before I'm called back into the world of exterior action, must jump from their laps and go about my adult responsibilities. But after such rests I find that [Jesus and Mary] come with me in a sense, enfolding me, holding my hand even when my hands are busy-busy-busy about many things. It's not a one-time event. It has to be renewed often—daily—and in my case hourly whenever the going gets rough.*

> *When I'm resting on Our Lady's lap in this way, I sometimes cry, sometimes laugh, but most often I just sigh and sink into that place of total protection and consolation... Then joy fills me and I can go out again to play like a child in the fields of the Lord, His beautiful created world, among all those whom He has given me to love.*[33]

These beautiful sentiments call us to rest in the Hearts of Jesus and Mary, which are bleeding from the lance's blade for love of us.

And we may wonder: *"What could be more cleansing than this blood? What more healing than this wound?"*[34] Let us penetrate into the Wound of Jesus' Heart, and into the Sorrowful Heart of His Mother, especially in Eucharistic Communion and through the contemplation of the Rosary. St. Catherine of Siena speaks of resting in the Heart of Christ: *"I say that the soul that rests there and considers... the Heart that is consumed and opened out of love, that soul receives such conformity within, **seeing itself so loved, that it cannot do anything but love.**"*[35] May we allow this exchange of love that will lead to joy. May we console the Lord and His Mother, telling them that we offer our life as a sacrifice of love, for souls and for sinners. Let us look into these Two Faces and say: *"Jesus, Mary, I love You; You are my life, my smile, my hope, my joy, my everything, now and forever! Save souls!"*

Thus, reader, let us look forward with HOPE to and dedicate our lives to bringing about **the coming Triumph and Reign of the Two Hearts, the great Era of Peace, and the establishing of the universal Kingdom of the Divine Will on earth**; and let us spread this 'good news' with urgency and love!

Post-Script: The End of Time & the Heavenly Jerusalem

The Book of Revelation gives some indication as to what will happen after the millennium of peace as humanity approaches the end of time. After *"a thousand years"* of the renewed humanity and of the era of peace, the devil will be released for a season, as a sign that the end of the world has arrived.

But even then, Satan will be defeated and thrown into the lake of fire to be tormented day and night forever and ever (Revelation 20), together with the cowardly, the faithless, the polluted, murderers, fornicators, sorcerers, idolaters, and all liars (Revelation 21).

Then will come the Second Coming of Christ at the end of time, and the righteous will reign with Christ forever in body and soul. *"He will wipe away every tear from their eyes, and death shall be no more, neither shall there be mourning nor crying nor pain any more, for the former things have passed away."*[36] In that final day, the glory of the heavenly city will be without a temple, for God Almighty and the Lamb will be its temple. God will dwell with His people and His people with Him in the beatific vision, in a communion of love forever. In the heavenly city, there will be no need for the sun or moon, for the glory of God the Lamb and His Mother will illuminate the holy city. Its gates will never be shut, and there will be no night there. Only those written in the Lamb's Book of Life will enter the glorious city of the beatific vision, ensuring that it remains free from any abomination and defilement (Revelation 21).

The end of time and of life on earth will come, and for all of us. *And when will the end of time come?* Only the Lord knows. Heaven is our eternal destiny! If we persevere to the end, we will reign forever with the Lamb Who was slain for *us* – with Jesus the Alpha and the Omega, the First and the Last, the Beginning and the End! As we enter His heavenly realm and behold His beatific vision, our hope now fulfilled, He will declare to us: *"Blessed are those who wash their robes (in faith and righteous deeds of love), that they may have the right to the tree of life and that they may enter the city... The Spirit and the Bride say, 'Come'"* (Revelation 22). God in Heaven awaits us! Alleluia!

Chapter Six
The Fruit of Reparation

Jesus, Mary, I love you, save souls.
Let us eternally adore the Holy Sacrament through Mary.
To the Two Hearts of Jesus and Mary be honor and glory.

Sacrifice Prayer of Fatima

O My Jesus, I offer this for love of You,
for the conversion of sinners,
in reparation for the sins and offenses
committed against the Immaculate Heart of Mary,
and for the conversion of poor sinners.
(Said when offering up personal sacrifices,
sufferings, and penances)

The Chaplet of Divine Mercy

On rosary beads, pray as follows:

1. Begin with the Sign of the Cross, 1 Our Father, 1 Hail Mary and the Apostles Creed.

2. Then on the Our Father Beads say the following:
   Eternal Father, I offer You the Body and Blood, Soul and Divinity of Your dearly beloved Son, Our Lord Jesus Christ, in atonement for our sins and those of the whole world.

3. On the 10 Hail Mary Beads say the following:
   For the sake of His sorrowful Passion, have mercy on us and on the whole world.

(Repeat step 2 and 3 for all five decades).

4. Conclude with (three times):
   Holy God, Holy Mighty One, Holy Immortal One, have mercy on us and on the whole world.

Hospitallers of Peace
Apostles of the Latter Times

☙

'Hallelujah!
For the Lord our God the Almighty reigns.
Let us rejoice and exult and give Him the glory,
for the marriage of the Lamb has come,
and His Bride has made herself ready;
it was granted her to be clothed
with fine linen, bright and pure' –
for the fine linen is the righteous deeds of the saints.
Revelation 19:6b-8

And have YOU spread through the world
what our heavenly Mother requested of you?
Our Lady of Fatima

"Today I invite YOU to become <u>missionaries of my messages</u>…
to transmit them to the whole world…
to be my joyful carriers of peace…
Through YOU, I wish to renew the world."
Our Lady of Medjugorje

WHAT TO DO? HOW TO BEGIN!

Pray – Pray to follow God's will, to live in His Divine Will.
Join – Go to <u>www.TwoHeartsPress.com</u> and

register as hospitallers (ambassadors/servants) of peace.
Priests can join as well.

Commit – Decide which growth commitment level to particpate in.

Spread – Become a missionary of the heavenly messages to others.
Share copies of this book! It is *the* Guide to the Era of Peace.

Three Levels of Growth

Level 1: The Call of Conversion

Pray daily for an increase of faith
Live the 10 Commandments with obedience
Pray to Jesus and Mary daily, with your heart
Pray the 5-Decade Rosary regularly (2-3 times a week)
Attend daily Mass regularly (2-3 times a week)
Go to Confession regularly
Make the First Friday Devotion to the Sacred Heart

Level 2: The Life of Consecration

Foster hope and be chaste
Wear the Brown Scapular daily with Marian devotion
Pray 5-decade Rosary daily
Pray the Chaplet of Divine Mercy regularly
Attend daily Mass each day
Make a Holy Hour of Adoration weekly
Make a Pleanary Indulgence daily, with prayers for the Pope
Pray with the Bible regularly (2-3 times a week)
Fast on Fridays
Go to Confession monthly
Practice works of mercy daily
Consecrate your life to Jesus through Mary
Draw other souls to authentic Marian devotion
Make the First Saturday Devotion to the Immculate Heart
Spread devotion to the Two Hearts
Promote the fifth Marian Dogma of Co-Redemptrix

Level 3: The Fruit of Reparation

Live continually *in* the Divine Will (Fiat), and pray for the Kingdom
    of the Divine Will on earth as it is in Heaven
Live in peace, and become ambassadors of peace and love
Carry the Rosary and Miraculous Medal with you daily
Pray 3-hours daily and foster a spirit of material poverty
Strive to pray the full 20-decade Rosary daily
Attend daily Mass everyday and live Eucharist to Eucharist
Pray the Chaplet of Divine Mercy daily during 3pm-hour
Pray with the Bible daily and other spiritual reading
Fast on Wednesdays and Fridays (and some Mondays)
Make Holy Hours of Adoration each week
Go to Confession at least monthly
Practice the 7 Virtues and the Evangelical Counsels
Offer up your daily tasks as a sacrifice in reparation for sins
Offer your life as a victim-soul in alliance of love with God
Foster special devotion to St. Joseph and your guardian angel
Practice the First Wednesday Devotion to the Heart of St. Joseph
Become saints!

FAMILY LIFE
Attend Mass together
Pray daily as a family, especially the Family Rosary
Enthrone home with the Two Hearts Image
Unite to the Holy Trinity
Model the Holy Family
Make and Renew regularly the Family Consecration

PAROCHIAL, PARISH & DIOCESAN LIFE
Celebrate the First Friday, Saturday, and Wednesday Devotion
Consecrate to the Two Hearts and promote the Devotion
Promote living in the Divine Will
Bring Dr. Bowring to be a speaker at your parish or event

Prayer of Consecration to the Divine Will

O adorable and Divine Will, here I am, before the immensity of Your Light, that Your eternal Goodness may open to me the doors, and make me enter into It, to form my life all in You, Divine Will.

Therefore, prostrate before Your Light, I, the littlest among all creatures, come, O adorable Will, into the little group of the first children of Your Supreme Fiat. Prostrate in my nothingness, I beseech and implore Your endless Light, that It may want to invest me and eclipse everything that does not belong to You, in such a way that I may do nothing other than look, comprehend and live in You, Divine Will.

It will be my life, the center of my intelligence, the enrapturer of my heart and of my whole being. In this heart the human will will no longer have life; I will banish it forever, and will form the new Eden of peace, of happiness and of love. With It I shall always be happy, I shall have a unique strength, and a sanctity that sanctifies everything and brings everything to God.

Here prostrate, I invoke the help of the Sacrosanct **Trinity**, that They admit me to live in the cloister of the Divine Will, so as to restore in me the original order of Creation, just as the creature was created.

Celestial Mother, Sovereign Queen of the Divine Fiat, take me by the hand and enclose me in the Light of the Divine Will. You will be my guide, my tender Mother; You will guard your child, and will teach me to live and to maintain myself in the order and in the bounds of the Divine Will. Celestial Sovereign, to your heart I entrust my whole being; I will be the tiny little child of the Divine Will. You will teach me the Divine Will, and I will be attentive in listening to you. You will lay your blue mantle over me, so that the infernal serpent may not dare to penetrate into this Sacred Eden to entice me and make me fall into the maze of the human will.

Heart of my highest Good, **Jesus**, You will give me Your flames, that they may burn me, consume me and nourish me, to form in me the life of the Supreme Will.

Saint Joseph, you will be my Protector, the Custodian of my heart, and will keep the keys of my will in your hands. You will keep my heart jealously, and will never give it to me again, that I may be sure never to go out of the Will of God.

Guardian Angel, guard me, defend me, help me in everything, so that my Eden may grow flourishing, and be the call of the whole world into the Will of God.

Celestial Court, come to my help, and I promise you to live always in the Divine Will. Amen.   (www.divinewill.org)

ABOUT THE AUTHOR

Kelly Bowring, S.T.D., received his masters in theology (M.A.) and Christian ministry, with advanced certification in catechetics, from Franciscan University of Steubenville, his licentiate in sacred theology (S.T.L.) from Dominican House of Studies (and the John Paul II Institute) in Washington, DC, and his pontifical doctorate in sacred theology (S.T.D.) from the University of St. Thomas Aquinas in Rome.

Dr. Bowring has received the theological *mandatum* to teach theology. He previously taught theology and directed an institute at St. Mary's College of Ave Maria University, and he has been a professor of sacred theology at Southern Catholic College, where he has overseen the theology program and has been the Dean of Spiritual Mission.

Dr. Bowring has written many articles, and his published books include *To Hold and Teach the Catholic Faith* with St. Paul/Alba House and various liturgical and prayer books with W. J. Hirten Co. His new book, *Your Life Redeemed*, is also being published with Two Hearts Press, LLC.

Dr. Bowring and his wife, Diana, have eight children.

List of minor updates/additions to text in recent printings:

Pg. 11 Added 2nd John Paul II quote on Medjugorje

Pg. 12 Added Medjugorje update

Pg. 13 Added last paragraph of Our Lady of America quotes

Pg. 18 Added Luisa Piccarreta update

Pg. 32 Added Medjugorje quote

Pg. 109 Added Luisa Piccarreta quote

Pg 114 Added Our Lady of All Nations reference

Pg 117 Added mention of reported Cuenca prophecy

Pg. 118 Added paragraph about the miracle of Guadalupe

Pg 142 Added Queen Mother summary sentence

Pg. 204 Added prayer given by Jesus, with imprimatur

Pg 218 Added Divine Will reference

Pg. 223 Added reference to Revelation 20

Pg 245 Added two Medjugorje quotes

Pg. 267, 269 Added Luisa Piccarreta quote to the subtitle on each page

Pg. 272 Added sentence on HOPE

Pg. 276 Added Medjugorje quote and call to *spread* the Message

Pg. 280 Updated Author page

ENDNOTES

Preface

[1] 1 Thessalonians 5:19-21

[2] http://campus.udayton.edu/mary/resources/aprtable.html

[3] http://www.spiritdaily.com/medjruling.htm

[4] http://www.ourladyofamerica.com/Approval.php

[5] For the Church's current position and Fr. Gobbi's good standing with the Church, see http://www.ewtn.com/expert/answers/MMP.htm

[6] Ecclesiastes 8:7

[7] John 16:13

[8] Karol Cardinal Wojtyla, *Wall Street Journal*, Nov. 9, 1978

[9] Our Lady to Fr. Gobbi of the Marian Movement of Priests, Message 501. His book, *"To the Priests, Our Lady's Beloved Sons,"* has received the *Imprimatur* of three Cardinals: the late Cardinal Echeverria of Ecuador, Cardinal Vidal of the Philippines and Cardinal Mikaï of Thailand. It also has the *Imprimatur* of many archbishops and bishops worldwide. Although the *Imprimatur* is not a declaration of authenticity, it does assure the reader that the book is free from doctrinal error - i.e. it does not contain anything which is contrary to Catholic faith or morals.
Unless reported apparitions or locutions have received an official declaration by the proper Church authorities that they are not supernatural, the faithful are free to accept them; hence, one who reads the messages given to Fr. Gobbi is in no way disobedient to the Church.
See http://www.mmp-usa.net/arc_defense.html

[10] Message of October 29, 1977

[11] Revelation 6:17

[12] Revelation 9:13-21

[13] Revelation 12:13-17

[14] Revelation 17:14

[15] Revelation 13:10, 14:12

[16] Our Lady to Fr. Gobbi, Message 412

[17] Our Lady to Fr. Gobbi, Message 389.

[18] *"The Teaching of the Catholic Church,' which bears the Church's required seals and was published in 1952 by a theological commission of qualified experts, clearly states that it is not contrary to Catholic teaching to believe or profess 'a hope in some mighty triumph of Christ here on earth before the final consummation of all things. Such an occurrence is not excluded, is not impossible, it is not all certain that there will not be a prolonged period of triumphant Christianity before the end.'"* (Fr. Iannuzzi, *The Triumph of God's Kingdom*, p. 75, cited from http://www.mmp-usa.net/arc_defense.html)

[19] Rich in Mercy 15

[20] 4/24/1994

[21] Joel 3:1-4; Acts 2:17-20

Chapter 1

[1] Cardinal Cipriano Calderón (Zenit 4/16/05)

[2] Quotes of John Paul II from Kelly Bowring, "The Great Jubilee: Unlocking Its Significance," in USCCB's *Jubilee 2000*, July/August 1999.

[3] From his book, *Truth or Weak Faith: Dialogue on Christianity and Relativism* (Italian), as cited in Zenit (12/17/06)

[4] www.ourladyofgoodsuccess.com 2/2/1611.
Bishop Salvador de Ribera of Quito gave ecclesiastical approval of this devotion on Feb 2, 1611, the day of the formal institution of the official devotion.
This message, particularly the novena prayer, again received ecclesiastical approval recently by Archbishop Carlos Maria of Quito (July 31, 1941).

[5] Excerpts from www.michaeljournal.org

[6] See Revelation 11:11.

[7] CCC 478

[8] *Haurietis Aquas* 106

[9] Pope St. Gregory the Great, *Liber Sacramentum: In Nativitate S. Joannes*

[10] *Commentary on St. John I*, 4:23

[11] *Legatus Divinae Pietatis*, Bk IV, Ch 4

[12] *Adversus Haereses* III, 24, 1

[13] *Dialogue* 135, 5

[14] *Opera Omnia*, vol. V

[15] St. Josemaria Escriva

[16] Diary 48, 742

[17] Matthew 6:12

[18] Matthew 7:2

[19] John 13:34

[20] James 2:17

[21] See Revelation 3:15

[22] Diary 429

[23] Diary 848

[24] Diary 965

[25] Diary 1146

[26] Diary 1160

[27] Diary 1588

[28] Diary 635

[29] Acts 2:46-47

[30] CCC 1389

[31] *De Sancta Virginitate* 3

[32] For more information on the Alliance of the Two Hearts organization with their promotion of the First Friday/First Saturday Devotion, the Communions of reparation, and their call for the Feast of the Two Hearts and the Consecration of the world to the Two Hearts, see http://www.allianceoftwoheartsgeorgia.com

[33] Pius IX, *Ineffabilis Deus*

[34] Benedict XV AAS 10 (1918): 182; OL 267

[35] Arellano, *A Definitive Covenant*, 245

[36] Ibid., 246-247

[37] *Inseg* IX: 2 (1986): 699-700; ORE 959:12

[38] Fr. Edgardo M. Arellano, *A Definitive Covenant: The Magisterial Stand on the Alliance of the Hearts of Jesus and Mary* (Two Hearts Media, 1998), Prologue

[39] From the book *Rosary Meditations: Loving Jesus With the Heart of Mary*

[40] Arellano, *A Definitive Covenant*, 69

[41] Arellano, *A Definitive Covenant*, 73

[42] Jesus to Catalina (1/9/1996) at www.greatcrusade.org

[43] *From Sinai to Calvary: The Testimony of Catalina*

[44] http://www.salvemariaregina.info/Message.html

[45] Frere Michele, *The Whole Truth About Fatima Vol. II*, 410

[46] http://www.ourladyofamerica.com/explanation.php

[47] Luke 1:48

[48] *Mother Teresa: Come Be My Light*, edited with commentary by Brian Kolodiejchuk, M.C. (NY: Doubleday, 2007), 99

[49] http://www.sancta.org/eyes.html

[50] See Denis Nolan, *Medjugorje and the Church* (Queenship Publishing). The publisher states as follows:

*Did you know that for the first time in Church history the Vatican removed the jurisdiction over an apparition from the local Ordinary when the investigation into Medjugorje was taken away from the then-bishop of Mostar, Bishop Zanic? Did you know that the **Vatican's current Secretary of State Cardinal Tarcisio Bertone wrote an official letter confirming that pilgrimages to Medjugorje are permitted and that the opinions on Medjugorje of Bishop Ratko Peric, the current Bishop of Mostar, are to be treated strictly "as his personal opinion" with no authority**? Did you know that the Vatican responded with an implicit rebuke of Bishop Peric's widely publicized June 15, 2006, condemnation of Medjugorje when Cardinal Vinko Puljic, president of the Bosnia and Hercegovina Bishops Conference and Archbishop of Sarajevo, announced on July 15, 2006, that "The Catholic Church is starting a new commission that will look into the Medjugorje events" thus reiterating the Vatican's position that the apparition does not fall under Bishop Peric's jurisdiction? Did you know that in his own hand **Pope John Paul II wrote, "I thank Sophia for everything concerning Medjugorje. I, too, go there everyday as a pilgrim in my prayers"**? Did you know that **Blessed Mother Teresa, again in her own hand, wrote: "We are all praying one Hail Mary before Holy Mass to Our Lady of Medjugorje!"**? Did you know that the world's foremost exorcist, **Fr. Gabriele Amorth, official exorcist of the Diocese of Rome who has performed more than 30,000 exorcisms, wrote, "Medjugorje is a fortress against Satan. Satan hates Medjugorje because it is a place of conversion, of prayer, of transformation of life"**? Did you know that hundreds of cardinals and bishops, and tens of thousands of priests, have either personally visited Medjugorje as pilgrims or expressed their appreciation for this fountain of grace, and that the vast majority explicitly proclaim that the Blessed Mother is appearing in Medjugorje? Did you know that bishops and cardinals of the universal Church from Africa to Asia to the Americas have built and consecrated Medjugorje shrines, recognized new religious orders inspired by Our*

Lady of Medjugorje and officially sanctioned new congregations whose mission is to live and spread Our Lady's messages? In Medjugorje and the Church you will find the truths that have been suppressed by the traditionalists and the liberals. Numerous bishops and cardinals have expressed appreciation for this book. For example, **Cardinal Francis Arinze has written from the Vatican: "May God Bless you for the great diligence put into producing this well documented work which I shall read with great interest."**

[51] www.medjugorje.org/overview.htm

[52] Message of October 13, 1987

[53] These secrets of Our Lady of La Salette were recently published in April, 2002, in a book, with *imprimatur,* entitled *Discovery of the Secret of La Salette,* by Fathers René Laurentin and Michel Corteville, intended for the general public on authenticity of the Secret of La Salette.

[54] Message 389

[55] See Message 389

[56] Our Lady spoke through Fr. Gobbi, saying: *"I have been able to hold back the chastisement because of the prayers and sufferings of many of my children."* (December 31, 1977, 142g)

[57] Through Fr. Gobbi, Our Lady said: *"The times will be shortened, because I am Mother of Mercy, and each day I offer, at the throne of Divine Justice, my prayer united to that of the children who are responding to me with a 'yes' and consecrating themselves to my Immaculate Heart."* (September 29, 1995, Feast of the Holy Archangels, 553c)

[58] *Divine Mercy in My Soul, Diary of St. Faustina,* # 1160

Chapter 2

[59] Message of January 21, 1984

[1] Benedict XVI, *Jesus of Nazareth* (NY: Doubleday, 2007), 86-87

[2] Benedict XVI, 87

[3] http://www.ave-ourladyofamerica.com/Messages.html (May 29, 1954)

[4] *Haurietis Aquas*

[5] *The Life of Mary As Seen By the Mystics*, compiled by Raphael Brown (Tan 1951), 243

[6] Our Lady to Fr. Gobbi, Message 435 e and f

[7] See http://www.kolbenet.com/pages/our_spirituality/ for more information on St. Kolbe.

[8] From Sheen's autobiography, *Treasury in Clay*

Chapter 3

[1] *Garabandal Journal* Special Edition, 3

[2] *Garabandal Journal*, 10

[3] http://www.garabandal.org/warning.shtml Visionary Conchita was received in a private audience with Pope Paul VI, who said: *"Conchita I bless you and with me the whole Church blesses you."*

[4] Messages of March 28, 1945, Aug. 15 and Nov. 15, 1951, March 20, 1952, Oct. 11, 1953

[5] Message 383

[6] http://www.garabandal.org/miracle.shtml

[7] The book, *"Synthesis of the Messages from the Apparitions of the Blessed Virgin Mary Guardian of the Faith"* has received an imprimatur (2009) from the Archdiocese of Cuenca.

[8] http://www.garabandal.us/prph_other.html

[9] July 12, 1982

[10] *Garabandal Journal*, 14-15

[11] *Diary of St. Faustina*, 83, 1588

[12] http://www.garabandal.org/punish.shtml

[13] August 7, 1971

[14] On April 22, 1984, after an investigation of over ten years, *"After the investigation conducted up to the present day, I recognize the supernatural character of a series of mysterious events concerning the (weeping) statue of the Holy Mother Mary . . . Consequently, I authorize . . . the veneration of the Holy Mother of Akita."* Bishop John Shojiro Ito of Niigata declared: The Bishop also stated: *"As for the content of the messages received . . . when one thinks of the actual state of the world, the warning seems to correspond to it in many points."*
In Akita, Sr. Agnes Sasagawa received messages from her guardian angel and Mary from June 24, 1973, through May 1, 1982.
The wooden statue of Our Lady at Akita, which shed human blood, sweat, and tears, is the image of the Church-approved apparition of *"Our Lady of All Nations"* in Amsterdam.

[15] Message 501

[16] Messages 332, 464, 442

[17] Information from World Apostolate of Fatima

[18] http://members.tripod.com/~Fabio001/Monarch.txt

[19] *Compendium of Social Doctrine of the Church* 395-396

[20] *Compendium of Social Doctrine* 140

[21] *Compendium* 407

[22] *Compendium* 407, citing John Paul II's Encyclical *Centesimus Annus* 46

[23] Dupont, *Catholic Prophecy* 44-45

[24] Father Sudac received the stigmata in the form of a cross on his forehead. In a series of tests, the cross was cut out at the Vatican hospital, and it reopened in front of the surgeon. Father later received the five wounds of Christ on his hands, feet, and side.

[25] Mobius Rex, *Prophecy: A History of the Future,* 1986; see also Dupont, *Catholic Prophecy*, 40-44

[26] Message of June 14, 1980

[27] On October 4, 1997, the Bishop and Auxiliary Bishop of the Diocese of Haarlem-Amsterdam declared the following: *"I am pleased to support the veneration of Mary under the title "LADY OF ALL NATIONS", which Bishop Bomers and myself have approved for the Diocese of Haarlem-Amsterdam. I am furthermore pleased to encourage the ACTION OF THE LADY OF ALL NATIONS, the goal of which is*

spreading her image and prayer throughout the world. This prayer has already received more than sixty imprimaturs and is translated into over sixty languages." Jozef M. Punt, Auxiliary Bishop, Diocese of Haarlem-Amsterdam, Haarlem, Netherlands, October 4, 1997.

On May 31, 2002, Msgr. Jozef M. Punt, bishop of Haalem/Amsterdam, officially recognized the supernatural origin of the apparitions, thereby approving the apparitions, saying: *"In light and virtue of all these recommendations, testimonies, and developments, and in pondering all this in prayer and theological reflection, I have come to the conclusion that the apparitions of the Lady of All Nations in Amsterdam consist of a supernatural origin... The devotion to the Lady of All Nations can help us, in my sincere conviction, in guiding us on the right path during the present serious drama of our times, the path to a new and special outpouring of the Holy Spirit, Who alone can heal the great wounds of our times."*

[28] LG 10, 57, 58, 61

[29] *Inter sodalicia* (May 1918)

[30] From *Octobri Mense (1891)*, cited in ND 710

[31] *Ad Diem Illum* (1904), cited in ND 712

[32] Cited from ND 716a

[33] CCC 967

[34] CCC 969

[35] Message 204

[36] October 7, 1992, Feast of Our Lady of the Rosary, 479m

[37] VS 120

[38] http://www.mmp-usa.net/arc_mother.html

[39] June 14, 1980, Feast of the Immaculate Heart of Mary, 201f

[40] July 13, 1980, Anniversary of the Third Apparition of Fatima, 203mn

[41] September 15, 1987

[42] For a detailed explanation of this proposed Marian dogma, see Mark Miravalle, STD, *Mary: Coredemptrix, Mediatrix, Advocate* (Santa Barbara: Queenship Publishing, 1993), 1-24. In June, 1997, a theological commission issued a negative opinion on the possibility of defining a dogma on Mary's maternal mediation. It seems they did not think it was the right time to do so. At that time, the movement seeking for the Pope to pronounce this dogma had received nearly 7 million petitions and the endorsements of 43 cardinals and over 550 bishops worldwide from the Universal Church. In 1997, the Holy See made the following statement: *"There is no study underway **at this moment in time** by the Holy Father Pope John Paul II or the Congregation for the Doctrine of the Faith on the subject of the possibility of a papal definition on this theme."* However, this statement hints at the possibility for such a study and actual declaration in the future. For more information about the movement seeking the Magisterial proclamation of the fifth dogma of Mary, see www.voxpopuli.org

[43] 5/31/1979

[44] *Cardinals Lead – Time for Us to Follow,* Catholic Exchange 3/30/2008 http://www.catholicexchange.com/node/71066

[45] Message 404, May 14, 1989, Feast of the Pentecost

[46] Message 405

[47] Message of May 13, 1976

[48] The Sacred Congregation for the Doctrine of the Faith renewed its position on Masonry in its Declaration on Masonic Associations, Nov 26, 1983, as follows: *The question has been raised whether the Church's position on Masonic associations has been altered, especially since no explicit mention is made of them in the new Code of Canon Law, as there was in the old code ...* **The Church's negative position on Masonic associations ... remains unaltered**, *since their principles have always been regarded as irreconcilable with the Church's doctrine. Hence joining them remains prohibited by the Church. Catholics enrolled in Masonic associations are involved in* **serious sin** *and may not approach Holy Communion. Local ecclesiastical authorities do not have the faculty to pronounce a judgment on the nature of Masonic associations which might include a diminution of the above-mentioned judgment... The Supreme Pontiff John Paul II approved this declaration, deliberated at an ordinary meeting of this sacred congregation, and ordered it to become part of public law... (signed) Joseph Cardinal Ratzinger, Prefect*

[49] #382

[50] Message 406

[51] Message 407

[52] Message 405, June 3, 1989, Milan, Feast of the Immaculate Heart of Mary

[53] Message 405

[54] Message of May 13, 1990

[55] Message 407

[56] Message of September 8, 1989

[57] Message of June 14, 1980

[58] Message 407

[59] Our Lady of La Salette

[60] Ephesians 6:12

[61] Fulton J. Sheen, *Communism and the Conscience of the West* (Bobbs-Merrill, 1948), 24-25

[62] CCC 675

[63] Message of November 22, 1992

[64] The last version of the secret, the longest as it is cited here, that of 1879, received the *imprimatur* of Bishop Zola, bishop of Lecce, Italy. These secrets of Our Lady of La Salette were recently published in April, 2002, in a book, with *imprimatur,* entitled *Discovery of the Secret of La Salette,* by Fathers René Laurentin and Michel Corteville, intended for the general public on authenticity of the Secret of La Salette.

[65] Amos 8:11

[66] *Crossing the Threshold of Hope* (Alfred A. Knopf: New York, NY, 1995) 221, 228-229

[67] See Daniel 9:27

[68] Message of 12/31/1992

[69] Yves Dupont, *Catholic Prophecy* (Tan Books and Publishers, 1973), 22

[70] Dupont, 29

[71] Dupont, 23

[72] Messages to Fr. Gobbi (October 2, November 22, December 8, 1992)

[73] Message of March 28, 1975 and April 9, 1982 (Good Friday)

[74] Matthew 24:29

[75] Dupont, 44-45

[76] The visionaries of Medjugorje have said that Our Lady has not given *them* messages about the three days of darkness. It seems the three days of darkness will take place only *after* the 10 secrets of Medjugorje occur.

[77] The last version of the secret, the longest as cited here, that of 1879, received the *imprimatur* of Bishop Zola, bishop of Lecce, Italy.

[78] Paul Thigpen, "Rapture Fever May Be Injurious To Your Spiritual Health" http://www.paulthigpen.com/apologetics/rapturefever.html

[79] See CCC 676

[80] Messages of September 29, 1981 and October 2, 1992

Chapter 4

[1] RM 48

[2] *True Devotion to Mary* #120-121

[3] *True Devotion* #120

[4] Message of September 29, 1995, Feast of the Holy Archangels, 553c

[5] http://www.ourladyofamerica.com/explanation.php (August 1957)

[6] *Rosarium Virginis Mariae* (2002) 38-39

[7] 10th edition, p. 240 and 319

[8] Message of October 13, 1989

[9] From Cardinal Ratzinger's interview with Vittorio Messori, cited in Barbaric's *Fast with the Heart*, 225

[10] *Fast with the Heart*, 4.28

[11] *Fast with the Heart*, 10.5

[12] Cited from Barbaric's *Fast with the Heart*, 10.5

[13] EV 100

[14] 5/25/1987

[15] *True Devotion to Mary*, #47-59

[16] Our Lady of La Salette

[17] Paul VI, *Homily* (June 29, 1972)

[18] Paul VI, *Christi Matri*

[19] Romans 5:20

[20] 2 Timothy 4:6-8

Chapter 5

[1] Message of December 8, 1990

[2] Dupont, *Catholic Prophecy*, 33

[3] Message of October 27, 1980

[4] See Messages to Fr. Gobbi, July 3 and August 21, 1987

[5] http://veritas-catholic.blogspot.com/

[6] Message of October 7, 1983

[7] Message 479

[8] Dupont, *Catholic Prophecy*, 29

[9] http://www.bosconet.aust.com/2columns.html Although I disagree with the interpretation of the dream on this web site as events that occurred in the nineteenth century, it was helpful in giving a detailed and accurate account of the dream itself.

[10] In 1886, Canon John Bourlot, who had been a seminarian in 1862 and heard Don Bosco's original narration, retold the parable at dinner in the presence of Don Bosco, and he placed a third Pope in the narrative.

[11] Message of August 28, 1973

[12] Sermo 5, *Adventu Domini*, 1-3

[13] See Fr. Iannuzzi, *The Triumph of God's Kingdom*, p. 29-30

[14] *The Catholic Encyclopedia*, Volume 1, "Antichrist," Robert Appleton Co. 1907, 561

[15] www.divinewill.org; January 29, 1919 Volume 12 and September 11, 1922 Volume 14. On 29 October 2005, Archbishop Giovan Battista Pichierri concluded the Diocesan phase for the Cause of Beatification and Canonization of the Servant of God, Luisa Piccarreta, Little Daughter of the Divine Will. The Cause has now been officially transferred to the Vatican for the Roman phase of the beatification process. St. Hannibal Mary di Francia was her extraordinary confessor for over 17 years and the ecclesiastical censor of her writings.

[16] *Biografia Andreucci*, p. 515

[17] CCC 686

[18] *The Teaching of the Catholic Church*; cited from *The Splendour of Creation*, Fr. Joseph Iannuzzi, 86

[19] Revelation 20:1-2, 4

[20] Message 413

[21] See http://www.mmp-usa.net/arc_defense.html

[22] 546hi

[23] See CCC 1042-1048

[24] See Revelation 21

[25] Message 383, 389

[26] Message 505

[27] Message 435, 186

[28] *TTP, August 8, 1986, 330B*

[29] *TTP, August 8, 1986, 330C*

[30] *TTP, December 31, 1997, 604opq*

[31] Messages of February 26 and August 15, 1991

[32] *The Life and Kingdom of Jesus in Our Lady*, trans. Trappist Fathers (NY: Trappist Fathers, 1946), 271

[33] *Meditations on Various Subjects* (NY: Trappist Fathers, 1947), 240

[34] Ibid., 240

[35] *Angelus* 9/15/1985

[36] *Angelus* 6/24/1979

[37] Benedict XVI, SC 33

[38] Fr. Stefano Maria Manelli, FI, *The Bread of Our Heavenly Mother*, Mother of All Peoples Weekly Ezine (7/16/05)

[39] Binet, 23

[40] St. Bernardine of Siena, *Serm. De S. Joseph*, 3; Suarez, *De Incarnat.*, p. 2, 8, 2; St. Francis de Sales, *Entretien* 19

[41] Binet, 133

[42] Binet, 141

[43] Excerpts taken from www.michaeljournal.org

Chapter 6

[1] Colossians 1:24

[2] John Paul II, *Salvifici Doloris (Apostolic Letter on the Christian Meaning of Human Suffering)* 38

[3] LG 62

[4] Luke 9:23-24

[5] Pius XII, *Haurietis Aguas* 2

[6] Benedict XV, *Inter Sodalicia*

[7] RM 39

[8] LG 62

[9] Acts 4:20

[10] 1 John 1:3-4

[11] January 22, 1989, July 24 and August 4, 1988

[12] Our Lord to St. Faustina, Diary #699

[13] Medjugorje Message 6/5/86

[14] Medjugorje Message 6/25/02

[15] Medjugorje Message of 2/25/95; 6/25/95; 10/25/96

[16] *Compendium of Social Doctrine* 488

[17] Judges 6:24

[18] *Compendium* 519

[19] Diary 1320, 1572

[20] Diary 699

[21] Diary 1777

[22] Encyclical *Miserentissimus Redemptor*

[23] CCC 616

[24] *Angelus* 9/10/1989

[25] See Pius XI's Encyclical *Miserentissimus Redemptor*

[26] http://www.vatican.va/roman_curia/congregations/cfaith/documents/rc_con_cfaith_doc_20000626_message-fatima_en.html

[27] See www.peterkreeft.com

[28] Leviticus 16: 10

[29] http://www.littleaudreysanto.org/

[30] www.directionforourtimes.com Message of 4/1/09

[31] www.divinewill.org

[32] Weigel, *Letters to a Young Catholic*, 117

[33] Michael D. O'Brien, *Fatherhood and the Prodigal Son*, Mother of All Peoples Ezine (7/29/05)

[34] Augustine, *Tractatus in Joannem* IX, 10

[35] Catherine of Siena, *Letters*, 97

[36] Revelation 21:4